MONEY AND ECONOMIC GROWTH

Tilburg studies in economics
Vol. 17

Money and economic growth

JAC. J. SIJBEN
Tilburg School of Economics,
Social Sciences and Law,
the Netherlands

Martinus Nijhoff Social Sciences Division
Leiden 1977

ISBN 90 207 0655 1

Photoset in Malta by Interprint (Malta) Ltd

Printed in the Netherlands by Intercontinental Graphics.

To the memory of my father
To Ria and Léon

Preface

In monetary theory the paramount problem posed by many economists was always whether monetary variables had a certain influence on the real variables in the economy, so that money would not be neutral but influence the economic process. In this way the outcome would differ from that of a barter economy. The outcome of this development was that money could no longer be regarded as an accommodating item like in many out-dated text-books but as an autonomous factor, the influence of which is explicitly analyzed. When, after the Second World War, the 'real' side of economics developed into growth economics, it was quite natural that efforts were made to integrate both lines of thought so that the effect of the rate of increase of money on the rate of growth of real national income could be studied.

Dr. Sijben gives the full and thorough story of these efforts in a way that enables economists to compare the different approaches more easily than was possible up to now. More specifically the various models are made comparable by the use of the same symbols for the same variables all over the book. After the introductory chapter Tobin's outside-money model in a neo-classical framework is discussed. What is income in this respect? Tobin argues that real disposable income is real net national income plus the real value of the increase in monetary balances. Johnson holds the view that cash balances are so convenient that they are a part of real consumption and of real income as well. Levhari and Patinkin analyse the consequences of this refinement of theory of which practical applications will not be available in the short term.

The Keynes–Wicksell approach, discussed in chapter three is more truly dynamic and leaves more room for disequilibria, as it deals with excess demand and excess supply of commodities. Institutional market arrangements come into the picture. On the basis of a synthesis of both neo-classical and Keynes–Wicksell approaches in chapter four the conclusion is reached that outside the equilibrium situation the Keynes–Wicksell is more relevant and that within this situation the neo-classical analysis is the best to explain the process of monetary growth.

In the final chapter Dr. Sijben has given an evaluation of the findings in the preliminary survey. Some theories are dependent on assumptions that are so subtle and rather far from reality that they cannot be regarded as reliable guidelines for practical policies. Much can be done however to improve the practical significance of these theories: the traditional notion of money can be extended in the direction of the notion of liquidity and money substitutes. Situations of less than full employment could be taken into account more than has been the case up to now, balance of payments problems can be included in the model, as well as the influence of the government budget connected with the problem of inside and outside money. It is Dr. Sijben's opinion that the aspect of the money supply is neglected too much in the theories that were dealt with in the foregoing chapters.

Summarizing I think that Dr. Sijben, by an extensive study of all the relevant literature, has given a fair and clear exposition of the relevant theories, making them more comparable than up to now. For this part of monetary theory it is an indispensable guide to further developments in this field of economic theory.

Dr. H. W. J. Bosman
Professor of Money and Banking,
Tilburg School of Economics,
Social Sciences and Law,
the Netherlands

Contents

Introduction

In economic literature the essence and significance of money for the issue of the economic process has always drawn a great deal of interest since the origins of the economic sciences. Especially the change-over from the exchange economy to a monetary economy, in which process transactions come about with the use of money as a medium of exchange, has ever since actuated many researchers to trace the fundamental differences between the two exchange economies.

In this study we will examine how conceptions about the meaning of money for real economic activity have been evolved from the quantity-theoretical thinking in the classical period till the modern capital-theoretical approach in the monetary theory in the post-Keynesian period. It is safe to say that till the end of the nineteen fifties economic literature strongly emphasized the feature of the neutrality of money in a comparative-static sense. This means that changes in the money supply will exercise no fundamental influence on the real issue of the economic process.

The changes mentioned can perhaps exercise some influence on the economic activity in the short run through changes in the rate of interest and the expenditure, but on the contrary for the structural development of the real economic variables money is of a negligible significance.

In other words the idea of money as a veil has dominated theoretical economy till recently.

We intend to review in this study the present state of monetary theory, as it appears from the literature. We shall be focusing on the question whether money maintains the feature of neutrality even in a framework of growth theory so in a comparative-dynamic sense.

In other words the question emerges whether changes in the rate of growth of the quantity of money can affect the equilibrium values of the real variables, compared with a growth path with another rate of monetary growth.

Before these central questions can be answered the reader must have a good understanding of the traditional classical and Keynesian monetary theories.

In the first chapter the central question mentioned above is modified and formulated as follows. What are the consequences for the development of the equilibrium values of the real variables in the long run, if the capital-theoretical views from modern monetary theory are integrated in the real growth theory?

On the basis of existing conceptions in the literature we shall try to give an answer to this question. We should like to point out explicitly that our theoretical analysis will always refer to the economic relations in a closed economy, in which the government's task is merely limited to a department, which takes care of the money supply. By that we are thoroughly conscious of the fact that the economic environment is in fact much more complicated and that the analysis in a more realistic sense is considerably reduced by the extreme simplification.

However we hold the view that if we wish to trace the meaning of money in a growth theoretical framework and the links between the monetary and the real sector, a start will have to be made with the most simple analysis, in order to understand the complicated economic interrelations properly.

Contemporary literature comprises two main approaches to the central problem mentioned above, viz. the neo-classical variant and the Keynes–Wicksell variant in the monetary growth theory. In the second chapter the most simple two-asset model is presented first of all. This is the Tobin model. Tobin was a pioneer in this field of economic theory. Next this analysis is extended by taking account explicitly of the functions of money as a consumer and as a producer good.

Further in the third chapter the Keynes–Wicksell analysis is represented, an approach in which the meaning of the disequilibria in the goods markets is centred and which is more suitable for a description of the monetary growth process in the short run.

In the fourth chapter we try to give a synthesis model of the neo-classical and the Keynes–Wicksell analyses. In that model the actual rate of inflation has been made dependent on the expected rate of inflation and as well on the existing disequilibria in the goods markets.

Finally a critical evaluation of the present monetary growth theory is given in the fifth chapter and an attempt is made to indicate in which direction theoretical research will have to move if significant recommendations are to be possible for practical monetary policy, based on the theoretical models.

1. General introduction to the monetary growth theory

It is a well-known fact that the classical authors consider money predominantly as a technical expedient to eliminate frictions which might come about when commodities are exchanged.

Money is an indifferent, neutral element with respect to real transactions of goods. The classical economists consider it sufficient to explain the relations in the real sector, because money does not affect the factors which determine the equilibrium in the real sector of the economy. These economists believe that if one thinks in real economic variables, there is no need to integrate monetary theory and real economic theory. The monetary problem manifests itself only in answering the question how the monetary system has to be organised in the most appropriate way, in order to make money function well as a medium of exchange. Failure to integrate the two theories is, in our opinion, too great an abstraction of reality. For in a realistic analysis the monetary phenomena are not merely reflections of and reactions to activities and changes in the real sector.

It is more realistic to say that an autonomous monetary mechanism exists which exceeds the ideas of the naive quantity theory. In modern economies all economic activities are in fact characterized by real, as well as by monetary aspects.

Although in the Keynesian theory a start was made towards integration of the real and the monetary sectors, by introducing money as an asset, in these reflections the comparative-static approach remains the focal point.

In economic theory, the question has regularly arisen as to how far the growth rate of the money supply and the rate of inflation, could influence the development of the economy in the long run. This boils down basically to the question whether money – dynamically considered – is neutral or not.

The fact is, one can wonder whether and – if so – how an alternative rate of growth of the money supply influences the equilibrium values of the real variables in the long run. In spite of the large number of publications after the second World War dealing with capital accumulation and economic growth problems, very little attention has been paid to integration of the monetary factors in the growth process.

In economic literature, the idea prevails or has prevailed till recently that the growth theory is one of real variables. Most growth models are real models in that they concentrate almost exclusively on the real economic variables and pay little or no attention to the monetary aspects of the growth process. This is fully justified, if it can be indicated that the monetary factors exercise no influence at all on the development of the real course of the economic process, in other words: that money is neutral in the long run. The models we refer to which have been developed during the last decades, explaining the process of capital accumulation, technical progress and economic growth, omit or minimize the influence of the monetary aspects.[1]

The neo-classical standard growth model with one sector confines itself to the case of a real economy, in which the economy will converge in the long term to a rate of growth, which is determined by the autonomous supply factors, viz. the rate of population growth and of technical progress. In the long run, economic growth acquires the character of an equilibrium growth process in that national product and capital have the same growth rate. An equilibrium and constant capital-output ratio results from this.[2]

The operation of the price mechanism will always take care that effective demand tallies with the production which comes about at full employment. Abstraction of the monetary variables in the traditional growth model is, in our opinion, more of a temporary simplification of the problems than a permanent omission.

It is safe to say that until the mid-sixties the theory of economic growth concentrated mainly on the building of real models. During

1. For a good survey of the real growth theory readers are referred in this context to F. Hahn and R. Matthews, The theory of economic growth, a survey, *The Economic Journal*, December, 1964, pp. 779–902. A book which provides good insight into the real growth models of the Harrod-Domar type, the neo-classical and the Cambridge growth models (Kaldor, Champernowne and others) is D. Hamberg's, *Models of economic growth*, 1971.

2. F. de Roos and D. Schouten, *Groeitheorie*, 1962 and J. Meade, *A neo-classical theory of economic growth*, 1961.

the fifties and sixties the theoretical publications about economic growth referred especially to modifications and expansions of either the Keynesian complementarity and demand models of Harrod and Domar, or the neo-classical supply models in which a substitution of factors of production is supposed (Solow, Meade and others). These modifications and expansions of the basic model emerged in the introduction of endogenous technical progress, the different suppositions with regard to saving behaviour, the developing of "more-sector" models, the introduction of the concept of heterogeneous capital goods, and so on.

For the first time in 1955, Tobin made an attempt to insert monetary factors into theoretical discussions about the growth of the economy. He laid the foundation for one of the approaches in the monetary growth theory, viz. the neo-classical monetary growth theory, which comes up for discussion in detail in the following chapter. Johnson assumes at the end of his meanwhile very well-known and comprehensive article 'Monetary theory and policy' in 1962, 'almost nothing has yet been done to break monetary theory loose from the mould of short run equilibrium analysis conducted in abstraction, from the process of growth and accumulation and to integrate it with the rapidly developing literature on economic growth'.[3] The challenge implied in this proposition has not remained unanswered by theoretical researchers. Since the second half of the sixties the situation on the 'model market' has changed considerably. From that time in growth theory, the monetary variables have been emphasized to an increasing degree and ingenious thoughts have been developed to illustrate in a great number of aspects the significance of the monetary sector in the growth process.

The aim of the monetary growth models, which have been brought out in the past decade, is to provide some insight into the operation and the influence of monetary policy in a growing economy. Thus the monetary growth theory has a double function. First of all it tries to create a theoretical framework, enabling us to bring about a significant integration of the monetary growth theory and the real growth theory. Next it enables us to trace the possible consequences of this integration for the long-term problems in monetary policy.

3. H. Johnson, Monetary theory and policy, *American Economic Review*, June, 1962, p. 377–378.

The monetary growth theory deals with the introduction of monetary factors when the growth process is explained.

In other words: the monetary growth theory studies the influence of money and monetary policy on the development of nominal and real variables in a growing economy and can be considered as such as a new field or a further specialization within the broad framework of the growth theory.

In recent years much attention has been paid to the monetary growth theory in economic literature. This has led to a great variety in presuppositions, definitions, interpretations and theoretical results, which have been brought out in publications concerning the integration of the monetary and the growth theories.

It is our purpose to survey in the following chapters the development and the present state of affairs in this new field of theoretical economics. Referring to the distinction made by Stein at the conference 'On money and economic growth' in 1968, we shall base our study on two aspects. On the one hand, a more neo-classical view, focusing on the concept of equilibrium growth and in which capital accumulation is always equal to ex-ante savings; on the other hand an analysis, which can be indicated as the Keynes-Wicksell model.[4]

In the last-mentioned theory, in which disequilibrium-dynamics are the very focal point, the demand for goods is emphasized more and the analysis supposes an independent saving and investment function. Further in this analysis it is postulated that prices will only change, if a discrepancy exists between total demand for and total supply of goods in the economy. In other words: prices change only when the markets are not in equilibrium (Walrasian excess-demand hypothesis). This variant of the monetary growth theory can be considered as a generalization of the well-known short run macro-models in a growing economy.

Though in many well-known growth theories possible monetary influences are pointed out, the essential part is still an analysis of the real variables and only indirect significance has been attached to the monetary factor. This shift in emphasis goes so far that even though the adjustment process in the neo-classical model implies

4. J. Stein, Introduction, *Journal of Money, Credit and Banking*, May 1969, pp. 131–137. The conference was held in June 1968 at Brown University, Providence, Rhode Island.

true monetary phenomena, they are not explicitly brought out in the model. This one-sided emphasis on the real variables might perhaps be explained by the fact that as a rule the money supply is assumed to be completely elastic and does not, therefore, form a restrictive factor in the growth process, as may be the case with the factors of production. Besides, the production of money occupies the production capacity to a negligible extent, so that from this point of view money does not restrict the growth of real production either.[5]

Another explanation for the slight interest in the monetary factors is related to the time-period. Growth theoretical analysis concentrates consciously on the long-run aspects of economic development. The period (corresponding to the length of the business-cycle in which the influence of the monetary variables is expressed) is left out of consideration. Then a separation comes about between the short and the long run theories, between the business cycle and the structural development of the economy. Next – in connection with the above mentioned – the real growth theory will mostly proceed from the conception of equilibrium growth by which on the one hand the analysis can be simplified considerably, on the other hand the model becomes more sophisticated.

This is particularly apparent when the government authorities become 'growth-conscious' and demand practically applicable recommendations from the theorist to stimulate economic growth.

From the point of view of practical economic policy it is more necessary to study disequilibrium growth and dynamic adjustment processes to attain a synthesis of the business cycle theory and the growth theory. If one wishes to analyse adjustment processes in the short and medium-long term or disturbances of the growth process, an obvious step is to add money to the real variables as an essentially determining factor for the issue of the economic process. This is confirmed by the discussions on the effectiveness and significance of monetary measures in the framework of a stabilization policy.[6]

As has been stated before, Tobin developed in 1955 a dynamic model, which in its structure is neo-classical, but also contains Key-

5. A. G. Chandavarkar, Money and economic growth, *Economia Internazionale*, 1965, p. 85–93.
6. H. Abele, Ueber geldwirtschaftliche Wachstumsmodelle, *Zeitschrift für Nationalökonomie*, Band 30, 1970, p. 125–158.

nesian elements in that two investment alternatives are distinguished, viz. money and real capital goods.[7] In the modern capital theoretical approach of monetary theory the asset function of money is emphasized. The neo-quantity theory of the Chicago school (Friedman c.s.) and the modern portfolio-theory of the University of Yale (Tobin c.s.) have some features in common. According to the conceptions of both schools, monetary theory has become an integrated part of a general theory of choices, or otherwise expressed, of a general theory of the holding of wealth assets. This implies that the demand for money can be analysed as a decision concerning the composition of the portfolio. Money is considered as an asset and bears in this way a competitive, or substitutive relation to the other wealth assets (real capital goods, financial assets and so on) when decisions are made as to the composition of the portfolio. In Tobin's theoretical analysis the economic agents can choose holding their savings, and so their total wealth, in one of the two assets. This not only requires decisions on the absolute amount of savings from the available income (wealth accumulation), but also a decision with regard to the composition of the portfolio (wealth composition). Tobin expresses all this as follows: Fisher and Keynes, among others, have drawn the useful and fruitful analytical distinction between choices affecting the disposition of income and choices affecting the disposition of wealth. The first set of choices determines how much is saved rather than consumed and how much wealth is accumulated. The second set determines in what forms savers hold their savings, old as well as new'.[8] Whereas in the real growth theory savings determine the capital accumulation (the only wealth asset), in the monetary growth theory it rather holds that the capital goods as a wealth component have assumed a competitive position with other assets as a component in the portfolio.

Now it is necessary to introduce a behaviour relation which represents the choice problems mentioned above. Tobin uses the analysis developed by Markovitz concerning the optimum composition of the portfolio, by which the principle of marginal cost and marginal revenue is introduced in monetary theory. If one confines oneself

7. J. Tobin, A dynamic aggregative model, *Journal of Political Economy*, April 1955, p. 103–115.

8. J. Tobin, Money and economic growth, *Econometrica*, October, 1965, p. 671.

to equilibrium situations, one sees that, if the expected rates of return of both assets are equal, the economic agents are indifferent to the composition of the portfolio. This is the most simple conception of investor behaviour in the two asset-model in question.

Under these circumstances the portfolio will be composed one-sidedly, though the investor accepts any given combination of the assets. If, on the other hand, the rates of return are not equal, the portfolio will be composed one-sidedly of that asset with the highest rate of return, relatively speaking. With a more realistic approach, both assets will be hold, the division taking place according to the relative yields of the two assets. The degree of risk of the wealth components also plays a part when the portfolio is compiled.[9] If one starts from uncertainty with regard to the expected rate of return and/or from incomplete markets, one might postulate a higher rate of return of real capital goods than of money in order to achieve a balanced portfolio. This is due to the higher degree of liquidity of the cash-balances.[10] For, beside the real rate of return of money, which is equal to the rate of deflation, money has the advantage over real capital goods of a higher degree of liquidity. Particularly if uncertainties are taken into account this higher degree of liquidity must be expressed in the requirement formulated above. Regardless of the behaviour relation one applies the rates of return and the degree of risk of the two assets play a decisive part in the composition of the amount of the assets held.

Though no-one has yet succeeded in developing in an elaborate study a generally-accepted and a practicably-applicable monetary theory, which is at the same time an integral part of the general business cycle – and growth theory, the first key-stones for such a theory have been laid.

The intention in the following analysis is to present the main relations and results connected with the problem, and explain how a different rate of monetary expansion influences the real variables, particularly the equilibrium value of per capita income, of the real cash balances per head and of capital intensity. This comparative-

9. J. Tobin, *Econometrica*, October, 1965, op. cit. p. 676–679 and by the same author, *Journal of Political Economy*, April, 1955, op. cit. p. 106–107.

10. D. Levhari and D. Patinkin, The role of money in a simple growth model, *American Economic Review*, September, 1968, p. 715.

dynamic question concerns the neutrality of money in a framework of growth theory. Two different aspects are attached to the question of the neutrality of money. Firstly, the influence of a change in the absolute amount of money (and hence of the absolute price level) on the equilibrium values of the real variables as is the case in a comparative-static analysis. Secondly, the influence of a change in the growth rate of the nominal quantity of money (and hence in the growth rate of the price level) on the equilibrium values of the real variables in the system.[11]

We focus particularly on the latter comparative-dynamic aspect in our study, in the course of which we shall examine how far alternative growth rates of the quantity of money can influence the equilibrium values of the real variables. Under certain circumstances there can be a question of an optimum growth rate of the quantity of money, which – given the natural rate of growth – represents an optimum rate of inflation.[12]

In chapter 2 dealing with the neo-classical interpretation of the monetary growth theory, it will be indicated first of all how the introduction of money as a competitive asset, beside physical capital goods, can result in a lower equilibrium value of capital intensity and of production per head. ('Tobin-paradox'). Next it will be examined how a change in the rate of monetary growth can change the composition of the portfolio through a change in the rate of inflation. The resulting substitution process in the wealth-sector will, in turn, have repercussions for the equilibrium values of that real variables. Tobin's rather strange conclusion that a pure introduction of money as a wealth component would reduce the equilibrium value of capital intensity, is due to the fact that he only considers money in its function as an asset.

11. J. Tobin, The neutrality of money in growth models, a comment, *Economica*, February 1967, p. 69; A. L. Marty: The optimal rate of growth of money, *Journal of Political Economy*, July-August 1968, p. 869. D. Levhari and D. Patinkin *American Economic Review*, September 1968, op. cit. p. 732–733 and H. Abele, *Zeitschrift für Nationalökonomie*, 1970, op. cit. p. 132.

12. M. Friedman, The optimum quantity of money, in *The optimum quantity of money and other essays*, London 1969, p. 1–50. See also A. L. Marty, *Journal of Political Economy*, July-August 1968 op. cit. p. 860–873; J. Tobin, Notes on optimal monetary growth, *Journal of Political Economy*, July-August 1968, p. 833–859; E. S. Phelps, Comment, *Journal of Political Economy*, July-August 1968, p. 881–885.

The implications of money as a medium of exchange will be discussed in detail. On the one hand money will be considered as a consumer good, which yields services to the wealth-owner and can act as a substitute for the consumption of material goods and services, on the other hand the significance of money as a producer good will be analysed. It will transpire that an analysis of money as a consumer good and/or as a producer good resulting in the unambiguous positive relation between alternative growth rates of the quantity of money and the equilibrium value of capital intensity, as emerges in Tobin's model, ceasing to exist.

Finally in this chapter attention will be paid to the stability of the neo-classical monetary growth model. This stability proves to be critically dependent on the value of coefficient (β) in the price-expectations equation. This coefficient is an indication for the speed with which economic agents adapt their expectations concerning the rate of inflation if a difference has come about between the actual and the expected rate of inflation.

In Chapter 3 the conceptions existing in the literature with regard to the so-called Keynes-Wicksell model in the monetary growth theory will be reviewed. The essential feature of the Keynes-Wicksell analysis, as we said earlier, lies in the specification of an independent saving and investment function, and the explicit representation of a Walrasian price equation. With this we mean that prices will only change as far as disequilibrium on the commodity markets exists. This supposition contrasts sharply with the neo-classical postulate of a continuous equilibrium on all markets. The neoclassical two-asset model assumes a price flexibility such that there will always be equilibrium between the demand for and supply of cash-balances. There is no need for a specification of an independent investment function, since all savings are transformed direct into real capital goods. Moreover the Keynes-Wicksell model distinguishes between three assets, viz. money, bonds and physical capital goods. From the Keynes-Wicksell analysis it will appear that, within the suppositions of the model, there is no unambiguous relation between alternative rates of growth of money supply and the equilibrium values of the real variables of the system.

In chapter 4 the neo-classical and the Keynes-Wicksell models will be brought together in one model, which in the equilibrium situation in the long run has the features of the neo-classical theory described in chapter 2, whereas in the analysis of the short run the features of the Keynes-Wicksell model are most salient.

We should like to point out that, for the sake of simpilicity, we shall not be discussing a number of important determinants of economic growth in our strictly theoretical expositions. For instance, the rate of population growth and population participation in the labour process are assumed to be exogenously given and constant.

The determinants of technological development are not discussed, nor is attention paid to certain limits which can be set to economic growth and are related to a given supply of raw materials and so on. The monetary growth theory at issue should preferably be considered, from the economic policy viewpoint, as a partial analysis of the problem of economic growth, the more so as important sociological and political aspects of this problem are not raised. For in practice there is an interaction between economic, sociological and political factors, which has an essential impact on practical economic policy.

Finally we must emphasize that the theoretical explanations always refer to a closed economy. This means that the monetary influence of the balance of payments, which can be very substantial in a system of fixed exchange rates, is omitted.

2. The neo-classical monetary growth theory

2.1. Introduction

As we pointed out in the general introduction to the monetary growth theory, the monetary growth models which have been developed in the last decade, can be divided into two categories: viz. the neo-classical and the Keynes-Wicksell analyses. Neo-classical analysis, which we shall be dealing with in this chapter, is characterized by the suppositions that the rate of capital formation is always equal to planned savings, and that equilibrium always exists on all markets, regardless of the degree of price change.[1] The monetary policy, expressed in changes in the rate of growth of money can influence – within the suppositions of the model – the equilibrium value of the capital intensity in the long run through the operation of the real cash-balance effect, which has been inserted as an argument in the consumption function.

If the real cash-balances are inserted in the production function, another mechanism is active, by means of which the monetary policy will be able to influence the real variables of the system.[2]

We can also express it in such a way that the monetary factor in the form of real cash-balances appears in the neo-classical mone-

1. The authors, who represent this neo-classical approach, include: J. Tobin: Money and economic growth, *Econometrica*, October, 1965, p. 671–684; and by the same author: The neutrality of money in growth models, a comment, *Economica*, February, 1967, p. 69–72. A. Marty, Notes on money and economic growth, *Journal of Money, Credit and Banking*, May 1969, p. 252–265 and by the same author: The optimal rate of growth of money, *Journal of Political Economy*, July-August 1968, p. 860–873. H. Johnson, The neo-classical one sector growth model: a geometrical exposition and extension to a monetary economy, *Economica*, August 1966, p. 265–287: M. Sidrauski: Inflation and economic growth, *Journal of Political Economy*, December 1967, p. 796–810; D. Levhari and D. Patinkin The role of money in a simple growth model, *American Economic Review*, September 1968. p. 713–755.
2. D. Levhari and D. Patinkin, *American Economic Review*, September, 1968, op. cit. p. 737.

tary growth theory, in accordance with the monetary tradition of the Chicago school, either as a consumer good, by which the services ('convenience services') of these cash-balances have been inserted in the disposable income, or as a producer good in the production function. In the neoclassical monetary growth theory, a dichotomy is brought about as it were with regard to the meaning of the real cash-balances. The questions facing us are, firstly, under which circumstances changes in the growth rate of the money supply, and so in the real cash-balances per head, will influence the consumption function. And secondly, how far the existence of real cash-balances can influence the production process.[3]

The view which underlies the latter conception is that these cash-balances make free factors of production for the proper production of goods and services, and these factors of production are used in a pure barter economy upon the direct exchange of goods and services. These freed factors of production perform a 'brokerage-function' in a pure barter economy, putting potential buyers and sellers in touch with each other. The introduction of money as an explicit medium of exchange enlarges the productivity as a consequence of the ensuing greater scope for specialization. Patinkin and Levhari say in this context: money is held only because it enables the economic unit in question to acquire or produce a larger quantity of commodities in the usual sense of the term.'[4]

Before moving on to this more advanced theory, it is desirable to present Tobin's analysis (1965). This analysis, worked out in detail by Johnson, has formed the basic principle for the models developed later on.

Tobin's monetary growth theory starts from the supposition that three markets can be distinguished in the economy: the commodity market, the labour market and the money market. It is supposed that the labour market is always in equilibrium. In the analysis the producer households are not considered as separate decision units, but form – as it were – one whole with the consumer households. The latter category forms the savings, which can be used for expan-

3. J. Stein, Monetary growth theory in perspective, *American Economic Review*, March 1970, p. 87.
4. D. Levhari and D. Patinkin, *American Economic Review*, September 1968, op. cit. p. 737.

sion of the physical capital goods and of the real cash-balances. The interactions of the households on the different markets are explained by a Walrasian 'tâtonnement'' process, which means that equilibrium always exists on all markets together. In other words: the validity of Walras' law is taken as a starting point.

Tobin, as an important representative of the neo-classical monetary growth theory, joins money and government bonds in his analysis and works with one representative financial asset, outside money or government money. This procedure is justified by the fact that within the framework of economic growth with inflation and deflation, the wealth-assets can be divided into assets with a fixed nominal value (money and government bonds) and assets for which this does not hold, viz. goods.

This distinction has been based upon the possible risk of changes in wealth as a consequence of price changes.

Thanks to this method of aggregation the problem of equilibrium concerning the composition of the portfolio is reduced to a weighing out process on the margin of monetary wealth and physical capital goods. In this respect Tobin closely follows the monetary tradition of the Cambridge School (Lavington and Pigou) according to which bonds and money were also joined and a choice was made, for wealth composition, between money and capital goods.[5] The demand functions for the two assets, physical capital goods and real cash-balances (outside-money) are not independent of each other, due to the given budget constraint, which implies that the value of the total real wealth is always equal to the sum of real cash-balances and physical capital goods. This means that in the neo-classical monetary growth theory it is sufficient to specify one of the two demand functions, because the other can be derived from the budget constraint. In other words: the portfolio behaviour of the private sector is completely described by specifying for instance the demand function for real cash-balances. In Tobin's view this means that a decrease in the demand for real cash-balances, for instance as a consequence of a relative decrease in the real rate of return of this asset or as a consequence of a relative increase in

5. A. Leyonhufvud, *On Keynesian economics and the economics of Keynes*, New York, 1968, p. 143.

the yield of capital, is fully reflected in an equal increase in the demand for capital goods.

It is now fairly simple to analyse how an increase of the quantity of money acts upon the portfolio balance. The monetary impulse will lead initially to an increase of the real wealth, from which an excess-supply of real cash-balances and an excess-demand for real capital goods results. The price level (price of existing capital goods) will increase in order to restore the equilibrium in the portfolio.

The supposition in the neo-classical monetary growth theory (Tobin, Sidrauski, Johnson, Levhari, and Patinkin) that there is always an equilibrium on all markets, including the market for wealth-assets, implies that the price level is so flexible that possible excess-demand and excess-supply situations on the markets are immediately eliminated.

Finally, there are many variants of the neo-classical monetary growth theory in the literature. This often makes it difficult to trace the relations between the different models, the more so as some authors (Tobin and Johnson) prefer a verbal and graphical interpretation of the theory, whereas other authors stand for a more mathematical presentation (Levhari, Patinkin and Sidrauski). Considerable abstraction from reality will occur to enable examination of certain aspects of the interaction of the real and monetary phenomena in an economic growth model. For example, it is always supposed that a constant financial structure of the economy exists. Consequently no attention is paid to the fundamental question how a monetary economy develops, to the institutional changes within the money and credit system, which influence the saving and investment process, and so on.

2.2. Tobin's monetary growth theory (implications of the asset-structure)

The views developed in this section are based especially upon the most simple version of the monetary growth theory, as was developed by Tobin (1965) and Johnson (1966). Tobin's original explanations, in which a second asset beside physical capital goods was introduced in the standard macro-economic model of the neo-classical growth theory, have had a stimulating influence on theoretical research concerning the integration of the monetary and the real growth theories since the middle of the sixties.[6]

First of all it is worth illustrating further the presuppositions upon which the analysis is based. In accordance with the traditional neo-classical growth models, we start from a linear, homogeneous production function and 'diminishing returns to substitution'. This means that the average as well as the marginal products can be expressed in terms of capital intensity. The relevant production function is:

$$Y = F(K, L)$$

in which the symbols stand for

Y : production
K : capital
L : labour

With this production function, per capita production can be expressed as a function of capital intensity:

$$y = f(k)$$

where

y : production per head
k : capital intensity

The marginal product of capital is positive and decreasing, the result being

$$f'(k) > 0 \text{ and } f''(k) < 0$$

Further it is supposed that as a consequence of full wage and price

6. Foley and Sidrauski did not start in their book from one, homogeneous, macro-economic good, but developed a (neo-classical) monetary growth model with two sectors, in which the relative price of capital goods is variable in terms of consumer goods and plays a crucial part in investment behaviour. See D. Foley and M. Sidrauski, *Monetary and fiscal policy in a growing economy*, New York, 1971.

flexibility, the available labour supply will always be completely used and that the population grows exponentially and exogenously at a fixed rate. We omit the problems concerning the technical progress.

Our theoretical reflections are based on a simple saving hypothesis, viz. a fixed savings ratio, taken over the disposable income. The savings can be held in the form of real cash-balances and real capital goods, the division or the composition of the portfolio being dependent on the real rates of return of both assets. Next, full competition on the markets of factors of production and goods is supposed.

Now Tobin introduces the monetary factor in the form of 'non-interest bearing outside money', as it is termed. This represents a completely liquid financial asset from the monetary authorities to private economic agents, who consider it as an addition to their net-wealth.[7] The government brings this money into circulation by means of transfer payments, and withdraws it from circulation by taxes. This is independent of the existing individual cash-balances, because otherwise the economic agents would consider the transfer payments as an interest payment pro rata their cash-balances. If the transfer payments were dependent on the existing individual cash-balances, changes in the rate of monetary expansion could not influence the desired real cash balances.

For in that case the real rate of return of real cash-balances (nominal rate of interest minus the rate of inflation) will not change, and consequently the substitution process between real cash-balances and capital goods cannot set in.

It is through the transmission mechanism of the relative rates of return of both wealth-assets that the monetary policy can influence the real variables in the neo-classical monetary growth theory.

The most important influence this government money can have on the operation of the economy is through the disposable income, which variable determines the savings of the economic agents. The

7. Pesek and Saving advance in their book *Money, Wealth and economic theory*, 1967, that the distinction between inside and outside money introduced by Gurley and Shaw is incorrect. They prove that both forms of money form net-wealth for the public, provided that the money is non-interest bearing. Readers are also referred in this context to H. Johnson, Inside money, outside money, income, wealth and welfare in monetary theory, *Journal of Money, Credit and Banking*, February 1969, p. 30–45.

disposable income, which is of fundamental importance in the Tobin growth model is equal to the sum of the income obtained from current production, plus the change in real cash-balances held by the economic subjects. Since the real cash-balances are considered as a net-wealth component, a fall in the price level at constant nominal cash-balances or a rise of the nominal cash-balances at one and the same price-level can be interpreted as an increase in wealth. This wealth increase is then added to the real income, from which the total disposable income results. The disposable income of the economic agents can be rendered as follows:

$$Y_B = Y + \frac{d\left(\frac{M}{p}\right)}{dt} = Y + \frac{M}{p}(\mu - \pi) \tag{1}$$

or in terms per head:

$$y_B = y + m(\mu - \pi) = f(k) + m(\mu - \pi) \tag{1'}$$

in which the following sense is attached to the symbols:

M = nominal quantity of money (outside money)
p = price level
μ = rate of growth of the money supply (rate of monetary expansion)
π = rate of growth of the price level (rate of inflation)
$m = \frac{M}{pL}$: real cash-balances per head
Y : national income
Y_B : disposable income

Otherwise formulated: real disposable income is equal to real national income plus the real value of the increase in the nominal quantity of money, ($\mu M/p$) minus the decrease of the real value of the existing balances as a result of an increase of the price level ($\pi M/p$).

Further, constant equilibrium is assumed to exist between the supply of and the demand for real cash-balances per head. This equilibrium in the monetary sector is brought about by adequate adjustments in the price level. For, if there are disturbances in the equilibrium the economic agents can immediately restore the desired real cash-balances. If an excess supply of real cash-balances exists, this surplus will be offered on the market, causing prices of goods to increase and the real value of the cash-balances to decrease. With an excess demand for real cash-balances a process will occur in an inverse direction. The price level determines the real value of the economic agents' wealth, as does its division over the two wealth components already mentioned in the introduction, viz. money and real capital goods. If the actual division agrees with the desired division, it is termed a portfolio-balance.

Tobin says in this context: 'portfolio balance is assumed to be the necessary and sufficient condition for price stability'.[8] As will appear later on, the above-mentioned supposition is of great importance in the framework of the stability of the neo-classical monetary growth model.

Tobin's model distinguishes between two kinds of assets which can be held by the economic agents, viz. physical capital goods and real cash balances. As we indicated in the introduction, the rates of return of these assets play an essential part when savings are divided among the two investment possibilities. The real rate of return of the capital goods (r) is equal, upon repayment of the factors of production in accordance with their marginal productivities, to the marginal product of capital, so that $r = f'(k)$.

The expected rate of return of the real cash-balances is determined by the expected rate of growth of the price level. The real rate of return of the real cash-balances ($-\pi$) is negative when a positive rate of inflation is expected, zero at a constant price level and positive at an expected rate of deflation. For the sake of simplicity, it is supposed that the expected growth rate of the price level or the expected rate of inflation is equal to the existing equilibrium value of the rate of inflation.

The last mentioned variable is determined by the growth rate of the nominal quantity of money per head.[9] In the equilibrium growth situation the real cash-balances per head (m) are constant. This

8. J. Tobin, A dynamic aggregative model, *Journal of Political Economy*, April 1955, p. 105.
9. H. Johnson, *Essays in monetary economics*, 1967, p. 162.

means, that the rate of inflation (π) is equal to the algebraic difference between the growth rate of the nominal quantity of money (μ) and the rate of population growth (n).

The following can be said as regards the demand function for real cash-balances. The economic agents hold part of the national income in the form of real cash-balances. This desired real cash-balance ratio (λ), defined as the real cash-balances in proportion to the national income, is negatively related to the opportunity costs attached to the holding of cash-balances. These opportunity costs can be represented as the difference between the real rate of return of capital goods (r) and the real rate of return of the cash-balances ($-\pi$). The opportunity costs can consequently be rendered as ($r + \pi$). If the foregoing is taken into account the following applies as a condition for a portfolio-balance.

$$\frac{M^s}{pL} = \frac{M^d}{pL} = \lambda(r + \pi)y$$

$$\text{in which } \lambda = \frac{M^d}{pY} = \lambda(r + \pi) \text{ and } \lambda'(r + \pi) < 0 \tag{2}$$

This equation shows that the demand for real cash-balances per head (M^d/pL) is proportionally related to the national income per head, in which λ acts as a proportionality factor.

An important supposition in the neo-classical monetary growth model lies in the continuous equality between the supply of and the demand for real cash balances (equation 2). According to a number of authors this means that changes in the price level are not explained. The equilibrium postulate with regard to the portfolio is, they argue, as a 'deus ex machina', from which the price level can be derived. Hahn remarks in this context: '. . . the price of money was changing because this was required for asset equilibrium and not because any reason was adduced why, in fact, it should change'.[10] What this crucial supposition amounts to in essence is that the price

10. F. Hahn, On money and growth, *Journal of Money, Credit and Banking*, May 1969, p. 183. J. Stein *American Economic Review*, March 1970, op.cit. p. 97 and M. Bolle, Geld Wachstum und Beschäftigung, *Zeitschrift für die gesamte Staatswissenschaft*, March 1973, p. 8–9.

level is not explained by the operation of some economic adjustment process, but only results from a formal equilibrium condition.

Relation (2) is of essential importance – as will appear later on – for the stability of the model. Starting from a constant savings ratio over the disposable income, total savings can be expressed as follows:

$$S_B = \sigma_B Y_B \tag{3}$$

in which σ_B represents the fixed savings ratio over the disposable income. These total savings can be apparent on the one hand in an expansion of capital goods, on the other hand in an enlargement of the real cash-balances, which are required in a growing economy. All this can be reproduced as follows:

$$S_B = S_M + S_K \tag{4}$$

in which:

S_B: total savings from the disposable income
S_M: savings used for expansion of the capital goods (dK/dt)
S_k: savings which are held in real cash-balances $(d\frac{M}{p}/dt)$

With an equilibrium growth, the need for real cash-balances for transaction purposes will increase in accordance with the natural rate of growth. A specified part of total savings is necessary to increase the real value of the cash-balances accordingly.

If λ represents the desired real cash-balance ratio and g the rate of growth of the national income, determined by the rate of population growth, we obtain the term for the increase of real cash-balances:

$$\frac{d\frac{M}{(p)}}{dt} = \lambda g Y$$

Therefore, if we take account of equation (1):

$$Y_B = Y(1 + \lambda g) \tag{5}$$

or in terms per head:

$$y_B = y(1 + \lambda g) \qquad (5')$$

If the above mentioned term for the change in the real cash-balances is taken into account, total savings per head can be derived from equations (3) and (4):

$$\sigma_B y_B = \frac{dK}{dt}\frac{1}{L} + \lambda g y \qquad (6)$$

By substitution of (5′) for (6) and taking account of equation (4), we obtain per capita savings, which are available for the expansion of per capita investments

$$\frac{S_M}{L} = \frac{dK}{dt}\frac{1}{L} = \sigma_B y\left[1 - \lambda g\left(\frac{1}{\sigma_B} - 1\right)\right] \qquad (7)$$

From the preceding we see that the real cash-balances on the one hand lead to greater total savings ($\sigma_B\ \lambda g y$), but that on the other hand from these total savings must be deducted the increase of the real cash-balances ($\lambda g y$) in order to obtain the savings which are intended for an extension of the real capital goods (S_M).

Since $1/\sigma_B > 1$, it can be concluded from equation (7) that part of the total savings is absorbed by the growth of the real cash-balances, so that the savings, which can be used for extending material capital goods, are smaller than in a pure real economy. Johnson maintains that, given the rate of economic growth (g), the larger the desired real-cash ratio (λ), the larger the absolute increase in real cash balances and, consequently, the drop in the real investment ratio will be.[11]

Assuming that the demand for real cash-balances is always in equilibrium with the supply, Tobin proves that the equilibrium value of the capital intensity (k_e) in this monetary model is repre-

11. H. Johnson 1967, op. cit. p. 164, Chapter IV. This volume of essays also includes the improved version of the article, published by Johnson in *Economica*, August 1966, op.cit. p. 265–287. See also J. Tobin's comment on this article in *Economica*, February 1967, op.cit. p. 69–72 and further H. Johnson, *Macro-economics and monetary theory, Lectures in economics*, I, 1971, p. 168–175.

sented by the equilibrium condition:

$$nk_e = \sigma_B y \left[1 - \lambda n\left(\frac{1}{\sigma_B} - 1\right)\right] \tag{8}$$

In the long-term equilibrium situation the rate of growth of the national income (g) will be equal to the rate of growth of the population (n). The above-mentioned equilibrium condition implies that the investments per head, which are required to provide the growing population with capital in order to maintain the equilibrium value of the capital intensity, are lower than in a real economy. In the real growth theory, real cash balances are not inserted, so that the second term between brackets in equation (8) is omitted and the equilibrium equation passes into the well-known relation:

$$nk_e = \sigma_B y. \tag{9}$$

With aid of equations (8) and (9) the relation between the equilibrium value of capital intensity in the real growth theory and the equilibrium value of capital intensity in the monetary growth theory can be reproduced by the term:

$$\frac{1}{1 - \lambda n\left(\frac{1}{\sigma_B} - 1\right)} > 1.$$

This term expresses the so-called Tobin-paradox, which implies that the equilibrium value of capital intensity in a monetary model is smaller than in a real model, because part of the total savings occurs in an accumulation of real cash-balances. Tobin assumes: 'Moreover it (the equilibrium capital intensity) is lower the higher the value of $b(= \lambda)$'.[12]

Because the desired real cash-balance ratio is a negative function

12. J. Tobin, *Economica*, February 1967, op.cit. p. 71, *Econometrica*, October 1965, op.cit. p. 681 and M. Sidrauski: *Journal of Political Economy*, December 1967, op.cit. p. 7. See also H. de Haan and S. Kuipers; Een onderzoek naar de invloed van monetaire factoren op het reële groeiproces in enkele traditionele theorieën van economische groei, *De Economist*, 1969, p. 292. **(Haarlem).**

of the rate of inflation (after all $\lambda' < 0$), the investment ratio will refer positively to this rate of inflation. This means that a more expansive monetary policy leads, given the natural rate of growth, to a higher equilibrium value of the rate of inflation and a lower real cash-balance ratio. The result of all this is a higher equilibrium value of capital intensity than the value belonging to a growth path with a lower rate of monetary growth. The above described relations can be further illustrated with the aid of the following graph, which has been quoted from Johnson.[13]

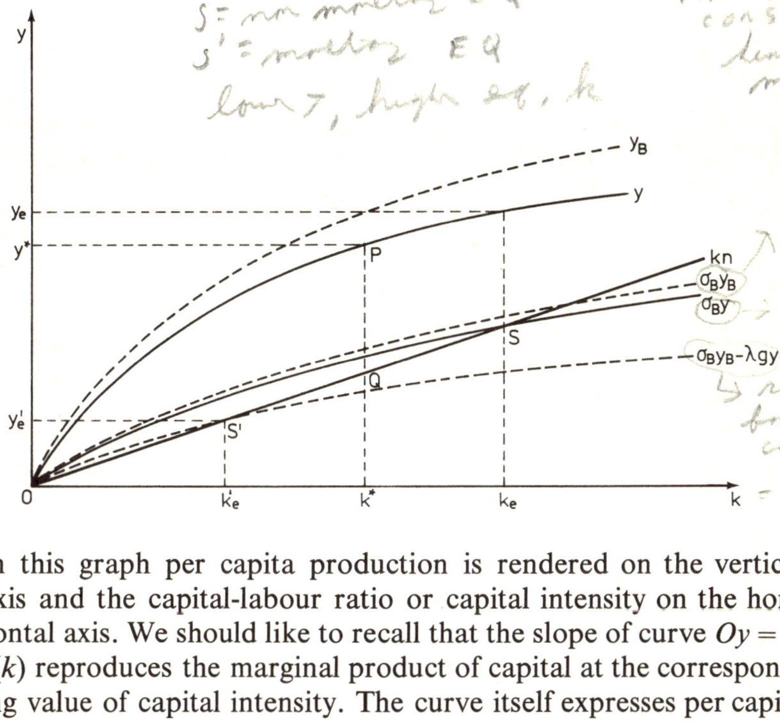

In this graph per capita production is rendered on the vertical axis and the capital-labour ratio or capital intensity on the horizontal axis. We should like to recall that the slope of curve $Oy = O$ $f(k)$ reproduces the marginal product of capital at the corresponding value of capital intensity. The curve itself expresses per capita income as a function of capital intensity. The vertical distance between the Oy-curve and the $O\sigma_B y$-curve represents consumption per head at the relevant value of capital intensity. Curve Okn, with the population growth rate as its slope, represents the rate of growth of capital goods required to maintain the equilibrium value of

13. H. Johnson, 1967, op.cit. p. 166 and D. Purvis, Introducing useful money into a growth model, *Canadian Journal of Economics*, August 1971, p. 377.

capital intensity. Equilibrium in the real model occurs where the curve of the savings which are fully transformed into real capital goods, cuts *Okn*-curve (*S*). In this point $kn = \sigma_B y$ or $n = \sigma_B y/k$ i.e. the rate of economic growth is equal to the savings ratio, divided by the capital output ratio. The equilibrium value of capital intensity and accordingly the production per head are Ok_e and Oy_e respectively. However, in the monetary model, equilibrium occurs in point S', at a lower equilibrium value of capital intensity (k_e'). and of production per head (y_e'). Because of the introduction of the monetary factor a new, higher curve arises for total savings ($O\sigma_B y_B$). If pure monetary savings are now subtracted, curve $O - (\sigma_B y_B - \lambda gy)$ results, which represents the available savings for expansion of real capital goods (see equation 7). The lower λ, the desired real cash-balance ratio, is (which will be the case at a lower rate of deflation or a higher rate of inflation) the higher the equilibrium value of the capital intensity will be. This means that the point of intersection of curve $O(\sigma_B y_B - \lambda gy)$ with curve *Okn* shifts more to the right. An upper limit arises in point *S*, where such a rate of inflation exists that the desired real cash balance ratio is reduced to a negligible amount.

The amount of real savings in the monetary model then tallies with that in the real model ($S_B = S_M$).

Johnson points out that in Tobin's analysis money is not neutral, in the sense that the degree of convergence to the equilibrium growth path depends on the rate of monetary expansion and that the features of this equilibrium growth path depend on the pursued monetary policy.[14] The author holds the view that within certain limits the monetary policy can be used to make the economy move to a growth path, in which the 'golden rule' is upheld and per capita consumption is maximised. This condition implies that the rate of profit (marginal product of capital) is equal to the natural growth rate of the economy and that the savings ratio equals the share of capital in total national income.[15] All this can be illustrated with the aid of the foregoing graph. Consumption per head can be raised

14. H. Johnson, 1967, op.cit. p. 167.

15. E. S. Phelps. The golden rule of accumulation, a fable for growthmen, *American Economic Review*, September 1961, p. 638–643. en C. C. von Weiszäcker, *Wachstum, Zins und Optimale Investitionsquote*, 1963.

by capital accumulation, if the marginal product of capital is larger than the natural rate of growth ($f'(k) > n$). Consumption per head is maximised in point P, where the marginal product of capital is equal to the natural rate of growth ($f'(k) = n$). The corresponding equilibrium value of capital intensity is k^* and consumption per head is PQ. Points on the production function to the right of point P, which corresponds to an equilibrium value of capital intensity which is larger than k^*, represent situations which are dynamically inefficient ($f'(k) < n$). Per capita consumption can be increased at any time by reducing savings and consequently by bringing about a lower equilibrium value of the capital intensity. If the saving behaviour in the economy is such that the real investment ratio according to the 'golden rule' condition is exceeded, this saving-surplus can be eliminated by bringing about a contraction in the money supply, producing a deflationary price development.

In our analysis the real cash-balance ratio will increase and lower savings will aim at enlarging the real capital goods. A reduction of the rate of monetary growth and the concomitant higher equilibrium value of the rate of deflation will lead to a substitution process in the portfolio, decreasing the equilibrium value of capital intensity with respect to the growth path with the higher rate of monetary growth. All this will lead to an increase of per capita consumption. In view of the suppositions on the economic agents' behaviour with regard to portfolio composition, a limit has been set to this deflationary policy. For investment in real capital goods will come to an end if the rate of return of real cash-balances exceeds the rate of return of the real capital goods.

On the other hand, if savings are such that the relevant optimum investment ratio, is not attained due to a great real cash-balance ratio (λ), and consequently too few savings are available for expansion of real capital goods, a more expansive monetary policy, accompanied by a higher equilibrium value of the rate of inflation can offer the solution of raising the investment ratio.

Under these circumstances the equilibrium value of capital intensity will be higher in comparison with the growth path with a lower rate of monetary growth. In this case too the monetary policy will result in an increase of consumption per head. The extreme limit is now formed by such a rate of inflation that the real cash-balances are reduced to a negligible amount so that savings in the economy are fully transformed into real capital goods. It is possible that the resulting investment ratio does not satisfy the condition of the 'golden rule' which maximizes consumption per head.[16]

We can conclude from Tobin's analysis that introduction of outside money, which forms an element of the economic subjects' net-wealth, beside the real capital goods, has a distinct influence on the real variables of the model through the amount of the real cash-balances. For, starting from an equilibrium growth path, a higher rate of monetary expansion will bring about a relative increase in the price level and a decrease in the real cash-balances per head, due to the rise in opportunity costs attached to the holding of these cash-balances. Because the real cash-balances have been inserted as an argument in the consumption function through the disposable income, the savings available for expansion of real capital goods will increase. Ultimately, compared with the starting situation, the economy will attain a new equilibrium growth path with a higher equilibrium value of capital intensity and per capita production. In this situation the relative change in the price level or the rate of inflation (π) is equal to the difference between the growth rate of the nominal quantity of money (μ) and the rate of production growth, which corresponds with the natural rate of growth (n). This proposition can be interpreted as a long-run version of the quantity theory.

Tobin holds the view that if money and material capital goods are good substitutes in the portfolio of economic agents, alternative growth rates of the nominal money supply are not neutral, but will rather be of essential influence on the features of the equilibrium growth path.

It is safe to say that Tobin was merely interested in a growth model including a monetary factor, and compared this with a real growth model. Special attention was paid to the long term, in which the economy attains an equilibrium growth path. The essence of his analysis lies in the fact that, in a monetary economy, savings can take the form of physical capital goods and/or of an expansion of the real cash-balances. For this reason, the equilibrium value of capital intensity (and therefore of per capita production, of the rate

16. J. Tobin, Notes on optimal monetary growth, *Journal of Political Economy*, July–August 1968, p. 838–839. A. L. Marty *Journal of Political Economy*, July–August 1968, op. cit. p. 860–863.

of profit and so on) has become dependent on the composition of the portfolio. Under these circumstances the equilibrium value of capital intensity in a monetary economy will be lower than in a real economy because of the pure introduction of an additional asset. However, a higher rate of monetary expansion will lead, ceteris paribus, to a drop in real cash-balances and a higher equilibrium value of capital intensity, given the behaviour hypothesis with regard to the different investment possibilities ($\lambda' < 0$). According to Tobin's analysis a change in the equilibrium value of the capital intensity can be brought about by influencing the wealth structure in the economy.

Tobin only analyses the asset which he introduces in its function as a store of value; it will naturally disappear if money can no longer perform this function well. This will be the case if the rate of inflation has attained such a value that the real rate of return of money as an asset has become negligible. At that moment the economy will be again in a situation which existed before the introduction of that asset. The economic agents' wealth will consist once more of physical capital goods only, as is the case in the real growth theory.

Tobin's model does not, therefore, give a clear distinction between the operation of a barter economy and a monetary economy. Tobin is aware of this, as is apparent from his remark to Johnson 'a comparison of a barter and a monetary economy in this fashion is probably unfair, since it leaves unanswered the question of how the barter economy performs the functions of money in a monetary economy.'[17] Presumably Tobin refers here to the function of money as a medium of exchange when transactions are performed. This function does not emerge explicitly in his analysis.

Tobin's conclusion that in a monetary economy the equilibrium value of the capital intensity (read: income per head) would be lower than in a barter economy, quite rightly comes Levhari and Patinkin, Johnson, Purvis and others to wonder why money will be introduced in the economy. Patinkin and Levhari wonder: 'Where are the vaunted advantages of a monetary economy?[18] It is as well to recall that the fact that the equilibrium value of capital intensity in the

17. H. Johnson, 1967, op. cit. p. 173, footnote 2, and D. Purvis, *Canadian Journal of Economics*, op. cit. p. 379.
18. D. Levhari and D. Patinkin, *American Economic Review*, September 1968, op. cit. p. 717.

monetary model is lower, does not necessarily need to imply that the relevant equilibrium value in a monetary economy is lower than that in a barter economy. The traditional real, 'non-monetary' growth models do really relate to a monetary economy. They are 'non-monetary' in that models are involved for a monetary economy, but the monetary factors are left out of consideration. Hahn remarks in this context: 'Present growth models which make no allowance for money are not barter models. No attention is paid to the economics of transactions and one must suppose that in this world the 'mediating' function of money is performed costlessly by some outside agency.'[19]

Patinkin and Levhari try to find a rational explanation for the holding of cash-balances by the economic subjects. Money must be able to perform other functions beside that of a store of value, if it is to be attractive for the economic agents to hold. Tobin's paradox finds its ultimate explanation in the fact that money is not considered as a consumer good nor as a producer good.

In the following two paragraphs we will go into the analysis developed in economic literature about the meaning of the real cash-balances in the consumption and the production sectors. It will then prove possible to solve the Tobin paradox, albeit that an unambiguous positive relation will no longer exist between the rate of monetary growth and the equilibrium value of capital intensity. Finally we wish to point out that for the sake of analytical simplicity we have chosen to deal separately with money as a consumer good, and as a producer good. However, this does not mean that money could not perform both these functions at the same time.

2.3. The implications of real cash-balances as a consumer good

2.3.1. Immaterial consumption of real cash-balances

Several results of Tobin's analysis have been changed by the theoretical view-points of the authors Johnson, Levhari and Patinkin.[20] These authors use another definition of disposable income and

19. F. Hahn, *Journal of Money, Credit and Banking*, May 1969, p. 172.
20. H. Johnson, 1967, op. cit. chapter IV, D. Levhari and D. Patinkin *American Economic Review*, September 1968, op. cit. p. 717–737.

consumption by explicitly taking account of the utility which the services of the cash-balances yield for economic subjects.

In the income conception in the preceding paragraph, real cash-balances have been inserted, which are related with the growth of the economy. The supposition of a demand for real cash-balances, implies according to Johnson, that these cash-balances yield a stream of 'convenience services' for the owners, non-physical yields, in the form of convenience, higher liquidity, certainty and so on, which are a component of real consumption as well as of real income.[21] The services of these cash-balances are added to the income from current production in the same way as the imputed income, resulting for example from the services of owner-occupied homes. In this context the disposable income per head is equal to the income per head obtained from the current production, plus the real value of the increase in money supply, corrected for the decrease of the real value of existing cash-balances, plus the value of the services of real cash-balances.

The equation of the disposable income from the preceding paragraph is then changed as follows:

$$Y_B = Y + \frac{M}{p}(\mu - \pi) + U \tag{1}$$

The imputed income which results from the amount of the real cash-balances is represented by the factor U. Johnson takes the line that the imputed part of income is fully consumed.

An important question, which immediately emerges concerns the valuation of the non-physical yields of real cash-balances (U) in the income definition.

Opinions on this are strongly divided in the relevant literature. Levhari and Patinkin hold the view that corresponding to the principles of welfare economics the imputed income of cash-balances has to be valued against the opportunity costs attached to the holding of the cash-balances.[22] As we have seen before, these costs are equal

21. H. Johnson, 1967, op. cit. p. 168, J. Stein, *American Economic Review*, 1970, op. cit. p. 94–95 and R. Crouch, A new approach to the monetisation of neo-classical growth models in A. Powell and R. Williams, *Econometric studies of macro and monetary relations*, 1973, p. 289–291.

22. D. Levhari and D. Patinkin, *American Economic Review*, September 1968, op. cit. p. 717.

to the difference between the real rate of return of the competing asset, real capital goods, (r) and the real rate of return of real cash-balances ($-\pi$). The opportunity costs attached to holding real cash-balances are then equal to ($r + \pi$), in Fisher's terms the nominal rate of interest. According to this approach the relevant function of the disposable income per head can be represented as follows:

$$y_B = y + m(\mu - \pi) + m(r + \pi). \tag{1'}$$

The real disposable income per head consists now of the following components: real national income per head, the change in the real cash-balances per head and the utility expressed in income, of the existing real cash-balances per head. The method of imputation used by Levhari and Patinkin has certain consequences. As emerges in the above equation the imputed income depends on the nominal interest-sensitivity of the demand for real cash-balances. If the demand for real cash-balances is interest inelastic/elastic, a higher rate of inflation, given the rate of return of capital, will enlarge/reduce the imputed income. An increase in opportunity costs for holding real cash-balances consequent on a higher rate of inflation will then lead to a less or to a more than proportional decrease in the demand for real cash-balances.

However Johnson has pointed out that assessment of the imputed income according to the principle of opportunity costs can lead to paradoxical results. As we know from the behaviour hypothesis with regard to the demand for money in the preceding analysis, the desired real cash-balance ratio (λ) varies inversely with the opportunity costs of holding cash-balances. This means that if the demand for real cash-balances is inelastic with regard to the opportunity costs, the method of valuation implies that the lower the cash-balance ratio (λ) the higher the imputed income will be. Besides, the imputed income share and so the disposable income would be lower if the demand for real cash-balances had reached satiety level (i.e. the opportunity costs of the real cash-balances have become equal to zero, if $-\pi = r$), that if this level had not yet been attained.[23] For this reason Johnson holds another view with regard to the

23. H. Johnson, 1967, op. cit. p. 171–172 (footnote 1) and A. H. Meltzer Money, intermediation and growth, *Journal of Economic Literature*, March, 1969, p. 45.

method of imputation. He values the non-physical returns of real cash-balances by means of the integral under the linear demand curve for real cash-balances. The demand curve indicates the relation between the opportunity costs and the demand for real cash-balances. This method implies that if the opportunity costs of holding real cash-balances are equal to zero, satiety level has been attained and the imputed income share is maximal (the consumer's surplus is maximised).

2.3.2. *Influence of the immaterial consumption effect according to Johnson*

Now we will examine the consequences of the two methods of assessing these non-physical returns of real cash-balances in determining the influence of the monetary factor on the real variables.

It is assumed in Johnson's analysis, as well as in that of Levhari and Patinkin, that the non-physical returns of these real cash-balances form a substitute for the consumption of physical goods and services. The insertion of non-physical returns of real cash-balances in the definition of the disposable income, as well as in that of the total consumption, leads to quite opposite conclusions on the influence of monetary policy on the real variables to those reached by Tobin. In his analysis the change in the amount of real cash-balances is considered as an income component, which is fully marked as saving, by which fewer savings are available for real capital accumulation. A more expansive monetary policy, which is expressed in a higher rate of growth of the money supply, has a growth-stimulating effect through a decrease in real cash-balances and an increase in real investments. Several rates of growth of the nominal quantity of money lead to a different degree of price rise, which is reflected in the opportunity costs attached to the holding of real cash-balances. The higher the rate of inflation, the fewer the economic agents' real cash-balances will be in relation to the real income.

In that real cash-balances have been included as an argument in the savings function, this relative decrease of the monetary wealth will result in a relatively higher physical investment ratio.

If, on the contrary, we start like Johnson, from the fact that the non-physical returns of existing real cash-balances are an income component, which is fully consumed, the consumption of physical goods and services can be smaller and the material investment ratio can be enlarged accordingly, with a fixed savings ratio over the disposable income.

This supposes partial replacement, as it were, of material consumption by immaterial consumption of the services of the real cash-balances. In this way, additional real savings will be formed, which are further used for expansion of material capital goods.

It is a well-known fact that at a given level of per capita production and a corresponding rate of profit, the desired real cash-balance ratio will vary inversely with the rate of inflation through the opportunity costs ($r + \pi$) for holding real cash-balances.

Consequently, if sole account is taken of the immaterial consumption-effect of non-physical returns of real cash-balances, the real savings and investment ratio will be higher, as the monetary authorities pursue a less expansive, or a more restrictive monetary policy. The lower rate of inflation and the concomitant greater real cash-balances imply higher non-physical returns of real cash-balances and will lead to a reduction of consumption of physical goods and services.[24] Johnson concludes that, as monetary policy is less expansive, which is expressed in a lower equilibrium value of the rate of inflation, the economy will attain an equilibrium situation with higher production per head. This proposition must again be qualified, as was the case in Tobin's analysis: the rate of deflation (the real rate of return of real cash-balances) may not exceed the real rate of return of material capital goods, because otherwise the investments will recede to a negligible amount.[25]

If, moreover we take account of Tobin's analysis and the influence of the real cash-balances as a component of the disposable income, from which total consumption (including immaterial consumption of the non-physical returns of the real cash-balances) is formed, one monetary policy leads to opposite effects concerning the influence of an alternative growth rate of the money supply on the real savings which are used for real capital accumulation. This influence has not been unambiguously established either.

Starting from a more expansive monetary policy, the real savings and investment ratio is influenced in two ways. On the one

24. H. Abele, Über geldwirtschaftliche Wachstumsmodelle, *Zeitschrift fur Nationalökonomie*, Band 30, 1970, p. 136.
25. H. Johnson, 1967, op. cit. p. 169.

hand, in a positive sense, through a change in the desired real cash-balances (Tobin's portfolio-effect), on the other hand in a negative sense through the influence of non-physical returns of real cash-balances (Johnson's consumption-effect). A higher rate of inflation resulting from a more expansive monetary policy will diminish desired real cash-balances, which form part of the disposable income, and so total consumption. However, a higher rate of inflation will reduce imputed income and immaterial consumption resulting from the amount of real cash-balances, and this will cause the material consumption of physical goods and services to increase and real savings (which consequently can lead to real investments) to decrease. On the one hand with a higher rate of inflation a growth-stimulating effect sets in (an increase of the equilibrium value of long-term production) as a result of the drop in desired real cash-balances; on the other hand we encounter a growth-retarding effect (a decrease of the equilibrium value of long-term production) as a result of the drop in non-physical returns of real cash-balances.

An analysis taking explicit account of the non-physical returns of wealth in the form of real cash-balances reveals two opposite influences on the equilibrium values of real variables when there is an exogenous change in the rate of growth of money.

In the first place for instance as a result of a lower rate of growth of the nominal quantity of money an increase of the desired real cash-balances will set in, having an adverse effect on the real savings-ratio. Further the greater real cash-balances will imply an increase in non-physical returns. From this an immaterial consumption-effect results, which has a positive effect on the real savings and investment ratio.

These effects are, however, determined by several factors. The portfolio-effect (Tobin), which has a negative effect on real savings depends on the relative rates of returns of both wealth components (real cash-balances and physical capital goods). On the other hand the immaterial consumption effect, with a positive effect on real savings, is determined by a process of marginal appraisal of the utility-yields of the services of real cash-balances and of physical consumer goods. The effects of a change in the rate of monetary expansion on the equilibrium value of capital intensity and of the other real variables can no longer be determined unambiguously, as was the case in Tobin's analysis. The ultimate influence has become dependent on the relative intensity of the two, above-mentioned effects, which work in opposite directions.

The relations described above between income from current production, disposable income, consumption and the meaning of the real cash-balances can be illustrated by the following graph.[26]

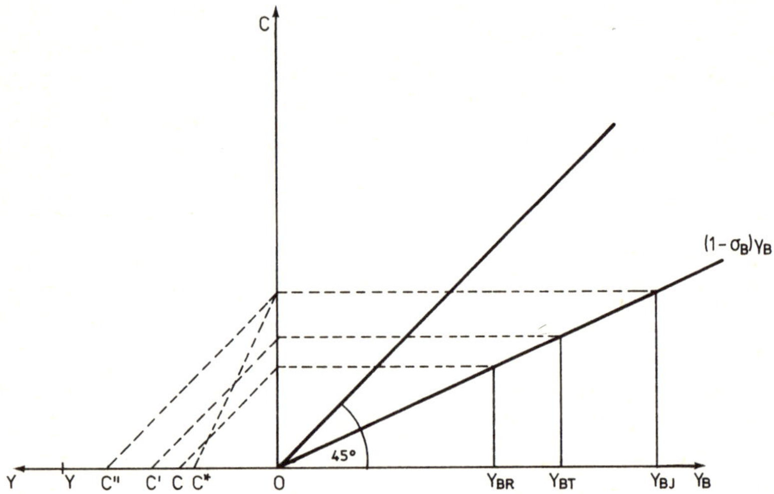

Production (Y) and the total consumption ratio $(1 - \sigma_B)$ are given and constant. The consumption function is represented by line $(1 - \sigma_B)\ Y_B$, because consumption is determined by the disposable income (Y_B). On the horizontal axis three different levels of the disposable income have been indicated, viz.:

(a) $Y_{BR} = Y$ (real economy)

(b) $Y_{BT} = Y + \dfrac{d\left(\dfrac{M}{p}\right)}{dt}$ (the Tobin model)

(c) $Y_{BJ} = Y + \dfrac{d\left(\dfrac{M}{p}\right)}{dt} + U$ (the Johnson model)

26. This graph is taken from H. Abele, *Zeitschrift für Natinalökonomie*, Band 30, op. cit. p. 125.

In the negative direction on the horizontal axis constant production has been reproduced, which corresponds with the disposable income. The distance between the given amount of production and total consumption – also indicated in the horizontal axis in a negative direction – indicates the amount of real investments. This means, for example, for the real model that the amount of investments (current production minus consumption) can be represented by line $YC\,(= OY - OC)$

OC = material consumption in the real model
OC' = material consumption in Tobin's model
OC'' = total consumption, including immaterial consumption of the services of the real cash-balances in Johnson's model.
OC^* = material consumption in Johnson's model.

If disposable income is increased, as in the Tobin analysis, by allowing for changes in the real cash-balances $(dM/p)/dt$, then a decrease of the investments results, viz. $YC > YC'$. If immaterial consumption in the form of the non-physical returns of the existing real cash-balances is included in the analysis, represented by line $Y_{BT} - Y_{BJ}$, a total consumption of CC'' results. Because these non-physical returns are however fully consumed, material consumption from current production diminishes to the same extent, represented by line $C''C^* = Y_{BT}Y_{BJ}$, so that the material consumption amounts to OC^*. This means that real investments increase to the same extent and amount to YC^* $(= OY - OC^*)$.

If we now suppose that the non-physical returns of the real cash-balances as a part of the income is an increasing function of the real cash-balance ratio, which can be represented by $u = u(\lambda)$, in which $u' > 0$ and $u'' < 0$, the equations from section 2 will be changed as follows. The disposable income per head is:

$$y_B = y(1 + \lambda g + \mu(\lambda)) \tag{1}$$

The savings per head which are available for increasing of real investments per head can be reproduced, as follows, taking account of equation (6) from Section 2.[27]

$$\frac{S_M}{L} = \frac{dK}{dt}\frac{1}{L} = \sigma_B y \left[1 - \lambda g\left(\frac{1}{\sigma_B} - 1 - \frac{\mu(\lambda)}{\lambda g}\right)\right] \tag{2}$$

Unlike the situation with Tobin's analysis, it is no longer possible to determine unambiguously that the curve representing real savings will cut line -*Okn* at a point to the left of equilibrium point *S* and that consequently the equilibrium value of capital intensity will be lower in the monetary model than in the real model (see the graph on page 23).

This Tobin paradox will only come about in the analysis in question if the effect of additional real cash-balances on the real savings (portfolio-effect) outweighs the effect of non-physical returns of real cash-balances (immaterial consumption-effect). In algebraic terms this condition holds if

$$\left(\frac{1}{\sigma_B} - 1\right) > \frac{\mu(\lambda)}{\lambda g}$$ [28]

In the reverse case, in which the immaterial consumption-effect dominates: $(1/\sigma_B - 1) < u(\lambda)/\lambda g$, the investment ratio will be larger than in the real model and the equilibrium value of capital intensity will in the long run be accordingly higher.

The point of intersection of the curve representing real savings with line -*Okn* is in that case to the right of point *S*. If both effects compensate each other exactly, investments per head will be equal to savings per head which emerge in the real growth model. The

27. We must point out that the definition of $u = u(\lambda)$, as given by Johnson in his Essays in monetary economics, 1967, page 171, is incorrect. Johnson defines $u = u(\lambda)$ as the imputed income as a part of real per capita income, instead of the imputed income as a part of total real income. From the income definition $Y_B = Y + \lambda gY + U$, in which U represents the imputed income of cash-balances, we can derive per capita income: $y_B = y + \lambda gy + U/L$ or $y_B = y(1 + \lambda g + U/Y)$. From this results: $y_B = y(1 + \lambda g + u(\lambda))$.
In correspondence with Johnson he informed us that he could agree with our definition.

28. B. C. Cohen, The Johnsonian savings function and the rate of inflation, *Economia Internazionale*, February 1971, p. 97–99. This author gives the mathematical proof for the condition mentioned in the text.

curve of real savings will then cut line -Okn in equilibrium point S.

The preceding explanations have consequences for the maximization of per capita consumption too. After all, a higher rate of monetary growth, accompanied by a higher equilibrium value of the rate of inflation will reduce the desired real cash-balances. If the immaterial consumption-effect dominates, real savings will be reduced and the equilibrium value of capital intensity will decrease. If the economy has not yet reached the 'golden rule' path, a decrease in material, as well as in immaterial consumption will set in. In the reverse case, in which the portfolio-effect dominates, the expansive monetary policy will lead to a higher equilibrium value of capital intensity and an increase in physical consumption per head. If, in the initial situation, the equilibrium value of capital intensity exceeds the 'golden rule' value, the following reasoning holds: the desired real cash-balances will decrease even then. If the immaterial consumption-effect dominates and real savings decrease, there will be a movement towards the 'golden rule' path, causing physical consumption to increase. If the portfolio-effect dominates, real savings and real capital accumulation will increase, causing the economy to recede further from the 'golden rule' path.

2.3.3. Levhari and Patinkin's analysis

2.3.3.1. Influence of the rate of monetary growth on the equilibrium value of capital intensity

As we have already stated, valuation of the non-physical returns of real cash-balances occurs in Levhari and Patinkin's monetary growth theory according to the principle of opportunity costs. It is worth noting that this principle is, in essence, a decision criterion for one individual, which now is applied to the analysis of the behaviour of all individuals. In other words, there is always, ceteris paribus, a marginal appraisal between real cash-balances and real capital goods. The application of this principle runs up against difficulties in macro-economics.

For the method of valuation does correspond with the usual method for calculating the national income. One might nevertheless wonder how all individuals together can consider real cash-balances as a form of investment which can be converted into real capital goods, and how the conversion must take place, if all individuals wish to do this at the same time.[29]

Patinkin and Levhari make a distinction between total consumption, including the immaterial consumption which results from the ownership of real cash-balances, and the material or physical consumption which determines the amount of real investments. The method of valuation mentioned above and consequently the imputed income ($M/p(r + \pi)$) which results from the ownership of real cash balances leads in Levhari and Patinkin's explanations to the following definition of disposable income:

$$Y_B = Y + \frac{M}{p}(\mu - \pi) + \frac{M}{p}(r + \pi) = Y + \frac{M}{p}(r + \mu) \qquad (1)$$

Here we see that Patinkin and Levhari use in essence one and the same definition of income as Johnson. The total consumption, dependent on the disposable income, is then equal to

$$C_T = (1 - \sigma_B)\left[Y + \frac{M}{p}(r + \mu)\right] \qquad (2)$$

In order to find the savings which will be transformed into real capital goods, real production is reduced by material consumption (C_M).

As in all versions of the neo-classical monetary growth theory it is also supposed that the price level is flexible in such a way that a continuous equilibrium exists between demand for and supply of real cash-balances. Algebraically expressed:

$$\frac{M^d}{p} = \lambda Y = \frac{M^s}{p}, \text{ where } \lambda = \lambda(r + \pi) \text{ and } \lambda'(r + \pi) < 0 \qquad (3)$$

The desired material consumption can now be written as the difference between the total desired consumption from the disposable income and the immaterial consumption of the imputed income

29. H. Abele, *Zeitschrift für Nationalökonomie*, Band 30, 1970, op. cit. p. 138.

component.

$$C_M = (1 - \sigma_B)\left[Y + \frac{M}{p}(r + \mu)\right] - \frac{M^d}{p}(r + \pi) \qquad (4)$$

The amount of investments can be defined as the difference between income from current production and material consumption of goods and services.

$$\frac{dK}{dt} = Y - \left\{(1 - \sigma_B)\left[Y + \frac{M}{p}(r + \mu)\right] - \frac{M^d}{p}(r + \pi)\right\} \qquad (5)$$

The third term in this equation represents the immaterial consumption of the services of the real cash-balances. The following analysis is strongly based on the reflections which Levhari and Patinkin devoted to the monetary growth theory in the second part of their well-known article in the 'American Economic Review', September 1968.[30]

It is assumed that the supply of labour and the nominal quantity of money increase annually by a constant percentage n or u, respectively. The long-term equilibrium growth path is characterized by a constancy of capital intensity (k) as well as of real cash-balances per head (m). From this results the following relation for capital intensity:

$$\frac{dk}{dt}\frac{1}{k} = \frac{dK}{dt}\frac{1}{K} - \frac{dL}{dt}\frac{1}{L} = \frac{dK}{dt}\frac{1}{K} - n = 0 \qquad (6)$$

In other words: the capital intensity is constant if the growth rate of capital has become equal to the exogenously-given rate of growth of the labour supply. Further on the equilibrium growth path we can write for the relative change in real cash-balances per head:

$$\frac{dm}{dt}\frac{1}{m} = \frac{dM}{dt}\frac{1}{M} - \frac{dp}{dt}\frac{1}{p} - \frac{dL}{dt}\frac{1}{L} = \mu - \pi - n = 0 \qquad (7)$$

30. D. Levhari and D. Patinkin, *American Economic Review*, September 1968, op. cit. p. 717–737.

From equations (6) and (7) it can be concluded that in the equilibrium growth situation, physical capital and real cash-balances increase by one and the same percentage, which is equal to the rate of growth of the labour supply (= rate of growth of the national product). It also holds on the equilibrium growth path that for exogenously given values of μ and n the rate of inflation (π) is constant, as is the rate of profit ($r = f'(k)$). For in this situation the rate of inflation is equal to the growth rate of the nominal quantity of money per head.

If we substitute (3) for (5) and take (6) and (7) into account the following equation can be derived:

$$\frac{Y}{K}\{\lambda n - \sigma_B[1 + \lambda(n + \pi + r)]\} + n = 0 \tag{8}$$

With the aid of this last equation, in which we also made use of the characteristics of the production function in section 2, the equilibrium value of capital intensity can be derived from the following equilibrium condition (9).

$$nk = \{\sigma_B[1 + \lambda(n + \pi + r)] - \lambda n\} f(k) \tag{9}$$

We already said in section 2 that Tobin pointed out that an essential characteristic of a monetary economy in the framework of the growth theory is that part of total savings out of the disposable income (S_B) will be aimed at the accumulation of real cash balances (S_K). In this analysis this implies that the savings which are available for expansion of physical capital goods (S_M) can be reproduced as follows:

$$S_M = \sigma_B\left[Y + \frac{M}{p}(r + \mu)\right] - \frac{M}{p}(\mu - \pi) = \tag{10}$$

$$= \sigma_B[Y + \lambda Y(r + u)] - \lambda Y(\mu - \pi).$$

The second component in the right-hand term is equal to the amount by which the income from the current production was enlarged in Tobin's analysis, viz. the change in the real cash balances held by the economic agents.

If we take account of equations (3), (6) and (7) we can write for the material savings in the equilibrium situation

$$S_M = \sigma_B Y\,[1 + \lambda(n + \pi + r)] - \lambda Y n \tag{11}$$

After division by income (Y), the material savings ratio (σ_M) results, and its value is equal to the coefficient of $f(k)$ in equation (9).

$$\sigma_M = \frac{S_M}{Y} = \sigma_B[1 + \lambda(n + \pi + r)] - \lambda n. \tag{12}$$

If we take account of equation (9) the equilibrium condition in a growing economy comes about: $\sigma_M f(k) = nk$, which is completely analogous to the condition obtained in the traditional neo-classical real growth theory. For this relation implies that, in a situation of equilibrium growth, per capita savings must equal per capita investments required to maintain the equilibrium capital intensity.

We can conclude from the foregoing reflections that even if the savings ratio from a disposable income (σ_B) is constant, this is not valid for the material savings ratio (σ_M). For the latter variable depends on the desired real cash-balance ratio (λ), which is, in turn, determined by the opportunity costs attached to holding cash-balances ($r + \pi$). The material savings ratio is in this way ultimately dependent on the capital intensity (k) and the rate of inflation (π).

The material savings ratio can now be represented as follows:

$$\sigma_M = \sigma_M(k, \pi) \tag{13}$$

Further, Patinkin and Levhari take the line that the savings ratio out of the disposable income is variable and dependent on the respective rates of return of both assets in which total savings can be held. This supposition is expressed as follows:

$$\sigma_B = \sigma_B(f'(k), -\pi), \text{ where } \sigma_{B1} > 0 \text{ en } \sigma_{B2} > 0. \tag{14}$$

From equation (12) we can further conclude that the material savings ratio need not necessarily be smaller than the total savings ratio, out of the disposable income. This did prove to be the case in Tobin's analysis. In terms of the graph depicted in section 2, it is possible that the curve representing material savings cuts line -*Okn* at a point to the right of *S*, whereby the equilibrium value of capital intensity in a monetary economy can be larger than in a real economy. Patinkin and Levhari further point out that even if, in the monetary economy, a lower equilibrium value of capital intensity were to result than in a real economy (Tobin), the prosperity of the economic agents need not be affected.

The loss of utility which results from lower material consumption per head is compensated by an increase of utility, which is connected with the immaterial consumption of the holding of real cash-balances.

If we analyse the influence of a change in the rate of monetary expansion on the equilibrium values of capital intensity and of the other real variables, the equilibrium condition in equation (9) can first of all be rewritten, (allowing for equation 12):

$$\frac{f(k)}{k} = \frac{n}{\sigma_M(k, \pi)} = A(k), \text{ in which } A'(k) < 0 \tag{15}$$

This equation represents a well-known proposition from the neo-classical real growth theory and implies that, in the equilibrium growth situation, average capital productivity ($A(k)$) is related positively to the natural rate of growth and negatively to the material savings ratio. As was indicated earlier in the equilibrium growth situation it holds that the difference between the rate of monetary expansion (μ) and the rate of population growth (n) is equal to the rate of inflation (π). Hence a differentiation of equation (15) to π can provide insight into the influence of a change in the growth rate of the money supply on the equilibrium value of capital intensity. From this the following equation results.[31]

$$\frac{dk}{d\pi} = \frac{\sigma_{M\pi}}{-\frac{\sigma_M^2}{n}A'(k) - \sigma_{Mk}} \tag{16}$$

This last equation shows how very important it is to examine the

31. $\sigma_{M\pi}$ and σ_{Mk} are the partial derivatives of σ_M with regard to π and k.

influence of changes in capital intensity and in the rate of inflation on the material savings ratio.

In other words, signs σ_{Mk} and $\sigma_{M\pi}$ are of crucial significance in answering the question how changes in the rate of monetary growth affect the equilibrium values of the real variables. Some mathematical exercises are necessary if an exact pronouncement is to be made.

Partial differentiation of equation (12) to the variables k and π leads to the following result.[32]

$$\sigma_{Mk} = \sigma_{B1} f''(k)\left[1 + \lambda(n + \pi + r)\right] + \\ + \lambda\sigma_B\left[1 + \frac{\lambda'}{\lambda}(r + \pi)\right] f''(k) - (1 - \sigma_B)\lambda' f''(k)n \qquad (17)$$

$$\sigma_{M\pi} = -\sigma_{B2}\left[1 + \lambda(n + \pi + r)\right] + \lambda\sigma_B\left[1 + \frac{\lambda'}{\lambda}(r + \pi)\right] + \\ -(1 - \sigma_B)\lambda' n. \qquad (18)$$

The expression $\lambda'/\lambda\,(r + \pi) = \varepsilon$ in the second part of the right-hand term is equal to the interest-sensitivity of the demand for real cash-balances. In accordance with various results of empirical research it is supposed that this elasticity has an absolute value of less than one.[33] Based upon this supposition with regard to the interest-sensitivity of the demand for money and taking account of the signs of the other variables, it can be deduced from equations (17) and (18), that σ_{Mk} is negative and $\sigma_{M\pi}$ is undetermined.

It is useful from an economic point of view to interpret the results shown in equations (17) and (18), in order to properly understand the interdependences between the different variables. An increase in capital intensity (k) and/or in the rate of inflation (π) can affect the material savings ratio in two ways. On the one hand, by a change

32. The results were obtained by taking account of the following relations: $\sigma_B = \sigma_B(f'(k), -\pi)$ and $\lambda = \lambda(r + \pi)$ by which $r = f'(k) > 0$, $f''(k) < 0$, $\lambda' < 0$, $\sigma_{B1} > 0$, $\sigma_{B2} > 0$ and $0 < \sigma_B < 1$.

33. For this we refer to studies of R. Teigen, Demand and supply functions in the United States, some structural estimates, *Econometrica*, October, 1964, p. 477–509; and D. Laidler, The rate of interest and the demand for money, some empirical evidence, *Journal of Political Economy*, December 1966, p. 543–555, and by the same author, *The demand for money: theories and evidence*, 1973, part III, p. 89–110.

in total savings at a given amount of physical production (overall-savings-effect), on the other hand, by a change in the proportion in which these savings can be held (portfolio-effect).

The overall-savings-effect is directly dependent on the savings ratio out of disposable income, and on the amount of the imputed income component resulting from the retained real cash-balances. The determinants of the overall-savings-effect emerge in the first two terms of equations (17) and (18), whereas the portfolio-effect is expressed in the last term of the equation concerned.

The operative mechanisms can be described as follows. On the one hand, an increase in capital intensity starting from the characteristics of the production function, will reduce, the real rate of return of capital and consequently the savings ratio out of disposable income. ($\sigma_B f''(k) < 0$). This means that future consumption is replaced by consumption at this time. On the other hand, the relative decrease in the nominal rate of interest (opportunity costs for holding money) – starting from an interest-inelastic demand for real cash-balances – will lead to a less than proportionate increase in real cash-balances, causing the imputed part of disposable income to decrease; in other words $(1 + \varepsilon)f''(k) < 0$. From this follows that the ultimate influence of an increase in capital intensity on total savings out of disposable income is negative. Further, as far as the portfolio-effect is concerned, regardless of the interest-sensitivity of the demand for real cash-balances, the decrease in opportunity costs for holding this asset will mean that a greater part of total savings is held in the form of real cash-balances, i.e. $-(1 - \sigma_B)\lambda' f''(k) < 0$. In other words, the portfolio-effect will produce a monetary 'deepening' in the portfolio. The net-effect of an increase in capital intensity means – within the suppositions of this analysis – a decrease in the material savings ratio (σ_M). The influence of a change in the equilibrium value of the rate of inflation on the material savings ratio cannot yet be determined unambiguously from the three terms in equation (18). The influence on material savings of such a change can be split up in the following three components. The rise in the nominal rate of interest $(r + \pi)$ brings on a portfolio-effect, $(-(1 - \sigma_B)\lambda' n > 0)$, in that a smaller part of total savings will be held in the form of real cash balances. Material savings will, as such, increase. The overall-savings-effect is undetermined, since two opposite forces are now active. For, starting from an interest-inelastic demand for real cash-balances, the relative rise in the nominal rate of interest will enlarge the imputed income (M/p $(r + \pi)$) and therefore the disposable income, resulting in a positive effect on total savings ($\lambda\sigma_B(1 + \varepsilon) > 0$), given the savings ratio. The negative effect on total savings results, however, from the fact that an increase in equilibrium value of the rate of inflation reduces the real rate of return of the real cash-balances ($-\pi$) and hence the savings ratio out of disposable income ($-\sigma_{B2} < 0$). The negative effect is caused by the negative influence emanating from the higher equilibrium value of the rate of inflation on savings activity, because the value of the flow of services from future consumption decreases compared with the value of present consumption.[34]

The change in the total savings ratio, caused by a change in the real rate of return of real cash-balances, reflects a substitution process of future for present consumption.

If we take account of the economic interpretation mentioned above, the following can be noticed with regard to equation (16), which expresses the influence of a change in the rate of monetary expansion on the equilibrium value of capital intensity. The fact that it is not possible to indicate the ultimate direction of a change in the material savings ratio (σ_M) resulting from a change in the rate of inflation (π), is the most important reason for the indefinite influence of a change in the rate of monetary growth on the equilibrium value of capital intensity. This can be illustrated as follows. If the demand for real cash-balances is interest-inelastic, the equilibrium value of the capital intensity and of the material savings ratio will change in the same direction, because in that case the denominator of equation (16) is positive.[35]

The equilibrium value of capital intensity is only affected under these circumstances by a change in the equilibrium value of the rate of inflation (π), in as far as this change alters the material savings ratio; in algebraic terms, in as far as $\sigma_{M\pi} \neq 0$. If the influences of a change in the rate of monetary expansion (the overall-savings-effect and the portfolio-effect) compensate each other exactly, in other words $\sigma_{M\pi} = 0$, the equilibrium value of capital intensity will not

34. A. H. Meltzer, *Journal of Economic Literature*, March 1969, op. cit. p. 47–48.
35. Sign $dk/d\pi$ is equal to sign $\sigma_{M\pi}$.

change. If, on the contrary, the portfolio-effect dominates, it holds that $\sigma_{M\pi} > 0$ and $dk/d\pi > 0$.

Patinkin and Levhari conclude that the less sensitive the savings ratio out of disposable income is to changes in the real rate of return of the real cash-balances ($-\pi$), the more chance there is that the portfolio-effect will dominate. In the extreme case, in which $\sigma_{B2} = 0$ and/or σ_B is constant with regard to the respective real rates of return of the two wealth-assets (r and $-\pi$), the overall savings-effect will as a result of a higher rate of inflation, reinforce the positive influence of the portfolio-effect on the equilibrium value of capital intensity.[36]

The influence of a higher rate of inflation on the savings ratio out of disposable income (σ_{B2}) is in essence dependent on the economic agents' preferences with regard to consumption and wealth accumulation. The question emerges whether the economic agents accept the drop in wealth in the form of real cash-balances as a result of the higher equilibrium value of the rate of inflation.

One could imagine that they wish to compensate this drop in wealth by decreasing their consumption, thus actually realising more savings. Such behaviour could result in further reinforcement of the positive influence of the portfolio-effect.[37]

From our explanations the conclusion of Tobin emerges, who takes the line of a constant savings ratio (σ_B) out of disposable income and assumes that a more expansive monetary policy will lead unambiguously to an increase of the investment ratio and consequently to a higher equilibrium value of the capital intensity.[38]

36. D. Levhari and D. Patinkin, *American Economic Review*, September 1968, op. cit. p. 725, footnote 14. The authors prove that even handling the conception of the disposable income according to Tobin, the indefiniteness referred to in the text, remains. Sidrauski and Stein take the line in their reflections of a positive effect of the rate of inflation on savings, in other words $c_\pi < 0$. See M. Sidrauski, Rational choice and patterns of growth in a monetary economy, *American Economic Review*, May 1967, op. cit. p. 542, and in the same journal in September 1968, a comment by Stein, p. 947. The supposition of both authors will further reinforce the positive operation mentioned in the text, of the higher rate of inflation on the equilibrium value of the capital intensity.

37. R. Mundell, Inflation, saving and the real rate of interest in: *Monetary Theory*, 1971, chapter II, p. 14–22.

38. Sidrauski has given further theoretical foundation for the monetary growth theory. He analyses the problem of the neutrality of money in a growth-theoretical framework by taking account explicitly of the real cash balances as an argument in the utility function. The individual saving behaviour of economic agents is considered as a

The results of the preceding analysis can be summarized with the aid of the following schemes:

Influence of a change in capital intensity and in the rate of monetary expansion (rate of inflation) on the material savings ratio (σ_M)

	Overall-savings			
Increase of:	Influence through savings ratio	Influence through imputed income	Portfolio-effect	Total effect on material savings ratio (σ_M)
k	σ_B decreases	$M/p(r + \pi)$ decreases	M/p increases	σ_{Mk} decreases
π	σ_B decreases	$M/p(r + \pi)$ increases	M/p decreases	$\sigma_{M\pi}$?

Influence of a change in the rate of monetary expansion (rate of inflation) on equilibrium value of capital intensity

Increase in the equilibrium value of the rate of inflation	$\sigma_{M\pi}$	$\dfrac{dk}{d\pi} = \dfrac{\sigma_{M\pi}}{-\dfrac{\sigma_{M^2}}{n}A'(k) - \sigma_{Mk}}$
Portfolio-effect dominates	increases	increases
Portfolio-effect compensates the overall-savings-effect	zero	zero
Savings ratio (σ_B) is constant (Tobin)	increases	increases
Influence of the rate of inflation on savings ratio ($\sigma_{B\pi}$):		
$\sigma_{B\pi} = 0$	increases	increases
$\sigma_{B\pi} > 0$ (Mundell)	increases	increases

Footnote 38 (*continued*)
process of wealth accumulation, directed at maximization of utility over an infinite time-horizon, in which the constant subjective rate of time preference (δ) acts as a discounting factor. For each individual the following budget restrictions hold: on the one hand, wealth will be divided between physical capital goods and real cash-balances and on the other hand at any given moment it will apply that the disposable income equals the sum of consumption and savings. In this way the demand functions for consumer goods and both assets, viz. real cash-balances and physical capital goods are deduced. See M. Sidrauski, *American Economic Review* May 1967, op. cit. p. 534–544, and J. Stein's comments in *American Economic Review*, September 1968, op. cit. p. 944–950.

2.3.3.2. Influence of the rate of monetary growth on equilibrium value of real cash-balances per head

Finally we analyse the influence of a change in the rate of monetary expansion on the real cash-balances per head (m), the competing asset with physical capital goods in the portfolios of individuals.

Starting from equation (3) in the preceding sub-section these real cash-balances per head can be represented as follows:

$$m = \lambda(r + \pi)\ f(k) = \lambda[f'(k) + \pi]f(k) \tag{19}$$

In the preceding sub-section it emerged that, under certain circumstances, ($\sigma_{M\pi} < 0$), a higher rate of monetary expansion (read: a higher equilibrium value of the rate of inflation) can reduce the equilibrium value of capital intensity with regard to the growth path with the lower rate of monetary growth. If this is the case, the increase in the rate of inflation will decrease the equilibrium value of the real cash-balances per head unambiguously. The real rate of return of both wealth assets will change. The rate of profit or real rate of capital ($f'(k)$) and the rate of inflation (π) will augment opportunity costs for holding real cash-balances, causing the desired real cash-balance ratio to decrease in accordance with the presuppositions. Besides, it holds that, as a result of the lower equilibrium value of capital intensity, the corresponding decrease in per capita production ($f(k)$) will also lead to a drop in demand for real cash-balances per head.

When an increase in the rate of monetary expansion has a positive influence on the equilibrium value of the capital intensity ($dk/d\pi > 0$ if $\sigma_{M\pi} > 0$), the development of the real cash-balances per head can no longer be determined unambiguously. This indefinite equilibrium value for real cash-balances per head accompanying a change in the equilibrium value of the rate of inflation can be expressed as follows, after differentiation of equation (19) to π.

$$\frac{dm}{d\pi} = \lambda'\left[f''(k)\frac{dk}{d\pi} + 1\right]f(k) + \lambda f'(k)\frac{dk}{d\pi} \tag{20}$$

On the one hand, per capita production ($f(k)$) will increase in this case, because the equilibrium value of the capital intensity increases; on the other hand the rate of profit ($f'(k)$) decreases. There are now two possibilities. The increased equilibrium value of per capita production will lead to larger demand for real cash-balances. If the decreased rate of profit is subsequently not fully compensated by the increase in equilibrium value of the rate of inflation, opportunity costs will decrease, causing a rise in demand for real cash-balances. On balance the demand for real cash-balances will have been increased in the new equilibrium situation. If, however, the decrease in the rate of profit is more than fully compensated by the higher equilibrium value of the rate of inflation, then opportunity costs will increase and consequently the demand for real cash-balances will decrease. The ultimate effect for the equilibrium value of the real cash-balances per head is then undetermined.

If as a result of a higher rate of monetary growth the overall savings effect and the portfolio-effect compensate each other, so that no change sets in in the material savings ratio ($\sigma_{M\pi} = 0$), the equilibrium value of capital intensity will remain constant. As appears from relation (20), the equilibrium value of the real cash-balances per head will then still have decreased, due to the fact that the opportunity costs for holding real cash-balances have increased ($\lambda' f(k) < 0$). This result will be obtained if the savings ratio is very sensitive to inflation, which implies that economic subjects prefer consumption of goods and services to wealth accumulation. The influence of a change in the rate of monetary growth (rate of inflation) on the equilibrium value of the real cash-balances per head can be summarized as follows:

		Influence on the demand for real cash-balances		Total effect
$dk/d\pi$	opportunity costs $(r + \pi)$	income-effect $f(k)$	portfolio-effect $\lambda = \lambda(r + \pi)$	$\frac{dm}{d\pi}$ (equation 20)
decreases	increase	negative	negative	negative
increases	1. increase	positive	negative	indefinite
	2. decrease	positive	positive	positive
0	increase	0	negative	negative

2.3.3.3. Monetary neutrality in a growing economy

The preceding analysis also has implications for the neutrality of money in the framework of equilibrium growth. The relevant literature advances two interpretations for the question of neutrality. Firstly, the influence of the absolute amount of money (and so of the absolute price level). Secondly the influence of changes in the rate of monetary expansion and consequently in equilibrium value of the rate of inflation on the equilibrium values of the real variables in a growing economy.[39]

From the equilibrium condition in equation (9) it can be deduced that the equilibrium value of capital intensity is ultimately dependent on the rate of inflation (π). From this it follows that if the monetary authorities bring about an increase in the money supply in the equilibrium growth situation and further continue the previous rate of monetary expansion, the equilibrium value of the capital intensity will not change. From equation (20) it also results that the equilibrium value of the real cash-balances per head will not change. The increase in the money supply will generate a positive real cash-balance effect, causing the demand for goods and services to increase. For, starting from full employment, the initial excess supply of real cash-balances will lead to a rise in the price level.

This process of price adjustment goes on until the real cash-balances have again returned to the desired level. In other words: the monetary impulse goes on exercising its influence until the price level has once more brought about an equilibrium between the demand for and the supply of real cash-balances. The monetary authorities can therefore control in principle the amount of nominal cash-balances, but the real cash-balances are more likely to be determined endogenously by the public.[40] In the new equilibrium situation, only the absolute price level has been proportionally altered with the change in the nominal quantity of money. The equilibrium values of the rate of inflation, of capital intensity and of real cash-balances per head have remained constant. Accord-

39. H. Johnson, 1967, op. cit. p. 163. A. Marty: Inside money, outside money and the wealth effect. *Journal of Money, Credit and Banking*, February 1969, p. 107–108. Philip Cagan, The non-neutrality of money in the long run: a discussion of the critical assumptions and some evidence, *Journal of Money, Credit and Banking*, May 1969 p. 207–208; and D. Levhari and D. Patinkin, *American Economic Review*, September 1968, op. cit. p. 733.

40. C. K. F. Nieuwenburg, *Geld en economische activiteit*, (Money and economic activity) University of Utrecht, 1973, p. 21–22.

ing to this conception, the principle of neutrality corresponds with the implications of the traditional quantity theory. Cagan assumes in this context: 'In that sense money may be viewed as a veil in the long run, producing proportional changes in the price level that leave all the real quantities in the economy the same'.[41]

As equation (16) may have shown a change in the rate of monetary expansion (in contrast to an increase in the absolute amount of money) does, however, affect the equilibrium values of the real quantities in general. This is partly because different rates of growth of money imply different rates of return of the real cash-balances. Consequently, economic subjects will make different decisions with regard to the optimum composition of their portfolios (real cash-balances versus physical capital goods). In the preceding explanations it has appeared that only in the special case of the overall-savings-effect and the portfolio-effect compensating each other exactly ($\sigma_{M\pi} = 0$), will monetary neutrality be maintained according to the second interpretation. Though this monetary neutrality is valid for the equilibrium value of the capital intensity, we can deduce from equation (20) that under the special circumstances mentioned the real cash-balances per head will still diminish.

2.4. The implications of real cash-balances as a producer good

2.4.1. The productive services of real cash-balances

In this section the monetary factor, in the form of real cash-balances, is considered as a variable which provides so-called 'shopping-services'. With this we mean that the real cash-balances are retained, because in this way factors of production are saved, which with the very absence of this monetary variable in a barter economy would have been used to promote the exchange. This idea can already be found in Mill's writings, in which he states that the use of money means a saving in factors of production: 'there cannot be intrinsically a more insignificant thing in the economy of society than money' and further on 'except in the character of a contrivance for sparing time and labour.'[42]

41. Ph. Cagan, *Journal of Money, Credit and Banking*, May 1969 op. cit. p. 207.
42. J. S. Mill, *Principles of Political Economy*, London 1917, p. 488.

The fact that real cash-balances are held at existing positive opportunity costs implies that these costs are apparently offset by certain returns. The advantage of holding real cash-balances focused on the production sector, is formulated by Levhari and Patinkin as follows: 'In somewhat more concrete – and more familiar – terms we can assume that an economy without money would have to devote effort (read labor and physical capital) in order to achieve the multitude of 'double coincidences' – of buyers who want exactly what the seller has to offer – on which successfull barter is based. Hence the entrance of money into the production function reflects the fact that it frees labor and capital for the production of commodities proper'.[43] The authors point out here clearly the advantages of a monetary economy in comparison with the barter economy. For if the exchange process is divided into two exchange transactions with money as an intermediary, the transaction costs of the exchange connected with the time required to put buyer and seller in touch with each other in a barter economy, are reduced. These costs are incurred in obtaining and spreading the required information on the goods which are demanded and supplied. Introduction of the generally-accepted medium of exchange, money, makes it possible to organize the exchange better, to advance the labour division and achieve more efficient allocation of the factors of production. The production of goods and services can then attain a higher level or is reflected in more spare time than would be possible in a barter economy, whilst the amount of goods can be supplied as in the barter economy with much less time and labour.[44]

Contrary to the situation in the preceding section, in which the

43. D. Levhari and D. Patinkin, *American Economic Review*, September 1968, op. cit. p. 737–738. For reflections about the significance of the money as a producer good readers are referred to: L. Mc. Gregor and A. Walters, Real balances and output: A productivity model of a monetary economy, in A. Powell and R. Williams, 1973 op. cit. p. 233–259, D. Patinkin, *Money, interest and prices* 1965, p. 146–161, M. Friedman, The optimum quantity of money in *The optimum quantity of money and other essays*, Chicago, 1969, p. 1–50, H. Johnson, *Journal of Money, Credit and Banking*, February 1969, op. cit. p. 30–45, K. Brunner and A. Meltzer The uses of money: money in the theory of an exchange economy, *American Economic Review*, December 1971, p. 773–805, D. Purvis, *Canadian Journal of Economics*, August 1971, op. cit. p. 374–381.
44. H. Visser, *Monetary theory*, Leiden 1973, p. 3–5.

real cash-balances were considered as a consumer good yielding a flow of non-physical returns, real cash-balances are now considered as a good rendering direct productive services in the production process.

In order to illuminate better the significance of real cash-balances as a factor of production in our analysis, this section will by-pass the implications of real cash-balances as a consumer good (non-physical returns, imputed income and so on). One of the ways of analysing the demand for and the influence of real cash-balances as a producer good concerns application of the views developed by Baumol and Tobin in their optimum cash-balance theory.[45]

The well-known analysis by Baumol and Tobin concerning optimum cash-balances hinges on the question how the costs of obtaining and holding real cash-balances must be minimized, or, in other words, how to maximise portfolio returns. For there are costs attached to the holding of cash-balances and also to the conversion of interest-bearing, non-monetary assets into money. From a theoretical point of view, Baumol and Tobin's analysis is very attractive, since the consideration of money as a producer good evokes inventory control problems, which are of the same nature as those brought out by the authors mentioned. In imitation of Patinkin and Levhari, the further analysis leaves this inventory control approach aside, and for the sake of analytical simplicity money will be inserted in the form of a real cash-balance as an argument into the production function. Besides, this will simplify comparison with the preceding analysis concerning real cash-balances as a consumer good.

2.4.2. *Influence of a change in the rate of monetary expansion*

The following analysis is strongly based upon the reflections of Levhari and Patinkin, who for the first time in the literature have paid elaborate attention to the significance of the real cash-balances as a producer good in a growth theoretical framework. The real quantity of (outside) money, as was stated before, is inserted as an

45. W. Baumol, The transactions demand for cash; an inventory theoretic approach; *Quarterly Journal of Economics*, November 1952, p. 546–566 and J. Tobin, The interest elasticity of transactions demand for cash, *Review of Economics and Statistics*, August 1956, p. 241–247.

argument into the production function, which is again assumed to be linearly homogeneous in all variables and can be represented as follows:

$$Y = F\left(K, L, \frac{M}{p}\right). \tag{1}$$

Per capita production can then be expressed as a function of the capital intensity and of the real cash-balances per head, from which results:

$$y = f(k, m), \text{ where } f_k > 0 \text{ en } f_m \geqq 0^{46} \tag{1'}$$

The definition of disposable income which is now used is the same as the one represented in equation (1) in section 2. This means that the imputed income component attached to ownership of real cash-balances is not inserted into the disposable income, in order to prevent double counts. This results from the fact that the services of real cash-balances are now expressed in the production sector by way of an increase in current production.

Changes in real cash-balances as a result of shifts in the price level continue, however, to form a component of the individuals' disposable income as in Tobin's analysis.[47]

Capital accumulation is equal to the difference between income from current production and consumption from the disposable income and is expressed in the following equation:

$$\frac{dK}{dt} = Y - (1 - \sigma_B)\left[Y + \frac{M}{p}(\mu - \pi)\right] \tag{2}$$

If we further take account of the fact that in the equilibrium growth situation, real cash-balances per head are constant, the equilibrium value of the capital intensity can be reproduced as follows:

$$\sigma_B f(k, m) + (\sigma_B - 1)\, mn = nk. \tag{3}$$

46. A borderline case can occur in an economy with very highly-developed financial institutions, so that $f_m = 0$, i.e. an increase in real cash-balances, does not lead to further saving of factors of production in the production process and so to an increase in per capita production.

47. D. Patinkin, 1965, *op. cit.* p. 160–161.

Equations (2) and (3) correspond with equations (7) and (8) in section 2.

The material savings ratio (σ_M), which now also depends on the rates of return of both assets in which savings can be held, viz. real capital goods and real cash-balances, can be represented by reformulating equation (3):

$$\left[\sigma_B + \frac{(\sigma_B - 1)mn}{f(k, m)}\right] + f(k, m) = \sigma_M(k, \pi) f(k, m) = nk. \quad (4)$$

With regard to the equilibrium value of the real cash-balances per head the following can be said. The demand for real cash-balances as a producer good is determined in this analysis by the principle of marginal productivity.

This differs from the preceding explanations where $\lambda = m/y$, the desired real cash-balance ratio was assumed merely to depend on the opportunity costs ($r + \pi$) attached to the holding of real cash-balances. Otherwise expressed, in the preceding explanations the demand for real cash-balances was dependent on the capital intensity and the rate of inflation. Not only the physical marginal productivity of the real cash-balances (f_m), but also the marginal capital gains which arise owing to an expected relative price fall ($-\pi$) are now of importance as determinants of the demand for real cash-balances by the production households. The production households will have attained an equilibrium with regard to portfolio composition when the marginal rates of return of physical capital goods and of real cash-balances are equal. This equilibrium is reproduced by the following condition:[48]

$$f_k = f_m - \pi \text{ or } r + \pi = f_m. \quad (5)$$

The left-hand term of this equation is equal to the rate of return of real capital, whereas the right-hand term expresses the rate of return of the real cash-balances, which is equal to the physical marginal productivity of the real cash-balances, minus the rate of

48. H. W. Wan, Extensions of the neo-classical model: the inclusion of monetary assets, *Economic growth*, Cornell University 1971, p. 252. See in this context also J. Stein, The optimum quantity of money, *Journal of Money, Credit and Banking*, November 1970, p. 401–402.

inflation. Another interpretation of equation (5) is that the last monetary unit which is used as a real cash-balance (so as a factor of production) must have a rate of return corresponding to the rate of return of the last monetary unit invested in the physical capital goods. The marginal product of the real cash-balances is then equal to the algebraic sum of the rate of inflation and the marginal product of capital.

It is not possible – contrary to the analysis in the preceding paragraph – to deduce explicitly from equation (5) the demand for real cash-balances per head (m) as a function of the capital intensity (k) and the rate of inflation (π).

On the other hand, we can indeed say something about the development of the real cash-balances per head under the influence of a change in the capital intensity, or in the rate of inflation. For this we need an implicit differentiation of equation (5) to k and π, from which, after some mathematical operations, the following partial derivatives can be obtained:[49]

49. Assume $Q(k, m, \pi) = f_k(k, m) - f_m(k, m) + \pi = 0$

$$Q_k + Q_m \frac{dm}{dk} + Q_\pi \frac{d\pi}{dk} = 0 \tag{1}$$

$$Q_\pi + Q_m \frac{dm}{d\pi} + Q_k \frac{dk}{d\pi} = 0 \tag{2}$$

$$(f_{kk} - f_{mk}) + (f_{km} - f_{mm}) \frac{dm}{dk} + 1 \frac{d\pi}{dk} = 0 \tag{1'}$$

$$\therefore \frac{\partial m}{\partial k} = - \frac{f_{kk} - f_{mk}}{f_{km} - f_{mm}} = \frac{-Q_k}{Q_m} > 0$$

$$1 + (f_{km} - f_{mm}) \frac{dm}{d\pi} + (f_{kk} - f_{mk}) \frac{dk}{d\pi} = 0 \tag{2'}$$

$$\therefore \frac{\partial k}{\partial \pi} = - \frac{1}{f_{kk} - f_{mk}} = \frac{-Q_\pi}{Q_k} > 0$$

$$\therefore \frac{\partial m}{\partial \pi} = - \frac{1}{f_{km} - f_{mm}} = \frac{-Q_\pi}{Q_m} < 0$$

The signs of the partial derivatives in equations (6), (7) and (8) have been obtained, on the one hand, on the supposition of the theory of marginal productivity with regard to variables k and m, i.e. f_{kk} and f_{mm} are both negative, and on the other hand that $f_{km} = f_{mk} > 0$.

$$\frac{\partial m}{\partial k} = -\frac{Q_k}{Q_m} > 0 \tag{6}$$

$$\frac{\partial m}{\partial \pi} = -\frac{Q_\pi}{Q_m} < 0 \tag{7}$$

$$\frac{\partial k}{\partial \pi} = -\frac{Q_\pi}{Q_k} > 0 \tag{8}$$

Substitution of the rate of inflation from equation (5) into the expression for the disposable income gives the following result:

$$Y_B = Y + \frac{M}{p}(\mu - \pi) = Y + \frac{M}{p}(\mu + f_k - f_m) =$$

$$Y + \frac{M}{p}(\mu + r - f_m). \tag{9}$$

We see that the rate of inflation in this equation is no longer explicit. This is due to the fact that an expected relative price rise, for instance, brings about a capital loss with regard to the real cash-balances held which is equal to the productive return which can be awarded to these cash-balances. One and the same interpretation is implied in equation (1) in section 3.3., in which real cash-balances are considered as a consumer good and are inserted as imputed income in the definition of the disposable income.

In accordance with the procedure followed in the preceding section we can analyse with the aid of equations (3) and (5) the influence of a change in the rate of monetary expansion (μ) (= rate of inflation) on the equilibrium values of the capital intensity and of the real cash-balances per head.

Starting from a constant savings ratio (σ_B) out of disposable income, the following equations are obtained by implicit differentiation of equations (3) and (5) to the rate of inflation (π).[50]

$$[\sigma_B f_k - n]\frac{dk}{d\pi} + [\sigma_B f_m + (\sigma_B - 1)n]\frac{dm}{d\pi} = 0. \tag{10}$$

$$[f_{mk} - f_{kk}]\frac{dk}{d\pi} + [f_{mm} - f_{km}]\frac{dm}{d\pi} = 1 \tag{11}$$

50. See footnote p. 56.

The following result gives a solution according to Cramer's rule for the influence of a change in the rate of inflation on the equilibrium value of the capital intensity and of the real cash-balances per head.

$$\frac{dk}{d\pi} = -\frac{[\sigma_B f_m + (\sigma_B - 1)n]}{D} \tag{12}$$

$$\frac{dm}{d\pi} = \frac{\sigma_B f_k - n}{D} \tag{13}$$

the determinant being equal to:

$$D = [\sigma_B f_k - n][f_{mm} - f_{km}] - [\sigma_B f_m + (\sigma_B - 1)n] \tag{14}$$
$$[f_{mk} - f_{kk}] = [\sigma_B f_k - n]. - Q_m - [\sigma_B f_m + (\sigma_B - 1)n]. +$$
$$-Q_k.$$

The suppositions which have been made to determine the signs of partial derivatives Q_k and Q_m in equations (6) and (7), are not however sufficient to determine the signs of the numerators and consequently of the differential quotients in equations (12) and (13). From equation (5) representing the portfolio-balance, we can deduce – as was indicated earlier – for a given value of the rate of inflation (π), (equation 6) that the influence of a change in the capital intensity on the real cash-balances per head is unambiguously positive. ($dm/dk = -Q_k/Q_m > 0$). On the other hand, we can derive from equation (3), representing the equilibrium value of the capital intensity, and from the related equation (10) that the differential quotient dm/dk concerned is equal to $-\sigma_B f_k - n/\sigma_B f_m + (\sigma_B - 1)n$, which sign cannot be determined unambiguously. This indefiniteness can also be represented by a graph, which is quoted from Levhari and Patinkin.[51] In this graph the CC-curve represents the

51. D. Levhari and D. Patinkin, *American Economic Review*, September 1968, op. cit. p. 741. For another graphic presentation readers are referred to J. A. Frenkel and R. Dornbusch, Inflation and growth: Alternative approaches, in *Report 7135 of the Center for Mathematical Studies in Business and Economics*, Chicago July 1971, p. 6–11.
The latter article was also published in the *Journal of Money, Credit and Banking*, February 1973, p. 144.

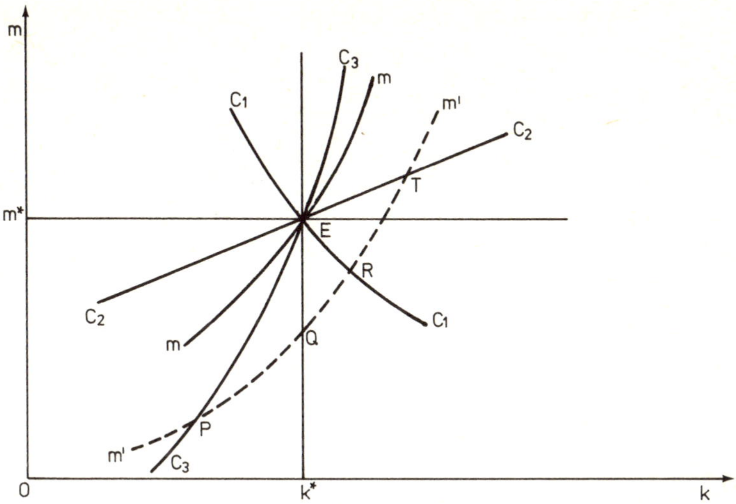

locus of all combinations of the real cash-balances per head (m) and the capital intensity (k) for which the conditions for an equilibrium growth on the long run hold (equation 3) and consequently the capital intensity is constant. The figure shows that the slope of the curve can be negative (C_1C_1) or positive (C_2C_2 and C_3C_3). The *mm*-curve is the locus of all combinations of the real cash-balances per head (m) and the capital intensity (k) for which a port-folio-balance exists (equation (5)), given the rate of inflation (π).

As has already been indicated, the slope of this curve is unambiguously positive. A higher capital intensity, given the rate of inflation, leads to a relative decrease in opportunity costs and a movement along the *mm*-curve, causing demand for real cash-balances to increase. An increase in the rate of monetary expansion, starting from equilibrium situation (E), leads to a shift in the *mm*-curve to the right ($m'm'$) (see equation (7)). This means that an increase in equilibrium value of the rate of inflation reduces the demand for real cash-balances per head, given the value of capital intensity. The *CC*-curves are not however influenced by a higher equilibrium value of the rate of inflation. The ultimate influence of an increase in the rate of monetary expansion on the equilibrium values of the real variables depends therefore on the one hand on the shape of the *CC*-curves and on the other hand on the points in which the new equilibrium situation will come about. (P, R and T).

As was indicated on page 48 (equation 20) a relation exists between the influence of a change in the equilibrium value of the rate of inflation on the equilibrium value of the capital intensity ($dk/d\pi$) and the influence of the change in the equilibrium value of the rate of inflation on the equilibrium value of the real cash-balances per head ($dm/d\pi$). The formal solution can be found by differentiating totally function $Q(k, m, \pi) \equiv 0$, which represents the equilibrium in the portfolio, to the rate of inflation (π), from which results[52]

$$\frac{dm}{d\pi} = -\frac{Q_k}{Q_m}\frac{dk}{d\pi} - \frac{Q_\pi}{Q_m} \tag{15}$$

$$\frac{dk}{d\pi} = -\frac{Q_m}{Q_k}\frac{dm}{d\pi} - \frac{Q_\pi}{Q_k} \tag{16}$$

There are various possibilities as regards the influence of a change in the rate of monetary growth (read: equilibrium value of the rate of inflation) on the equilibrium values of the capital intensity and of the real cash-balances per head. If an increased rate of monetary expansion (μ) has a negative influence on the equilibrium value of capital intensity ($dk/d\pi < 0$), the higher equilibrium value of the rate of inflation, taking account of equations (6), (7) and (8), will affect the equilibrium value of the real cash-balances per head negatively ($dm/d\pi < 0$). All this is apparent in the graph in a shift of the *mm*-curve to the right, and starting from the *CC*-curve, the new equilibrium point *P* results. So it follows from equation (16) that if the higher equilibrium value of the rate of inflation affects the equilibrium value of the real cash-balances per head positively ($dm/d\pi > 0$) the influence on the equilibrium value of the capital intensity will be positive too ($dk/d\pi > 0$). This case is also expressed in the graph in a shift of the *mm*-curve to the right and in equilibrium point *T*. If finally the equilibrium value of the rate of inflation has a positive influence on the equilibrium value of the capital intensity ($dk/d\pi > 0$), the influence on the equilibrium value of the real cash-balances per head is undetermined. This situation is expressed in the

52. From equation $Q(k, m, \pi) \equiv 0$ follows:

$$Q_k\frac{dk}{d\pi} + Q_m\frac{dm}{d\pi} + Q_\pi \equiv 0$$

graph by equilibrium points R and T. Conversely when the equilibrium value of the rate of inflation is negatively related to the equilibrium value of the real cash-balances per head ($dm/d\pi < 0$), the influence of the higher equilibrium value of the rate of inflation on the equilibrium value of capital intensity cannot be determined unambiguously (points P and R).[53]

Concluding, it can be said that if an increase in equilibrium value of the rate of inflation (π) brings about a new equilibrium situation with a lower equilibrium value of the capital intensity, point P, the equilibrium value of the real cash-balances per head will also have decreased with regard to the growth path with the lower rate of monetary growth. This result proceeds from the fact that in the situation concerned the opportunity costs attached to holding real cash-balances have increased. This increase is connected with the higher equilibrium value of the rate of inflation and – in as far as capital intensity has decreased in the new equilibrium situation – with the higher rate of return on capital. If on the contrary the higher equilibrium value of the rate of inflation leads to an increase in equilibrium value of capital intensity, the influence on the equilibrium value of the real cash-balances per head is indefinite (points R and T). And under these circumstances the development of opportunity costs cannot be determined unambiguously. If $m_k > m_\pi$, opportunity costs will have decreased on balance, which means a higher equilibrium value of the real cash-balances per head (point T).

If, on the contrary, $m_k < m_\pi$, opportunity costs will have increased on balance and a new equilibrium situation will be attained,

53. D. Levhari and D. Patinkin, *American Economic Review*, September 1968, op. cit. p. 742. In this context readers are referred to J. Harkness, The role of money in a simple growth model; comment, *American Economic Review*, March 1972, p. 177–179. Harkness proves that under special suppositions the growth model in which real cash-balances are merely considered as a producer good, is stable. So he comes to the conclusion that a higher rate of monetary growth will lead to a higher equilibrium value of the capital intensity and of the real cash-balances per head (see point T in the graph). The higher equilibrium value of the real cash-balances per head does not correspond with the conclusion in Tobin's monetary growth theory. The reason for this is that with Tobin the real cash-balances do not perform productive services. See in this context also: R. Ramanathan, The role of money in a simple growth model: comment, *American Economic Review*, March 1972, p. 180–184 and in the same issue of this journal: D. Levhari and D. Patinkin, The role of money in a simple growth model: reply, p. 185.

in which a decrease has set in in the equilibrium value of the real cash-balances per head (point *R*).

Stein too has examined the significance of the real cash-balances as a producer good in the neo-classical monetary growth model.[54] He emphasizes the negative effect emanating from a higher rate of monetary expansion on the real cash-balances per head. The drop in the last mentioned variable brings about a decrease in consumption expenditures as well as in production, by which the ultimate effect on material savings and so on the equilibrium value of the capital intensity is undetermined. The change in consumption expenditures can be ascribed to the operation of the real cash-balance effect. For consumption is also assumed to depend on the wealth of the economic agents, consisting of physical capital goods and real cash-balances per head. The influence of this real cash-balance-effect depends on whether the distinction between inside and outside money is relevant for determining changes in the economic agents' wealth position. If the quantity of money consists merely of outside money, which for the sake of simplicity is postulated in most theoretical analyses, each change in the rate of inflation brings on an opposed change in the net-wealth position of the economic agents. Stein apparently takes the line that economic agents do not accept the decrease of wealth in the form of real cash-balances as a result of the higher equilibrium value of the rate of inflation. They will prefer to compensate this capital-loss by charging it to consumption expenditures, thus actually achieving more savings. Besides, production will decrease due to the fact that the real cash-balances have decreased and these balances have been inserted into the production function. The influence on the equilibrium value of the capital intensity now depends on which of the two effects dominates.

If the marginal product of the real cash-balances per head is great, production decrease may exceed the drop in consumption expenditures, by which the capital intensity has been diminished in the new equilibrium situation. This situation tallies with point *P* in the above-mentioned graph. If, on the contrary, the marginal productivity of the real cash-balances is negligible ($f_m \rightarrow 0$), the decreasing effect of consumption expenditures will dominate and the equilibrium value of the capital intensity will be enlarged (point

54. J. Stein, *American Economic Review*, March 1970, op. cit. p. 91–93.

R). In this last case the conclusion of Tobin's original neo-classical monetary growth model results, albeit that Tobin did not include in his analysis the explicit distinction between real cash-balance as a consumer good and as a producer good.

2.5. The stability of the neo-classical monetary growth model

In the preceding analysis the line has always been taken that an equilibrium exists and that the system converges to a new equilibrium situation, if the original situation is disturbed for whatever reason. Otherwise formulated, it has always been presumed that stability of the equilibrium growth-path exists.

Tobin has paid attention to the stability process in a concise way. Let us assume that, for some reason or another the portfolio-balance is disturbed, because the rate of inflation for example decreases. A relative decrease in the rate of inflation implies a drop in the opportunity costs attached to holding cash-balances. This will induce economic agents to enlarge their real cash-balances, in order to maintain the equilibrium between the demand for and the supply of real cash-balances (portfolio-balance).

The excess-demand for real cash-balances implies an excess-supply of goods, from which a further fall in prices results. Two opposite effects can then be distinguished. On the one hand the price fall will lead, by way of the Pigou-effect, to an increase in the real value of the existing nominal cash-balances, by which a contribution is provided to restore the originally disturbed portfolio-balance. On the other hand, the Wicksell-effect causes a destabilizing effect to set in, in that the induced, higher rate of deflation will enlarge the real rate of return of the real cash-balances. Starting from the supposed investment behaviour, the demand for the monetary component in total wealth will further increase, enlarging the existing disequilibrium in portfolio composition. In this way a disturbance of the equilibrium as a result of the economic agents' dispositions can lead to a cumulative deflationary development. This adjustment process is connected, according to Tobin's views, with a decrease in equilibrium value of the capital intensity and an increase in the rate of return of capital. This development of the rate of return of capital leads to increased opportunity costs, which will form a stabilizing factor. Tobin further remarks: 'There is no a priori reason why one effect should be stronger than the other in the neighborhood of equilibrium'.[55]

He assumes that if the Pigou-effect dominates, a new equilibrium situation will ultimately, after a long period of deflation and a decrease in capital intensity, be possible. If there is a disturbance in the portfolio-balance, influenced by a relative increase in the rate of inflation causing opportunity costs to increase, the demand for real cash-balances will be reduced. The economic agents will change their dispositions in such a way that an excess-supply of real cash-balances results (excess-demand for goods) and a further increase in the rate of inflation will go on.

During this adjustment process the equilibrium value of capital intensity will increase and the rate of return of capital will decrease; this development forms in this case a stabilizing factor too.

The possible instability in the neo-classical monetary growth model lies in the supposition that equilibrium will always exist between the demand for and the exogenously given supply of real cash-balances. In other words the price level will be so flexible that the portfolio-balance will be maintained continuously.

$$\left(\frac{M^s}{pL} = \frac{M^d}{pL}\right).$$

The stability of the system is now determined crucially by price expectations. As we have said several times, real cash-balances per head are constant in the equilibrium situation ($m = M/pL$). This means that the equilibrium rate of inflation (π) is equal to the difference between the rate of growth of the money supply and the rate of population growth, or to the rate of growth of the money supply per head. In the usual notation this relation can be expressed as: $\pi = \mu - n$.

It is implicitly presumed that the expected rate of inflation (π^*) immediately adjusts to the existing equilibrium value of the rate of inflation (π) which is equal to the rate of growth of the nominal cash-

55. J. Tobin, *Econometrica*, October 1965, op. cit. p. 682–683.

balances per head. It is often suggested in the literature that Tobin's monetary growth model is characterized by a continuous equality of the expected and the actual (equilibrium) rate of inflation. This author indeed remarks in replying to Johnson, 'asset-holders correctly, expect the actually realized rate of inflation or deflation',[56] but in another publication he says: 'it will take time for the new rate of deflation to register in expectations and for wealth owners to try to adjust to new expectations.'[57]

In this analysis it will appear that this very adjustment of the expected rate of inflation with a possible difference between the actual and the expected value of this variable is of essential importance for stability in the neo-classical monetary growth theory. If we take the line that the expected rate of inflation (π^*) always agrees with the existing equilibrium value of the rate of inflation (π), the equilibrium between the supply of and the demand for real cash-balances can be reproduced as follows:

$$\frac{M^s}{pL} = \frac{M^d}{pL} = m = \hat{L}(k, \pi) \tag{1}$$

in which $\hat{L}_1 > 0$ and $\hat{L}_2 < 0$.

This equation implies that the demand for real cash-balances per head is on the one hand related positively to per capita income (demand for transaction money), which variable is determined by the capital intensity ($y = f(k)$), and is, on the other hand, related negatively to the opportunity costs attached to the holding of real cash-balances ($f'(k) + \pi$). In order to induce the economic agents (when there is a larger supply of real cash-balances) to hold more real cash-balances, given the capital intensity, the rate of inflation will have to decrease, starting from the behaviour hypothesis with regard to portfolio composition. In other words, the real rate of return of real cash-balances will have to increase. After an explicit solution of π from equation (1) the condition for the portfolio-

56. J. Tobin, *Economica*, February 1967, op. cit. p. 69, footnote 2.
57. J. Tobin, *Econometrica*, October 1965, op. cit. p. 683.

balance runs as follows:[58]

$$\pi = \pi(k, m); \pi_2 < 0. \tag{2}$$

In other words the rate of inflation must have a distinct value, in order to maintain – given the capital intensity – perpetual portfolio-balance between real cash-balances and capital goods.[59] The relative change in the real cash-balances per head is represented by the following equation:

$$\frac{dm}{dt}\frac{1}{m} = \mu - \pi(k, m) - n. \tag{3}$$

If the supply of real cash-balances deviates upwards from its equilibrium value, the rate of inflation will have to decrease given the capital intensity, in order to restore the portfolio equilibrium. The real rate of return of the real cash-balances $(-\pi)$ must be consistent with the 'asset equilibrium', the well-balanced composition of the portfolio. However from equation (3) it results that the supply of real cash-balances increases cumulatively and restoration of the equilibrium will not set in.[60] For:

$$\frac{\partial\left(\frac{dm}{dt}\frac{1}{m}\right)}{\partial m} = -\pi_2 > 0 \tag{4}$$

Solow remarks: '... It is asking for trouble to expect the currently experienced rate of inflation to maintain perpetual portfolio-balance'.[61] This author points out that by introducing an expectation hypothesis, a certain lag can be built in, in which a sudden

58. From relation $m = \hat{L}(k, \pi)$ it follows: $dm = \partial\hat{L}/\partial k\, dk + \partial\hat{L}/\partial\pi\, d\pi$. In the equilibrium situation it holds that $dm = 0$:

$$\frac{d\pi}{dk} = -\frac{\hat{L}_1}{\hat{L}_2} > 0 \text{ and } \frac{d\pi}{dm} = \frac{1}{\hat{L}_2} < 0$$

59. E. Burmeister and A. Dobell, *Mathematical theories of growth* 1970, p. 164. See also in this context M. G. Hadjimichalakis, Equilibrium and disequilibrium growth with money – The Tobin models, *Review of Economic Studies*, October 1971, p. 471–472.
60. J. Stein, *American Economic Review*, March 1970, op. cit. p. 96–97.
61. R. Solow, *Growth theory an exposition*, Oxford, 1970, p. 76.

change in the rate of inflation only brings about a small, immediate change in the expected rate of inflation and consequently in dispositions of the economic subjects. Cumulative disturbances, as described before, will then in all probability be slower to set in.

In the literature several authors point out that equilibrium in the neo-classical monetary growth theory has the features of a saddle point equilibrium.[62] This means that equilibrium is only stable if a disturbance causes the real cash-balances per head and the capital intensity to deviate from the equilibrium values in a distinct direction. If other deviations from the equilibrium are concerned, no convergence to the original equilibrium will set in.

Sidrauski has proved that the neo-classical monetary growth model (Tobin) is stable if adaptation of the expected rate of inflation comes about in a sufficiently sluggish way. Sidrauski's analysis interprets the Tobin-model more in the spirit than in the letter. This is due to the fact that Tobin himself remarks that it takes some time before the changed rate of inflation, or deflation, has been processed in the expectations and the economic subjects have adjusted their dispositions accordingly.[63]

Sidrauski uses in his analysis the well-known 'adaptive expectations function', which Cagan originally introduced.[64] Price expectations are assumed to be induced in the sense that the economic agents, in determing expectations with regard to a normal rate of inflation, take the past rate of inflation into account.[65] This normal rate of inflation is of essential importance for the decision on the amount of real cash-balances. If the actual rate of inflation deviates from the so-called 'normal' rate of inflation, the economic subjects will partially revise their expectations with regard to this variable. The relevant behaviour hypothesis expressing adjustment of the

62. K. Nagatani: A note on Professor Tobin's 'Money and economic growth', *Econometrica*, January 1970, p. 171–175; M. Sidrauski, *Journal of Political Economy*, December 1967, op. cit. p. 796–810, and, by the same author, *American Economic Review*, May 1967, op. cit. p. 538; M. Hadjimichalakis, Money, expectations and dynamics, an alternative view, *International Economic Review*, October 1971, p. 381–403.

63. J. Tobin, *Econometrica*, October 1965, op. cit. p. 683.

64. Ph. Cagan, The monetary dynamics of hyperinflation, in *Studies in the quantity theory of money*, Chicago, 1956. Cagan remarks, 'The expected rate of change in prices is revised per period of time in proportion to the difference between the actual rate of change in prices and the rate of change that was expected', op. cit. p. 37.

65. M. Sidrauski, *Journal of Political Economy*, December 1967, op. cit. p. 799.

expected rate of inflation, can be represented as follows:

$$\frac{d\pi^*}{dt} = \beta(\pi - \pi^*) \tag{5}$$

in which $\beta \geqq 0$ represents the 'expectations coefficient'. The value of this coefficient is an indication for the speed, with which the economic subjects will revise their expectations with regard to the rate of inflation. This relation indicates that the rate of adjustment of the expected rate of inflation depends on the error in estimating the actual rate of inflation. The equation above underlies the supposition that the economic subjects base their activities upon imperfect predictions with regard to the rate of inflation and deflation in the short run. Otherwise expressed, the adjustment of expectations is a linear function of the error in estimation. If $\beta = 0$ and $\beta = \infty$ one is either dealing with 'static expectations' or with 'perfect myopic foresight' with regard to the price development. Greater values for coefficient β mean a smaller lag in adjustment of the expected rate of inflation. The supposition that equilibrium will always exist between the supply of and the demand for real cash-balances, implies that at a possible difference between the actual and the expected rate of inflation immediate adjustments will take place in the last mentioned variable ($\beta = \infty$). In our preceding analysis it was always assumed that the expected rate of inflation is equal to the actual equilibrium rate of inflation, which was used for determining disposable income and opportunity costs. ($\pi^* = \pi$).

Nagatani speaks in this context of 'Tobin's assumption of 'myopic' price expectations'.[66]

In order to analyse the stability of the equilibrium growth path, we must examine which mechanisms set in with, and which influences emanate from changes in the endogenous variables, viz. capital intensity and expected rate of inflation on the development of the variables in question in the course of time. In other words, the question arises whether, when disturbances in equilibrium occur, forces will be present which restore the equilibrium. We will give in this paragraph a verbal interpretation of the problems concerned; the

66. K. Nagatani, *Econometrica*, January 1970, op. cit. p. 175.

mathematical implications come up for discussion in the appendix to this chapter.[67]

From the model represented in the appendix the following two basic-differential equations can be derived, which describe the dynamic system in question.

$$\frac{dk}{dt} = \sigma_B f(k) - (1 - \sigma_B)(\mu - \pi^*)\, m - nk. \tag{6}$$

$$\frac{d\pi^*}{dt} = \frac{\beta}{1 + \beta \dfrac{\hat{L}'}{\hat{L}}} \left[\mu - \pi^* - n - \frac{\eta}{k}\frac{dk}{dt}\right] \tag{7}$$

A rise in capital intensity above its equilibrium value will first of all reduce in (given the rate of inflation and a constant savings ratio out of disposable income) the average capital productivity and the savings per unit of capital. From this a stabilizing effect will emanate, given the rate of population growth, on the development of the capital intensity. Besides, the marginal product of capital and consequently opportunity costs $(f'(k) + \pi^*)$, will decrease as well, and so there results an increased demand for real cash-balances per unit of capital. Sidrauski takes the line that the economic subjects divide up their wealth depending on the rates of return of the two assets (viz. physical capital goods and real cash-balances).[68] As a result of the induced portfolio-effect, the savings which will be used for extending the material capital goods decrease. Both influences (overall-savings-effect and the portfolio-effect) will force capital intensity back to the original equilibrium level (see relation (12a) in the appendix).

On the other hand, an increase in the expected rate of inflation (π^*) will influence the disposable income in two ways. Firstly, capital losses will occur in the quantity of real cash-balances held. Sec-

67. M. Sidrauski, *Journal of Political Economy*, December 1967, op. cit. p. 804–807.

68. The demand function for real cash-balances per unit of capital is represented as follows.

$$\frac{M}{pK} = \frac{m}{k} = \hat{L}(f'(k) + \pi^*), \text{ in which } \hat{L}' < 0.$$

ondly, as a result of the increased opportunity costs, the desired quantity of real cash-balances per unit of capital will decrease. This drop in the disposable income will lead to a decrease in real consumption and consequently to an increase of capital accumulation. Sidrauski apparently assumes that the economic subjects wish to compensate the wealth decrease in the form of real cash-balances by charging it to consumption expenditures, by which more savings will come about for extending physical capital goods (see relation (12b) in the appendix).

Now a locus of all combination exists for the capital intensity and the expected rate of inflation, for which it holds that the change in the capital intensity is zero. The slope of the curve in the equilibrium situation (k_e, π^*_e) is represented by the following term:[69]

$$\frac{dk}{d\pi^*}\left|\frac{dk}{dt} = 0\right| = \frac{-\dfrac{\partial F}{\partial \pi^*}}{\dfrac{\partial F}{\partial k}} > 0.$$

The analysis from above is expressed in the graph below, which

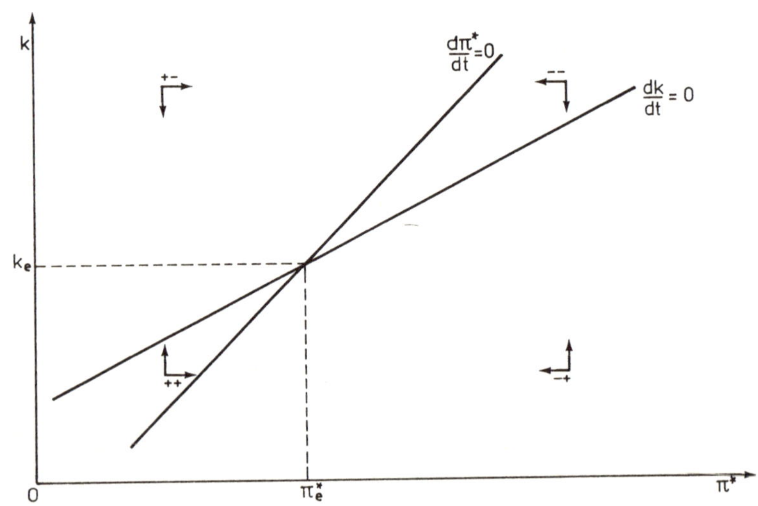

69. See appendix of this chapter.

has been taken from Sidrauski.[70] A deviation in the equilibrium situation expressed in a point above curve ($dk/dt = 0$), leads to an adjustment process in which the capital intensity decreases; whereas a deviation in the equilibrium expressed in a point below the curve will ultimately increase the capital intensity. This is represented by the arrows in the south and north directions and/or by the signs concerned. Further the influence of a change in the expected rate of inflation on this variable itself must be examined. Naturally the behaviour hypothesis with regard to adjustment of the expected rate of inflation is now of essential importance. In accordance with this behaviour relation, a positive difference between the existing rate of inflation (π) and the expected rate of inflation (π^*) will lead to an upward revision of the inflationary expectations. Under influence of the expected decrease in value of the real cash-balances, the economic subjects will diminish their demand for this asset. This results from the fact that the higher expected rate of inflation, given the capital intensity, enlarges the opportunity costs for the holding of real cash-balances.

The amount by which the demand for real cash-balances will decrease in order to make this demand tally with the changed expectations depends on the elasticity of the demand for real cash-balances with regard to the expected rate of inflation. An excess-demand for goods now occurs (excess-supply of real cash-balances) resulting in a larger actual or existing rate of inflation (π), assuming there is full employment. This will in turn result in a revision of the expected rate of inflation, in accordance with the so-called 'error-learning hypothesis', and the change in the expected rate of inflation will be further enlarged. This last development will reinforce the actual rate of inflation as a result of an adequate change in the dispositions of the economic agents. An ever-accelerating inflationary process will then be possible. Sidrauski says in this context: 'Given that we assume that there is no lag in the adjustment of the actual to the desired stock of cash, the stability of the system depends on the existence as well as the magnitude of the expectations lag'.[71] From

70. M. Sidrauski: *Journal of Political Economy*, December 1967 op. cit. p. 804–805. It is worth noting that when the author speaks of the stable situation he means figure 4 and not figure 3, as is stated in the text on p. 805. An analogous graph is developed by Nagatani for the combinations of capital intensity and real cash-balances per head. See Nagatani, *Econometrica*, January 1970, op. cit. 173.

71. M. Sidrauski, *American Economic Review*, May 1967, op. cit. p. 543.

relation (12d) in the appendix it appears that the development of the expected rate of inflation depends critically on the value of 'expectations coefficient' β. The smaller the value of β, the less quickly the economic agents will revise their expectations on the rate of inflation, thus reducing the effect of the actual rate of inflation on the inflationary expectations and the self-generating inflationary process. As far as the effect of a change in the capital intensity on the change in the expected rate of inflation in concerned, an increase in capital intensity will lead, as we have already said, to a decrease in the rate of capital accumulation. This means that a deviation in the equilibrium value of the capital intensity upwards, calls up forces which help to restore equilibrium. This development is linked with an increase in opportunity costs, which causes the demand for real cash-balances to decrease. Given a specific rate of monetary expansion the excess-supply of real cash-balances will result in a higher actual rate of inflation. Starting from the supposed behaviour hypothesis, the expected rate of inflation will then be adjusted in an upward direction (see relation (12d) in the appendix).

A curve can now be derived representing all combinations of the capital intensity and the expected rate of inflation for which it now holds that the change in the expected rate of inflation is zero. The slope of this curve (see the above-mentioned graph) in the equilibrium situation (k_e, π_e^*) is expressed in the following term.[72]

$$\left.\frac{dk}{d\pi^*}\right| \frac{d\pi^*}{dt} = 0 \left| = \frac{-\dfrac{\partial G}{\partial \pi^*}}{\dfrac{\partial G}{\partial k}} > 0.\right.$$

If the 'expectations coefficient' has the value:

$$0 < \beta < -\frac{\hat{L}}{\hat{L}'},$$

it holds that deviations in the equilibrium situation, expressed in points above curve ($d\pi^*/dt = 0$) lead to an adjustment process, in

72. See appendix. With the aid of equations 12a–12d it can be derived that the slope of curve $d\pi^*/dt = 0$ is larger than the slope of curve $dk/dt = 0$.

which the expected rate of inflation increases. For points below the curve, the adjustment process will result in a decrease of the expected rate of inflation. All this is indicated in the above-mentioned graph by the arrows in the east and west directions and/or by the signs concerned. If the adaptation coefficient takes the above-mentioned value, the system is asymptotically stable.

This means that regardless of deviations in the variables concerned (k, π^*), forces will be present which make the variables converge to the equilibrium situation (k_e, π_e^*). If the 'expectations coefficient' has the value $\beta > -\hat{L}/\hat{L}'$, the equilibrium in the neoclassical monetary growth model has the features of a saddle point equilibrium.

This means that the equilibrium point (k_e, π_e^*) will only be attained, if, as appears from the following graph, very distinct disturbances of the equilibrium are involved, e.g. (k_0, π_0^*).[73]

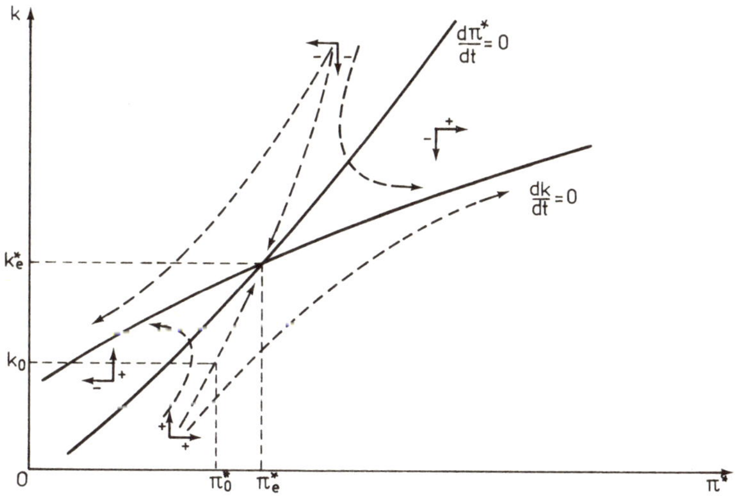

In all other cases an initial deviation in equilibrium values will lead to an adjustment process, which, depending on the starting situation, is characterized by a self-generating inflationary or deflationary process, with ever-more diverging values of the variables

73. H. Y. Wan speaks in this context of the 'razor's edge case', see H. Y. Wan, *Economic Growth*, 1971, p. 254.

concerned from the equilibrium point ($k\hat{e}$, π_e^*). It is worth noting that the faster the economic subjects adjust their expectations on the rate of inflation (in other words the greater the value of β) the more instable the system will be (see appendix). If we study the literature we will always discover that critical suppositions in the neo-classical monetary growth theory of a continuous equilibrium, on the one hand between the demand for and the supply of real cash-balances, and on the other hand between the actual and the expected rate of inflation will lead to instability of the economic system. This means that with an observed difference between the actual and the expected rate of inflation the last mentioned variable will be immediately and fully adjusted and accordingly dispositions will be taken with regard to the portfolio composition. All this can then result in a self-generating inflationary or deflationary process with consequences for real economic development.

Concluding it can be said that the neo-classical monetary growth model is always asymptotically stable, if the 'expectations coefficient' assumes such a value that the economic agents will revise the expected rate of inflation in a sufficiently sluggish way.

3. The Keynes-Wicksell monetary growth theory

3.1. Introduction

Economic literature contains a number of models which contrast markedly with the neo-classical monetary growth model. These can be characterized as the Keynes-Wicksell monetary growth theory.

As described in the preceding chapter, the neo-classical monetary growth theory starts from equilibrium dynamics, based upon the supposition that equilibrium always exists on all markets. On the contrary in the Keynes-Wicksell models disequilibrium situations are emphasized, finding expression in excess demand and supply situations on the commodity market.[1] This supposes that prices will only change if there is a discrepancy between total demand for goods and total supply of goods. Price changes reflect the demand and supply situations on the commodity markets. In other words, the rate of inflation is positively related to the excess-demand for goods and services, in accordance with this Walrasian excess-demand hypothesis. However the neo-classical monetary growth theory starts from the assumption that price flexibility is such that at any moment the excess-supply of real cash-balances or the excess-demand for goods is zero. In other words: equilibrium always exists on the assets market (real cash-balances and physical capital goods) and through Walras' law also on the commodity market. This means in fact that the price level adjusts immediately to the changed market situation and that exante-savings and investments are always equal. The different conceptions of the analysis method between the adherents of the neo-classical variant of the monetary growth theory on the one hand, and the adherents of the Keynes-Wicksell

1. Bent Hansen, *A survey of general equilibrium systems*, New York 1970, p. 109–125. Hansen speaks in this context of 'quasi-equilibrium systems' in contradistinction to the 'full equilibrium systems' which are expressed in the neo-classical models.

variant on the other are expressed by Hahn, when he says: '... one expects this (the rate of change in prices) to be a consequence of market disequilibrium. This makes equilibrium dynamics a doubtful procedure. In the foregoing the price of money was changing because this was required for portfolio equilibrium and not because any reason was adduced why in fact it should change.'[2] Hahn points out that the price changes are a signal for the existence of disequilibria on commodity markets and cannot be considered as a 'deus ex machina', as in the neo-classical models in order to maintain the equilibrium in the portfolio. If we study economic literature it will strike us that the adherents of the Keynes-Wicksell analysis use the Walrasian excess-demand hypothesis as an explanation of changes in prices of goods, but that this hypothesis is not applied consistently to all markets and to all prices. Stein does apply this hypothesis to the commodity market, but for the labour market and the market for financial assets he takes as his basis the equilibrium concept of the neo-classical authors. For he supposes such flexibility of the nominal wage rate and of the rate of interest that equilibrium on the labour market and on the market for financial assets is always maintained. Other authors start from the neo-classical hypothesis of continuous equilibrium on the labour-market, but suppose, on the contrary, a finite speed of adjustment of the prices of goods and the rate of interest with regard to disquilibria on the commodity market and on the market for financial assets.[3] Nagatani, however, applies the Walrasian excess-demand hypothesis to the commodity and the labour markets, but assumes a continuous equilibrium on the markets for financial assets.[4] The various authors cannot seem to agree on the specification of the adjustment mechanisms; in this respect empirical research is desirable in order to judge the practical value of the different models.

2. F. Hahn, On money and growth, *Journal of Money Credit and Banking*, May 1969, p. 183.
3. S. C. Tsiang, A critical note on the optimum supply of money, *Journal of Money, Credit and Banking*, April 1969, p. 274–275. A. Enthoven, A neo-classical model of money, debt and economic growth, in J. Gurley and E. Shaw, *Money in a theory of finance*, 1960, p. 328 and F. Takahashi, Money supply and economic growth, *Econometrica*, March 1971, p. 293.
4. K. Nagatani, A monetary growth model with variable employment, *Journal of Money, Credit and Banking*, May 1969, p. 191–192.

Further in the Keynes-Wicksell analysis it is postulated that savings are not automatically transformed into investments. On the contrary, the authors make use of a separate saving and investment function. This is connected with the fact that in the analysis concerned in contrast to the neo-classical models, the private sector is divided explicitly into production households and family households. Investment and saving decisions are based on totally different motives. This is particularly true in a monetary economy.

Investors are interested in the future flow of expected returns generated by physical capital goods. Savers, on the contrary, pursue rather the ownership of capital goods and are more interested in stable wealth assets, receiving for that purpose certain assets. In the Keynes-Wicksell model, it is supposed that if there is a positive difference between the marginal product of capital and the real rate of interest (nominal rate of interest on bonds minus expected rate of inflation) investment activity will be enlarged and newly-produced capital goods will be procured.

In the equilibrium situation the desired capital intensity will assume a value such that the marginal product of capital is equal to the real rate of interest. In other words a possible difference between desired capital goods and actual or existing capital goods will be eliminated through a change in the investment-demand. So we see that in this analysis decisions on investments are independent of decisions of family households on savings. This starting-point is – as will appear later on – of essential influence on the operation of the model.

A great number of the models developed by the adherents of the Keynes-Wicksell school can be considered as efforts to extend the synthesis, introduced by Patinkin in his well-known book 'Money, interest and prices', of monetary theory and macro-economic theory to the field of growth theory.

3.2. Suppositions

The following reflections are strongly based on the theoretical analysis of Stein, who developed a model in 1966 which still contains several elements from the neo-classical monetary growth theory, recorded in chapter 2.[5]

The analysis at issue starts from the production of one good, which can be used as a consumer and as an investment good. The production sector of the basic model is equal to that of the neo-classical monetary growth model. The production function is characterized by 'constant returns to scale' and 'diminishing returns to substitution', so production per unit of capital, or the average capital productivity ($Y/K = y$) and the rate of profit (r) can be expressed as a function of the labour-capital ratio or labour intensity ($\ell = L/K$).

Based upon the supposed linear homogeneity of the production function in both factors of production, capital and labour, the following technical relations can be distinguished:

$$y = \frac{Y}{K} = f(\ell), \text{ by which } f'(\ell) > 0 \text{ en } f''(\ell) < 0 \tag{1}$$

$$r = \frac{\partial Y}{\partial K} = f(\ell) - \ell f'(\ell) = r(\ell), \text{ by which } r'(\ell) > 0 \tag{1'}$$

Further it is assumed that full employment always exists and that the given natural growth rate has a constant percentage. ($n = dL/dt$ $1/L$).

It is a well-known fact that the traditional Keynesian income-expenditure model starts from the following four assets: money, government bonds, private financial assets and physical capital goods. The fact that in the theory concerned only two rates of return on assets emerge, viz. the rate of return on money, which is fixed at zero, and the rate of return on long-term government bonds, which is considered representative for the rates of return on the other assets (capital goods and private financial assets) means that

5. This analysis can, for instance, be found in the following publications by Stein: Money and capacity growth, *Journal of political Economy*, October 1966, p. 451–475; Stabilisation policies in a growing economy, *Review of Economic Studies*, April 1969, p. 165–183. Neoclassical and Keynes-Wicksell monetary growth models, *Journal of Money Credit and Banking*, May 1969 p. 162–171 and *Money and capacity growth*, New York – London 1971, chapters 3 and 4. See further A. Enthoven, 1960, op.cit. p. 303–359 and M. Beckman, A Wicksellian model of growth, *Revista Internazionale di Scienze Economiche e Commerciale*, March 1965, p. 201–210.

capital goods and bonds in the portfolio are considered as perfect substitutes for each other. By this implicit supposition the relation between existing capital goods and investment expenditures is not brought out explicitly.

The assumption that capital goods and bonds are completely interchangeable in fact reduces the choice to two assets when the portfolio is composed, viz. money and interest-bearing bonds. In other words, in the Keynesian theory no distinction is made between physical and financial non-monetary assets. The analysis at issue, with an independent saving and investment function, starts from three assets, in which the economic agents can hold their wealth: money, private bonds and capital goods, with the respective rates of return: the rate of deflation, the nominal rate of interest and the nominal rate of profit. It is the function of the financial markets to bring the demand for savings by employers in agreement with the supply of savings by the family households.

The savings per unit of capital are assumed to depend on the capital productivity (y) and the real cash-balances per unit of capital ($v = M/pK$). If we take account of equation (1) the savings-equation can be represented as follows.[6]

$$\frac{S}{K} = S^* \left[f(\ell), v\right] = S(\ell, v), \text{ by which } S_\ell > 0 \text{ en } S_v < 0 \qquad (2)$$

In this equation it is implied that exante consumption is relatedpositively to the income and the net wealth of the economic agents.

This net-wealth is equal to the sum of the capital goods and the net-claims of private economic subjects on the government. This last component of wealth, monetary wealth as it is called, consists of non-interest bearing government money. This interpretation means that interest-bearing government bonds are not considered

6. The total real wealth (W) of the private sector can be represented as the algebraic sum of physical capital goods (K) and monetary wealth, being the net-real claims of the private sector on the government (M/p). Then we can write:

$$W = K + \frac{M}{p} \text{ or per unit of capital: } \frac{W}{K} = 1 + \frac{M}{pK} = 1 + v,$$

so savings per unit of capital can be made dependent on the labour-capital ratio (ℓ) and the real cash-balances per unit of capital (v).

in this analysis as a net-wealth component of the private sector. This is based on the assumption that the economic agents fully capitalize the future tax liabilities resulting from the government debt-financing; this results in full compensation. Empirical research by Tanner has proved that in the Canadian economy in the 1951–1967 period a wealth effect was active, brought about especially by the quantity of circulating currency in the hands of the non-monetary sectors. The wealth effect connected with the interest-bearing government debt proves to be of negligible significance due to the capitalization mentioned above[7].

Just like the neo-classical monetary growth theory, the Keynes-Wicksell analysis supposes that the nominal quantity of money consists of so-called 'outside money', and that this grows by a constant percentage (μ). Changes in real cash-balances mean a similar change in the net-wealth position of the economic agents. The following can be said as regards investment behaviour, in which the Wicksellian element of the theory is apparent. Employers take investment decisions independent of the saving decisions by the other category of economic subjects, the family households.

Employers are now assumed to wish to maintain such capital intensity in the equilibrium situation that the marginal product of capital equals the real rate of interest, or otherwise expressed, that the nominal rate of return on capital tallies with the nominal rate of interest on financial assets (bonds). This desired capital-labour ratio will increase if a positive difference occurs between the marginal product of capital and the real rate of interest. In this Keynes-Wicksell analysis the following variables are inserted as arguments into the independent investment function.

On the one hand, investments are determined by the expected rate of profit, which is equal to the actual marginal product of capital, on the other hand by the expected real rate of interest (i^*) equal to the nominal rate of interest (i) on bonds, minus the expected rate of inflation (π^*). Otherwise expressed, with a positive difference be-

7. J. E. Tanner, Empirical evidence of the short run real balance effect in Canada, *Journal of Money, Credit and Banking*, November 1970, p. 473–485. In the literature in recent years much attention has been paid to the question which assets belong to the net-wealth components of the private sector. See in this context also the views of B. Pesek and T. Saving in their well-known work, *Money Wealth and economic theory*, 1967.

tween the expected nominal rate of profit ($r(\ell) + \pi^*$) and the nominal rate of interest (i), investment activity will be increased.[8]

Apart from that, Stein has still another explanation for the mentioned investment behaviour, which links up with the mechanism of the supply price of capital, the focal point in the portfolio-balance theory developed by the Yale school (Tobin c.s.).[9] He compares the market value of existing capital goods (discounted value of future returns of the capital good) with the supply price. If the market value of existing capital goods is higher than the price of newly-produced units, employers will extend the demand for investment goods, and vice versa.

The market value of existing capital goods is consequently related positively to the marginal product of capital (r) and the expected rate of inflation (π^*), and related negatively to the nominal rate of interest (i).[10] If the expected rate of profit ($r(\ell)$) has become equal to the real rate of interest (i^*) capital intensity, or inversely labour intensity, has attained its equilibrium value and capital goods will extend in accordance with the rate of population growth (n). This in order to maintain the equilibrium value of the capital intensity. The investment behaviour described above agrees with the views in the theory of marginal productivity. As we have seen in the preceding chapter, disturbances of portfolio equilibrium in the neo-classical monetary growth model (money versus goods) will lead to price changes. An increase in the money supply will bring about an excess-supply of real cash-balances through the increase of real wealth and will further lead to an excess-demand for goods, in this case capital goods. The price level (price of consumer good is price of investment good) will increase until the excess-supply of real cash-balances is eliminated and the equilibrium in the portfolio is restored.

In these reflections it is rather a question of an indirect mechanism, advanced by Wicksell, with the monetary influence manifesting

8. M. Beckmann, *Revista Internazionale di Scienze Economiche e Commerciale*, March 1965, op. cit. p. 201

9. See J. Tobin; *Essays in economics, Volume I, macro economics*, Amsterdam, 1971., W. Brainard and J. Tobin, *Pitfalls in financial model building*, Cowles Foundation Paper, No. 279, Yale University, 1968.

10. J. Stein, 1971, op. cit. p. 60.

itself through a difference between the market rate of interest and the natural rate of interest brought about by the authorities.[11] Here too an increase in money supply at the initial price level will make for an increase in real wealth.

The disturbance in the composition of the portfolio will in the first instance be felt on the bonds market and further on the commodity market by way of the assumed investment behaviour. An excess-demand will come about for bonds, causing the nominal rate of interest to decrease in order to restore equilibrium on the bonds market. The price level is now influenced in a more indirect way namely through an extension of investment activity and a corresponding excess-demand for goods. Under these circumstances a new equilibrium will be attained at a higher price level when the excess-demand for goods has been eliminated and the nominal rate of interest again equals the natural rate of interest.

The desired investments per unit of capital can be expressed by the following equation:

$$\frac{I}{K} = I\left[(r(\ell) + \pi^*) - i\right] + n. \tag{3}$$

The real rate of interest (i^*) can be considered as the opportunity costs attached to investment. From equation (3) it can be deduced that development of capital intensity is positively related to the difference between the expected nominal rate of profit and the nominal rate of interest. However it is not so that investment activity immediately brings about equality between the marginal product of capital (expected rate of profit) and the real rate of interest. Some time will pass before that difference leads to a change in investment policy ('decision lag'). For the employers wish to ascertain whether the difference between the nominal rate of profit and the nominal rate of interest is of a more enduring nature. One of

11. The classical authors, Ricardo and Thornton, have already pointed out the operation of this mechanism. Wicksell says: '... The normal rate of interest (at which the exchange value of money and the general level of commodity prices have no tendency to change) is determined by the current natural rate of interest, the real return of capital in production. If the rate of interest on money deviates downwards, be it ever so little, from this normal level prices will, as long as the deviation lasts, rise continuously; if it deviates upwards they will fall indefinitely in the same way'. The influence of the rate of interest on commodity prices, *Selected Papers on Economic Theory*, Cambridge, Mass. 1958, p. 83.

the other lags in the investment process concerns the so-called 'gestation period', the time which passes between order and delivery of the capital goods concerned.

Besides several factors of uncertainty can play a part, preventing employers from responding immediately to the existing discrepancy between the two rates of return mentioned. Our analysis will not go further into this lag.

We already pointed out in the introduction that the relative change in price level or the rate of inflation is explained by appealing to the Walrasian excess-demand hypothesis, according to which the actual rate of inflation depends on the possible difference between demand for and supply of goods per unit of capital. This excess-demand is equal to the sum of planned consumption and planned investments, less production.[12] Otherwise expressed, the existing rate of inflation is proportionally related to the difference between planned investments and planned savings per unit of capital, in which coefficient α represents the speed of price adjustment.

$$\frac{dp}{dt}\frac{1}{p} = \pi = \alpha\left(\frac{I}{K} - \frac{S}{K}\right). \tag{4}$$

In an inflationary situation, which implies that there is an excess-demand for goods per unit of capital, the wishes of consumers and producers cannot be fulfilled completely if there is no immediate adjustment on the markets. The transactions which will come about on the market lead to prices which are not equilibrium prices. If, on the contrary, a zero excess-demand for goods exists, i.e. there is equilibrium on the commodity markets, consumers' and producers' wishes will be granted. In this formulation a rate of inflation means the simultaneous existence of an excess-demand for goods, and conversely deflation implies an excess-supply of goods. Coefficient α, which in this analysis has a finite value, represents the speed at which the growth rate of the price level responds to disequilibria on the commodity market. When α approaches infinity, the commodity market disequilibria will immediately lead to price changes, meaning that planned savings and planned investments are in equilibrium at all times. This latter conception underlies the neo-classi-

12. $C + I - Y = I - (Y - C) = I - S$, in other words an excess-demand for goods ($C + I > Y$) is equal to the positive difference between investments and savings.

cal growth models, which came up for discussion in the preceding chapter.

As far as the demand for real cash-balances per unit of capital is concerned, it depends on the one hand on the level of transactions and on the other hand on the opportunity costs attached to the holding of money as an asset. These costs consist of two components, viz. the nominal rate of return of bonds (i) and the expected nominal rate of return of capital goods ($r(\ell) + \pi^*$).

Further a complementary relation still exists between the demand for real cash-balances and the net-private wealth per unit of capital (v). In other words the wealth-elasticity of the demand for money is positive.

The transaction demand for real cash-balances is positively related to the planned real expenditures by the family and production households, which can be represented as the total effective demand ($C + I$). Because planned consumption expenditures are equal to $Y - S$, planned real expenditures can be expressed as $Y + I - S$. Tsiang points out that the demand for transaction cash-balances ('money to spend') is primarily a function of the planned expenditures and that this variable need not be equal to real production, because planned investments can diverge from planned savings. Tsiang assumes that the total available quantity of money can always be divided into active cash-balances ('money to spend') and idle cash-balances ('money to hold') and that total expenditures have in any case to be financed from the existing quantity of money.[13]

If account is taken of equation (4), the demand for real (transaction) cash-balances per unit of capital depends on the factor: $Y/K + I - S/K = Y/K + \pi/\alpha = f(\ell) + \pi/\alpha$.

The total demand for real cash-balances per unit of capital is then as follows:

$$\hat{L} = \hat{L}\left[f(\ell) + \frac{\pi}{\alpha}, r(\ell) + \pi^*, i, v\right] \text{ in which} \tag{5}$$

$\hat{L}_1 > 0, \hat{L}_2 < 0, \hat{L}_3 < 0, 1 > \hat{L}_4 > 0.$[14]

13. S. C. Tsiang, *Journal of Money, Credit and Banking*, May 1969 op. cit. p. 269. See in the article concerned also the footnote on page 274.

14. The supposition $1 > \hat{L}_4$ implies that a monetary impulse will not be held fully in the form of cash-balances. This means that an increase of the real cash-balances implies an excess supply of real cash-balances.

The first argument in this equation refers to the income-effect of the demand for money, the second argument refers to the substitution relation between real cash-balances and real capital goods and the third argument concerns the substitution relation between real cash-balances and bonds. Finally the fourth argument points to a complementary relation between the demand for real cash-balances and monetary wealth per unit of capital held by the economic subjects.[15]

In accordance with Walras' law the excess-demand for goods plus the excess-demand for real cash-balances and bonds is zero, because it is supposed that full employment always exists. If it is assumed that a possible excess-demand for bonds is immediately eliminated, the excess-demand for goods per unit of capital (π/α) can be said to equal the excess-supply of real cash-balances per unit of capital. Since supply of and demand for real cash-balances per unit of capital refer to stock-variables and consumption, investments and savings refer to flow-variables, the excess-supply of real cash-balances as a flow-variable is taken to be proportionate to the excess-supply of real cash-balances as a stock variable. On the basis of Walras' law it is then valid:

$$\frac{\pi}{\alpha} = \frac{I}{K} - \frac{S}{K} = h[v - \hat{L}], \text{ in which } 0 < h < \infty$$

acts as a coefficient of proportionality. Coefficient h is an indication for the degree in which a discrepancy between supply of and demand for real cash-balances per unit of capital is expressed in an opposite disequilibrium on the commodity markets and a corresponding change in the rate of growth of the price level. The relative change in the price level is now related positively to the excess-supply of real cash-balances per unit of capital and can be reproduced as follows:

$$\frac{dp}{dt}\frac{1}{p} = \frac{\pi}{\alpha} = h\left[v - \hat{L}\left(f(\ell) + \frac{\pi}{\alpha}, r(\ell) + \pi^*, i, v\right)\right]. \tag{6}$$

in which (v) represents the exogenously given supply of real cash-balances per unit of capital. From this equation we see that when

15. J. Stein, *Journal of Political Economy*, October 1966, op. cit. p. 454.

equilibrium exists between the demand for and the supply of real cash-balances ($\hat{L} = v$) the price level will not change. Tobin says in this context: '. . . portfolio balance is assumed to be the necessary and sufficient condition for price stability'.[16] If actual real cash-balances are larger than the desired balances, this difference will be expressed in a greater demand for goods, exerting an upward pressure on the price level. When an excess-demand for real cash-balances exists, an adjustment in the reverse direction will come about.

If the analysis above is taken into account, Walras' law can be expressed by the following equation:

$$\frac{\pi}{\alpha h} = v - \hat{L}\left[f(\ell) + \frac{\pi}{\alpha}, r(\ell) + \pi^*, i, v\right] \qquad (6')$$

$$0 < \alpha h < \infty^{17}$$

For simplicity it is supposed that the expected rate of inflation always agrees with the equilibrium rate of inflation, which is equal to the growth rate of the nominal cash-balances per head.

$$\pi^* = \pi = \mu - n. \qquad (7)$$

The expectations are based on experience from the past, with the actual rate of inflation converging to the rate of growth of the nominal quantity of money per head.[18]

In order to complement the Keynes–Wicksell monetary growth model three more equations are of importance. In the first place, the equation describing the actual rate of growth of capital goods, and further an equation representing the development of the labour-capital ratio. Finally there is a need for an equation representing the rate of growth of real cash-balances per unit of capital.

The matter of the actual growth rate of capital goods when the economy is not in equilibrium, for example when expenditure exceeds production capacity, presents a number of problems.

16. J. Tobin, A dynamic aggregative model, *Journal of Political Economy*, April 1955, p. 105.
17. J. Stein 1971, op. cit. p. 67–68.
18. For alternative functions with regard to the price expectations it is referred to Stein, 1971, op. cit. p. 65.

From equation (4) it can be concluded that during periods of changes in the price level, savings and investments are not equal.

In the neo-classical analysis the line is taken that actual capital accumulation is equal to the difference between production and planned consumption expenditures. The investment function then is not relevant in determining the rate of growth of capital goods, since planned savings are always equal to planned investments. In the Keynes–Wicksell analysis however the key question arises how the actual rate of growth of capital goods is determined, if the effective demand for goods exceeds the production capacity. What this in fact amounts to, as we said earlier, is that during periods of inflation (excess-demand for goods per unit of capital) the wishes of consumers and producers cannot be fully granted at the same time. It is of importance to indicate to what extent planned savings and to what extent planned investments are realised in reality. In other words the question arises whether planned savings or planned investments are crucial for the actual rate of growth of capital goods, or both to some extent. Stein puts a 'deus ex machina' on the scene, taking the line that the actual rate of growth of capital goods during periods of inflation, is a linear combination of planned savings and planned investments per unit of capital.

$$\frac{dK}{dt}\frac{1}{K} = \gamma\frac{I}{K} + (1 - \gamma)\frac{S}{K},$$

$$\text{in which } 1 > \gamma > 0 \text{ when } \pi > 0 \qquad (8)$$

[19]

Under these circumstances actual capital accumulation is smaller than planned investments, but larger than planned savings. By substitution of equation (4) into equation (8) the following equation is obtained for the actual rate of growth of capital goods.

$$\frac{dK}{dt}\frac{1}{K} = \frac{\gamma}{\alpha}\pi + \frac{S}{K}. \qquad (9)$$

This equation expresses that during periods of inflation, when there

19. J. Stein, Rational choice and patterns of growth in a monetary economy, A comment. *American Economic Review*, September, 1968, p. 948. If $\gamma = 1$ the actual rate of growth of capital goods is equal to planned investments per unit of capital; if $\gamma = 0$ the actual rate of growth of capital goods is determined by planned savings per unit of capital.

exists an excess-demand for goods, forced savings will set in, represented by the factor $\gamma\pi/\alpha$. This results from the fact that the ex-post consumption expenditures are smaller than planned consumption expenditures. This view has been expressed by Wicksell in the monetary literature of earlier date. The concept of forced savings means that a greater part of the available production capacity of the economy is used in the investment sector than the public had proposed on the basis of individual saving decisions. We leave out of consideration in our analysis the possibility that producers and/or consumers, for instance on the basis of a learning process, take account in the future of the fact that their plans are not always realised and that they will change their behaviour accordingly. If this possibility were taken into account, it would mean that the institutionally-determined division between planned and realised variables would be inserted into the saving and investment function. One could then imagine that employers would 'over-estimate' as it were, the planned investment demand would be larger than is represented in equation (3), because they take the line that only part of these planned investments will be realised ultimately. The abandoning of this supposed learning process in investment behaviour means that the rate of inflation will be accordingly smaller.[20]

Finally the theoretical model still contains a couple of differential equations for the development of labour intensity and of real cash-balances per unit of capital. Per capita investments can be considered as the sum, on the one side, of investments, required to maintain the existing equilibrium value of the capital intensity and, on the other side, of investments which bring about a change in the capital intensity. If we take equations (3) and (9) into account, the rate of growth of the capital intensity can be reproduced by the following differential equation:

$$\frac{dk}{dt}\frac{1}{k} = \frac{dK}{dt}\frac{1}{K} - n = \frac{\gamma}{\alpha}\pi + \frac{S}{K} - n. \tag{10}$$

The rate of growth of the labour-capital ratio can then be repre-

20. K. Jaeger, Ein Einfaches monetäres Wachstumsmodell mit Product- und Prozessinnovationen, *Zeitschrift für die gesamte Staatswissenschaft*, August 1973, p. 416–417.

sented as:

$$\frac{d\ell}{dt}\frac{1}{\ell} = n - \frac{dK}{dt}\frac{1}{K} = n - \frac{y}{\alpha}\pi - \frac{S}{K}. \tag{10'}$$

The other differential equation in the model relates to the rate of growth of real cash-balances per unit of capital.

This equation is equal to the algebraic difference between the rate of monetary expansion, the rate of inflation and the rate of growth of capital goods

$$\frac{dv}{dt}\frac{1}{v} = \mu - \pi - \frac{dK}{dt}\frac{1}{K}. \tag{11}$$

From equations (10′) and (11) it can be deduced that in the equilibrium growth situation, when labour intensity and real cash-balances per unit of capital are constant ($d\ell/dt\ 1/\ell = 0$ and $dv/dt\ 1/v = 0$) the rate of inflation is equal to the rate of growth of the nominal cash-balances per head ($\pi = \mu - n$).

The conclusion can also be interpreted in such a way that a monetary policy, aimed at price stability, must imply that given the economic agents' preference for liquidity, the nominal quantity of money is extended in accordance with the increase of real production determined by the rate of population growth.

The model mentioned above consists of eleven equations, which – given the exogenous variables, viz. the rates of growth of the money supply (μ) and of population (n), – give a solution for the eleven variables: capital productivity (y), labour intensity (ℓ), rate of profit (r), planned savings per unit of capital (S/K), planned investments per unit of capital (I/K), actual rate of growth of capital goods ($dK/dt\ 1/K$), real cash-balances per unit of capital ($v = M/PK$), real cash-balances per unit of capital ($\hat{L}$), nominal rate of interest (i), actual rate of inflation (π) and expected rate of inflation (π^*).

3.3. The short-term model

3.3.1. The IS–FM equilibrium

As we have already seen in the preceding analysis, the essence of the Keynes–Wicksell monetary growth model lies in the fact that savings and investments come about independently of each other and that price changes are a reflection of the disequilibria on the commodity market.

Analysing the influence of a change in the rate of monetary expansion on the different real variables in the short run in which the labour-capital ratio has been taken as constant, we start from the following relations.[21] In the first place it is postulated, that the rate of inflation is related proportionally to the excess-demand for goods, which is equal to the difference between planned investments and planned savings per unit of capital. All this is expressed in the following equation.

$$\frac{dp}{dt}\frac{1}{p} = \pi = \alpha\left(\frac{I}{K} - \frac{S}{K}\right) \tag{1}$$

After substitution of equations (2) and (3) from the preceding section into the above, the excess-demand equation for goods can be represented as follows:

$$\frac{\pi}{\alpha} = n + r(\ell) + \pi^* - i - S(\ell, v). \tag{1'}$$

Further, starting from the supposition that equilibrium always exists on the market for financial assets (bonds) Walras' law (excess-demand for goods plus excess-demand for real cash-balances is zero) can be formulated as follows:

$$\frac{\pi}{\alpha} + h\left\{\hat{L}\left(f(\ell) + \frac{\pi}{\alpha}, r(\ell) + \pi^*, i, v\right) - v\right\} = 0 \tag{2}$$

With regard to price expectations the line is taken that the equilibrium value of the expected rate of inflation (π^*) is equal to the current rate of inflation in the short run (π), which agrees in the equilibrium situation with the algebraic difference between the rate of monetary expansion (μ) and the rate of population growth (n) or with the rate of growth of the nominal quantity of money

21. J. Stein, *Journal of Political Economy*, October 1966, op. cit. p. 456–458 and by the same author 1971, op. cit. p. 88–98.

per head.

$$\pi^* = \pi = \mu - n. \tag{3}$$

Because a short-term analysis is involved, in which the labour-capital ratio (ℓ) is taken as constant, the relative change in the real cash-balances per unit of capital can be formulated as:

$$\frac{dv}{dt}\frac{1}{v} = \mu - \pi - \frac{dK}{dt}\frac{1}{K} = \mu - \pi - n^{22} \tag{4}$$

After substitution of equation (3) into equations (1′) and (2), short-term equilibrium can be represented by the following equations:

$$\frac{\pi}{\alpha} = n + r(\bar{\ell}) + \pi - i - S(\bar{\ell}, v) \tag{5}$$

$$\frac{\pi}{\alpha h} = v - \hat{L}\left[f(\bar{\ell}) + \frac{\pi}{\alpha}, r(\bar{\ell}) + \pi, i, v\right] \tag{6}$$

Equation (5), which is in a way analogous to the *IS*-curve in the standard Hicks-Hansen diagram, represents the combinations of the nominal rate of interest (i) and the real cash-balances per unit of capital (v), for which it holds that the excess-demand or excess-supply of goods per unit of capital is constant. In other words, each point on the curve mentioned represents a combination of the nominal interest rate and the real cash-balances per unit capital for which it holds that the equilibrium value of the rate of inflation in the short term remains constant.[23] The value of coefficient α determines the speed at which possible disequilibria on the commodity market are expressed in relative price changes. The slope of this curve is positive, which can be explained as follows. If, in the start-

22. We know that the relative change in labour intensity is equal to the algebraic difference between the rate of population growth and the rate of growth of capital goods. In symbols:

$$\frac{d\ell}{dt}\frac{1}{\ell} = \frac{dL}{dt}\frac{1}{L} - \frac{dK}{dt}\frac{1}{K} \text{ or } \frac{dK}{dt}\frac{1}{K} = n - \frac{d\ell}{dt}\frac{1}{\ell}$$

23. See in this context R. Mundell's analysis, Inflation, saving and the real rate of interest, in *Monetary theory* 1971, p. 16–23.

ing position, the rate of inflation is zero, it means that planned savings and investments per unit of capital are equal to each other, or that the excess-demand for goods is zero. An increase of the nominal rate of interest – starting from the described investment behaviour – will in these circumstances lead to a reduction of the planned investments.

Accordingly, a deviation will arise between planned investments and planned savings per unit of capital in that an excess-supply of goods will arise. The real cash-balances per unit of capital will have to increase, causing planned savings to drop too ($S_v < 0$) due to the wealth-effect in the savings function; the initial zero-excess-demand for goods is restored again. So we see a positive relation between the nominal rate of interest and the real cash-balances per unit of capital, conforming with equation (5).

If on the contrary the rate of inflation in the initial position is positive, which means that the rate of monetary expansion (μ) exceeds the rate of population growth (n), an excess-demand exists for goods per unit of capital, represented by π/α. A rise of the nominal rate of interest will reduce this excess demand by decreasing investment activity. Now too the real cash-balances per unit of capital will have to increase in order to maintain the excess-demand of the initial situation. Price stability will only result in the equilibrium situation on the short run when the nominal quantity of money per head is constant, i.e. if the nominal quantity of money grows in accordance with the increase of production.[24]

The positive relation between the nominal rate of interest and the real cash-balances per unit of capital can be derived by partial differentiation of equation (5) to the real cash-balances per unit of capital (v).

$$\frac{\partial i}{\partial v} = -\,S_v > 0 \qquad (7)$$

On the other hand equation (6) represents the algebraic expression of the so-called *FM*-curve for the short term and can be considered as an equilibrium condition for the market for financial assets.

This curve represents the different combinations of the nominal

24. J. Stein, 1971, op. cit. p. 90.

rate of interest (i) and the real cash-balances per unit of capital (v), for which it holds that the sum of the excess-demand for goods and the excess-demand for real cash-balances per unit of capital is equal to zero. This means that Walras' law holds and an equilibrium exists on the market for financial assets (bonds). The *FM*-curve is negatively sloped. If in a certain initial situation the rate of inflation is equal to zero, equilibrium exists between the demand for and the supply of real cash-balances per unit of capital; in other words, the excess-supply of real cash-balances per unit of capital is zero ($v = \hat{L}(\ldots)$). A rise in the nominal rate of interest will lead to a drop in the demand for real cash-balances per unit of capital ($\hat{L}_3 < 0$), by which a tendency arises to an excess-supply of real cash-balances. The supply of real cash-balances per unit of capital will have to decrease now in order to maintain the equilibrium on the market in financial assets. One and the same reasoning holds when in the initial situation, the rate of inflation is positive. The excess-supply of real cash-balances per unit of capital is then $\pi/\alpha h$ according to equation (6). A rise in the nominal rate of interest will further increase the already-existing excess-supply of real cash-balances and the rate of inflation. The supply of real cash-balances will again have to decrease in order to maintain the initial excess-supply of the real cash-balances $\pi/\alpha h$.[25] The negative relation between the nominal rate of interest and the real cash-balances per unit of capital, for which it holds that there is an equilibrium on the financial markets, is obtained by partial differentiation of equation (6) to the real cash-balances per unit of capital.

$$\frac{\partial i}{\partial v} = \frac{1 - \hat{L}_4}{\hat{L}_3} < 0. \qquad (8)$$

The *IS*-curve of the short run mentioned above can be deduced with the aid of the graph on page 94.

Starting from the investment behaviour described in the preceding section, the second quadrant reveals the negative relation between the nominal rate of interest and the excess-demand for goods per unit of capital. In the third quadrant the excess-demand hypothesis of the short run analysis is expressed, which implies that the actual

25. J. Stein, 1971, op. cit. p. 91.

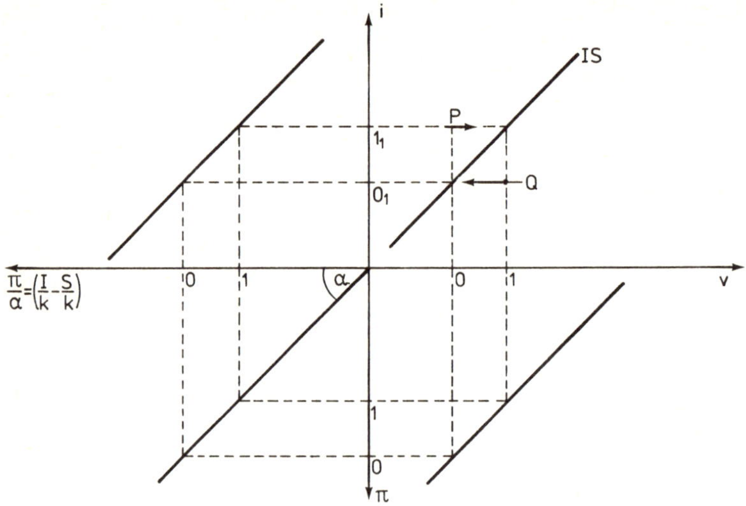

Figure 1a

value of the rate of inflation is related proportionally to the excess-demand for goods per unit of capital. Coefficient α represents the speed at which a disequilibrium on the commodity market is expressed in relative price changes. If the analysis starts from an equilibrium situation (i_0, v_0), with a corresponding excess-demand for goods $(\pi/\alpha)_0$ and a rate of inflation of π_0, a rise in the nominal rate of interest to i_1 will lead to the following adjustment process.

Because the nominal rate of interest has been inserted as an argument into the investment function, a decrease of the excess-demand for goods $(\pi/\alpha)_1$ will come about. The third quadrant indicates how the rate of inflation responds to the decrease in the excess-demand for goods, given the value of the adjustment coefficient. The real cash-balances per unit of capital – given the supply of money – will have to increase (v_1) as a result of the lower rate of inflation ($\pi_1 < \pi_0$) for the equilibrium condition to be fulfilled (equation 5). For the planned savings per unit of capital will decrease as a result of the increase in real cash-balances (negative wealth-effect in the savings function) induced by the lower rate of inflation. This causes the demand for goods and services to increase, whilst the excess-demand is maintained. We can now interpret the *IS*-curve as the locus of all combinations of the nominal rate of interest (i) and the real cash-balances per unit of capital (v) for which the excess-demand for goods per unit of capital remains constant.

Each point above the *IS*-curve, e.g. point *P*, means, starting from the equilibrium situation (i_0, v_0), such a nominal rate of interest (i_1) that the excess-demand for goods $(\pi/\alpha)_1$ no longer tallies with the rate of inflation π_0 belonging to the equilibrium value of the real cash-balances v_0. The real cash-balances per unit of capital will increase (v_1) under influence of the lower rate of inflation ($\pi_1 < \pi_0$), in order to restore the equilibrium (see movement to the right in point *P*).

The reverse is valid for points below the *IS*-curve (e.g. point *Q*). The arrows in the figure represent the movement of real cash-balances per unit of capital at deviations of the equilibrium situation.

The *FM*-curve can be deduced analogously. The equilibrium condition which underlies this curve is that the excess-supply of real cash-balances per unit of capital ($v - \hat{L}(\ldots)$) must be related proportionally to the excess-demand for goods per unit of capital ($\pi/\alpha h = I/K - S/K$).

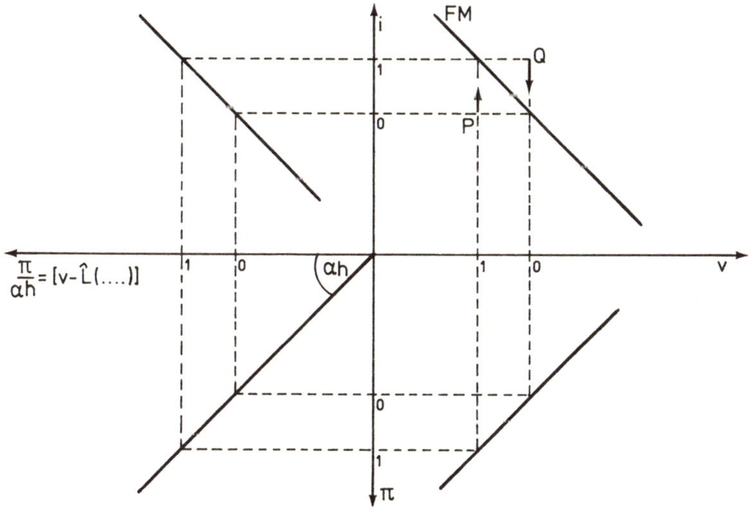

Figure 1b

This means that the market for financial assets (bonds) is always in equilibrium. This condition is expressed in equation (6) and in the third quadrant of the graph on page 95.

If the analysis starts from an equilibrium situation with regard to the bonds market, the nominal rate of interest i_0 and the real cash-balances per unit of capital amounting to v_0, and further the rate of interest is increased, i_1, greater excess-demand for real cash-balances per unit of capital will occur: $(\pi/\alpha h)_1 > (\pi/\alpha h)_0$. This results from the fact that demand for real cash-balances had decreased ($\hat{L}_3 < 0$). In accordance with Walras' law greater excess-demand for goods per unit of capital and consequently an increase in the rate of inflation will set in (π_1) given the equilibrium on the bonds market. Under influence of the increased rate of inflation the supply of real cash-balances (v_1) will adjust in order to maintain the equilibrium excess-supply of real cash-balances.

Points on the *FM*-curve represent combinations of the nominal rate of interest and real cash-balances per unit of capital, for which it holds that the market for financial assets (bonds) is in equilibrium. With regard to deviations in the equilibrium situations, which are expressed in points which are not situated on the *FM*-curve, the following can be observed. A point below the *FM*-curve (point P) will lead – starting from the equilibrium situation (i_1, v_1) – to an increase in the excess-demand for goods and for real cash-balances per unit of capital; (a decrease in excess-supply of real cash-balances per unit of capital with regard to equilibrium situation (i_1, v_1)). In accordance with Walras' law (excess-demand for goods plus excess-demand for real cash-balances = excess-supply of bonds) the excess-supply of bonds will increase, causing an interest-increasing effect to set in, in order to maintain the equilibrium on the bonds market. So a point above the *FM*-curve (point Q) will indicate an interest level which triggers off a decrease in the excess-demand for goods and for real cash-balances per unit of capital (an increase in the excess-supply of real cash-balances with regard to equilibrium situation (i_0, v_0)). Disequilibrium on the bonds market, expressed in a greater excess-demand for bonds, will bring about an interest-decreasing effect by which the equilibrium is restored again (see the direction of the arrows in the graph). With the aid of the graphs mentioned above and equations (5) and (6) the combination can now be derived from the nominal rate of interest (i_0) and the real cash-balances per unit of capital (v_0), in which both equations hold, given the labour-capital ratio (ℓ)[26]. All this can be reproduced graphically as follows:

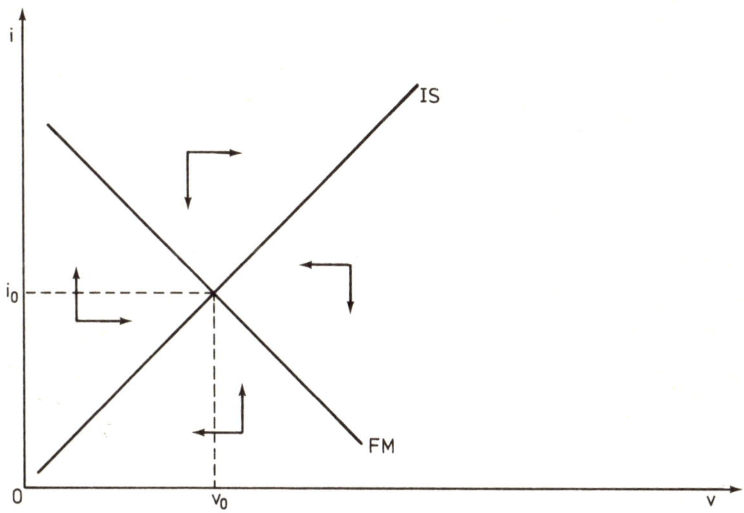

Figure 1

In equilibrium point (i_0, v_0) it holds that, given the labour intensity (ℓ) and the rate of growth of the quantity of money (μ), the excess-demand for goods per unit of capital (π/α) is equal to the excess-supply of real cash-balances per unit of capital ($h\,[v - \hat{L}(\ldots)]$), and also that the actual and the expected rates of inflation are equal to the rate of growth of the nominal quantity of money per head.[27] All this can also be formulated as follows. The equilibrium point (i_0, v_0) represents on the one side an equilibrium on the market for financial assets and given the concomitant equilibrium value of the nominal rate of interest, there results on the other hand such an

26. Readers should note that short-term equilibrium is assumed to be stable. A disturbance in equilibrium will always be accompanied by forces, which provide stability of the equilibrium.
27. J. Stein, 1971, op. cit. p. 92.

excess-supply for goods per unit of capital that the actual rate of inflation agrees with the equilibrium value of this variable ($\pi = \pi^* = \mu - n$). If the point of intersection of both curves implied a zero rate of inflation ($\pi = 0$), equilibrium would arise on the three markets at once, viz. the commodity market, the money market (demand and supply of real cash-balances) and the market for financial assets (bonds).

Otherwise formulated, in these circumstances the excess-demands on all markets will equal zero.

3.3.2. The influence of a change in the rate of monetary expansion

It is now interesting to analyse the influence of a higher rate of monetary expansion on the equilibrium value of the real cash-balances in the short run. As was propounded in the preceding chapter, an increase in the growth rate of the nominal quantity of money (μ) in Tobin's neo-classical model leads unambiguously to a reduction in the equilibrium value of the real cash-balances per unit of capital.

In the Keynes-Wicksell analysis this is no longer determined unambiguously. An increase in the rate of inflation, reflecting a disequilibrium on the markets, will lead to a drop in the quantity of real cash-balances per unit capital demanded ($\hat{L}_2 < 0$). Since continuous equilibrium between demand for and supply of real cash-balances is not assumed to exist now, and so the actual rate of inflation is not always equal to the equilibrium value of this variable, it cannot a priori be indicated how the supply of real cash-balances will develop (v). For this supply of real cash balances is dependent on the development of the actual rate of inflation. Besides the possibility is now left open that the expected rate of inflation (= equilibrium value of the rate of inflation) may deviate from the actual rate of inflation. In the foregoing analysis it has been already stated several times that with continuous equilibrium on the market for financial assets (bonds), the excess-demand for goods (π/α) is equal to the excess-supply of real cash-balances per unit of capital ($h[v - \hat{L}(\ldots)]$).

In algebraic notation:

$$\frac{\pi}{\alpha} = h\,[v - \hat{L}(\ldots)] \tag{9}$$

or

$$v = \frac{\pi}{\alpha h} + \hat{L}(\ldots). \tag{9'}$$

An increase of the rate of monetary expansion will, as we have seen, enlarge the (short-run) equilibrium value of the rate of inflation ($\pi = \mu - n$). The first term in equation (9′) will consequently increase, but what happens with the supply of real cash-balances per unit of capital (v) also depends on the size of the second term, the development of the demand for real cash-balances ($\hat{L}_1 > 0$, $\hat{L}_2 < 0$ and $1 > \hat{L}_4 > 0$). In other words, an increase in the rate of monetary expansion can enlarge, as well as reduce the equilibrium value of real cash-balances per unit of capital (v). In the short-term equilibrium situation it holds that the actual and the expected rates of inflation are equal ($\pi = \pi^*$). An increase in the expected rate of inflation (π^*) as a result of an increase in the growth rate of the nominal quantity of money per head ($\mu - n$), will enlarge investments per unit of capital, starting from an investment behaviour which increases the excess-demand for goods per unit of capital (see equation 1′). The extent to which this greater discrepancy between demand for goods and supply of goods has been passed on in an increased actual rate of inflation and so in the development of the supply of real cash-balances, depends on the adjustment coefficient of the price level (α) from the Walrasian excess-demand equation.

Two cases can now be distinguished. If $\alpha < 1$, the supply of real cash-balances per unit of capital will increase, because the actual rate of inflation increases less quickly than the equilibrium value of the expected rate of inflation ($\pi < \pi^* = \mu - n$).[28] An adjustment process will come about, in that as a consequence of the increased supply of real cash-balances and the corresponding wealth-effect in the savings function ($S_v < 0$), the initial excess-demand for goods will be reinforced. The actual rate of inflation will further increase, until in the equilibrium situation the actual rate of inflation has become equal to the new, higher equilibrium value of the concerning monetary variable ($\pi = \pi^* = \mu - n$). If we proceed from the constant labour-capital ratio, the relative change in the supply of real cash-balances per unit of capital will have become equal to zero (see equation 4).

28. See equations (1′) and (9′).

In the reverse case, with $\alpha > 1$, under influence of the initial increase of the excess-demand for goods per unit of capital, the actual rate of inflation will increase more quickly than equilibrium value (π^*), causing the supply of real cash-balances per unit of capital to decrease. The drop in expenditure which results from the operation of the wealth-effect in the savings function, will mitigate the increase in the actual rate of inflation. This process goes on until in the equilibrium situation such a decrease in the supply of real cash-balances and in the excess-demand for goods per unit of capital has set in, that the actual rate of inflation has been reduced to the new equilibrium value, which is equal to the growth rate of the nominal quantity of money per head ($\pi = \pi^* = \mu - n$).

It can be said that a higher rate of monetary growth, which manifests itself in an increased growth rate of the nominal quantity of money per head ($\mu - n$) may increase or decrease the equilibrium value of real cash-balances per unit of capital in the short-run analysis, depending on whether the adjustment coefficient of the price level (α) in the Walrasian excess-demand equation is smaller or larger than one.[29] In neo-classical equilibrium analysis, where adjustments come about very quickly, there will always be equality between the expected (= equilibrium value of the rate of inflation) and the actual rate of inflation. In other words, a continuous zero excess-demand for goods will exist, and accordingly, a zero excess-supply of real cash-balances. The implications of these explanations for the development of the labour-capital ratio come up for discussion in the following section.

3.4. Long-term equilibrium analysis

3.4.1. The relation between the rate of inflation and the nominal rate of interest

For analysis of the long-term equilibrium model the two differential equations (10′) and (11) in section 2 are of essential importance. One

29. The mathematical proof of this proposition is given by Stein on p. 97 in his book *Money and capacity growth*, 1971. The influence of a change in the equilibrium value of the rate of inflation in the short-term analysis on the equilibrium value of the real cash-balances per unit of capital ($dv/d\pi$) is ultimately determined by the value of the partial differential quotient ($\partial\pi/\partial\pi^*$) which represents the influence of a change in the expected rate of inflation on the actual rate of inflation.

describes the development of the labour-capital ratio (ℓ), the other refers to the rate of growth of the real cash-balances per unit of capital (v). If we take account of the fact that the rate of growth of capital goods during periods of excess-demand for goods is equal to the algebraic sum of savings per unit of capital ($S(\ell, v)$) and the forced savings per unit of capital ($\gamma\pi/\alpha$), equation (9) from section 2, the relevant differential equations can be written as follows:

$$\frac{d\ell}{dt}\frac{1}{\ell} = n - \frac{dK}{dt}\frac{1}{K} = n - \frac{\gamma\pi}{\alpha} - S(\ell, v) \quad (1)$$

$$\frac{dv}{dt}\frac{1}{v} = \mu - \pi - \frac{dK}{dt}\frac{1}{K} = \mu - \pi - \frac{\gamma\pi}{\alpha} - S(\ell, v) \quad (2)$$

For insight into the factors and mechanisms which play a part in the impact of a change in the rate of monetary expansion in the Keynes-Wicksell monetary growth model, represented by the differential equations mentioned above, it is necessary to express the actual rate of inflation in terms of labour intensity (ℓ), expected rate of inflation (π^*) and real cash-balances per unit of capital (v). This is possible with the aid of the following equations (1′) and (2) from the preceding section 3.1.

$$\frac{\pi}{\alpha} = n + r(\ell) + \pi^* - i - S(\ell, v) \quad (1')$$

$$\frac{\pi}{\alpha} + h\left\{\hat{L}\left(f(\ell) + \frac{\pi}{\alpha}, r(\ell) + \pi^*, i, v\right) - v\right\} = 0 \quad (2)$$

Equation (1′) can be reproduced graphically (by analogy with the short-term equilibrium analysis) as an *IS*-curve, with expresses the combinations of the nominal rate of interest (i) and the rate of inflation (π), given labour intensity (ℓ), real cash-balances per unit of capital (v) and expected rate of inflation (π^*), for which it holds that the excess-demand for goods per unit of capital is constant. Partial differentiation of the relevant equation (1′) to the rate of inflation (π) represents the slope of the *IS*-curve.

$$\frac{\partial i}{\partial \pi} = -\frac{1}{\alpha} < 0, \text{ by which } 0 < \alpha < \infty. \quad (3)$$

All this can be illustrated graphically from a four-quadrant system, upon which the *IS*-curve is based. In the second quadrant the relation between the nominal interest rate and the excess-demand for goods per unit of capital becomes evident, given ℓ, π^* and v.

The third quadrant expresses the proportional relation between the excess-demand for goods and the rate of inflation (Walrasian excess-demand hypothesis).

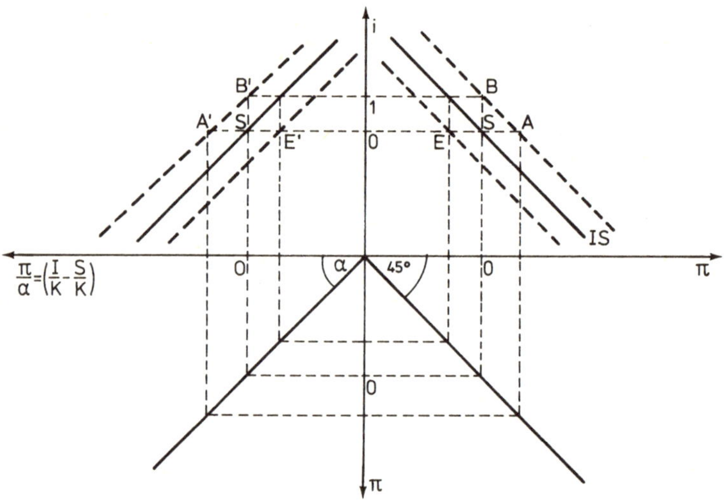

Figure 2

The negatively-sloped *IS*-curve can be explained as follows. A decrease in the nominal rate of interest (i) will result in extension of investments, thus enlarging the excess-demand for goods per unit of capital. Because the rate of inflation is related positively to excess-demand, the rate of inflation will increase. We can also put it in this way: an increase in the rate of inflation in the analysis at issue can only set in upon an increase in the excess-demand for goods per unit of capital. This can be brought about, given the expected rate of inflation, by a lower nominal rate of interest. Equation (2) from section 3.1. can be reproduced as the *FM*-curve, which expresses the combinations of the nominal rate of interest (i) and the rate of inflation (π) when the excess-demand for goods is equal to the excess-supply of real cash-balances.

This curve is an expression of Walras' law in which is likewise postulated that the market for bonds is always in equilibrium.

Partial differentiation of this equation (2) to the rate of inflation (π) provides the slope of this *FM*-curve:

$$\frac{\partial i}{\partial \pi} = - \frac{1}{\alpha \hat{L}_3} \left(L_1 + \frac{1}{h} \right) > 0. \tag{4}$$

If the rate of inflation increases, which implies in this analysis an increase in excess-demand for goods (π/α), the demand for real cash-balances for transaction purposes ($f(\ell) + \pi/\alpha$) will increase as well. The increased excess-demand for goods and real cash-balances implies, in accordance with Walras' law, an increase in the excess-supply of bonds. Because continuous equilibrium is assumed to exist on the market for financial assets, consequently the rate of interest will have to increase.[30]

All this can be illustrated graphically by the figure below.

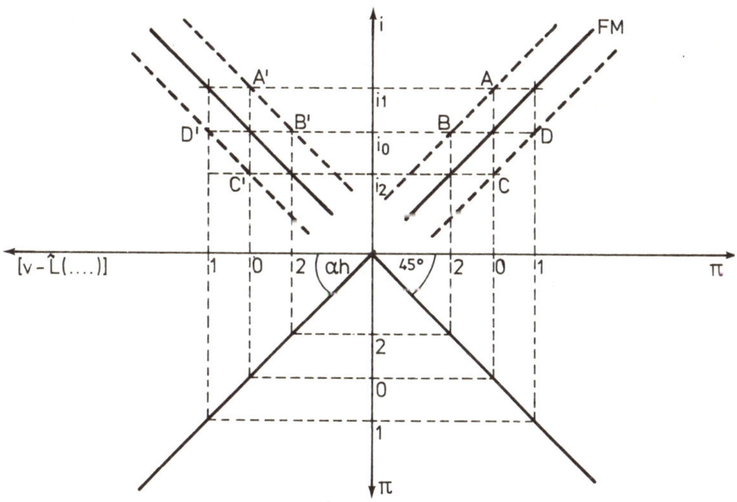

Figure 3

30. J. Stein, 1971, op. cit. p. 99–101.

The second quadrant expresses the positive relation between the nominal rate of interest and the excess-supply of real cash-balances per unit of capital, given ℓ, π^* and v. The third quadrant represents the relation between the excess-supply of real cash-balances per unit of capital (= excess-demand for goods) and the rate of inflation, on the assumption that equilibrium continuously exists on the market for financial assets (bonds). The graph can be interpreted as follows. If the nominal rate of interest increases, from i_0 to i_1 a greater excess-supply of real cash-balances will come about, which – given the equilibrium on the bonds market – results in a greater excess demand for goods and an accordingly higher rate of inflation ($\pi_1 > \pi_0$).

The point of intersection (S) of the two curves (i_0, π_0) in graph 4 represents the combination of the nominal rate of interest (i) and the rate of inflation (π) for which equations (1′) and (2) hold simultaneously. We might also say that combination (i_0, π_0) represents on the one hand an equilibrium on the markets for financial assets, and that on the other hand, given this equilibrium nominal rate of interest (i_0), such an excess-demand for goods results that the corresponding rate of inflation is equal to equilibrium value π_0.

The graph presents a certain similarity to the traditional *IS–LM* curves. In the well-known Hicks-Hansen diagram, the curves represent the combinations of rates of interest and national income, with equilibrium in the real sector (commodity market equilibrium) and in the monetary sector (money market equilibrium). In the analysis at issue the *IS–FM* curves refer rather to disequilibrium situations on the commodity and money markets (demand and supply of real cash-balances). So according to the *IS*–curve a lower nominal rate of interest means a greater excess-demand for goods and, according to the Walrasian excess-demand hypothesis, an accordingly higher rate of inflation.

On the other side, a lower nominal rate of interest implies according to the *FM*–curve, given the supply of real cash-balances, a smaller excess-supply of real cash-balances because the demand for real cash-balances will have increased ($\hat{L}_3 < 0$). This smaller excess-supply of real cash-balances means, starting from Walras' law and the supposed equilibrium on the market for bonds a smaller excess-demand for goods so the rate of inflation decreases. On the basis of equations (1′) and (2) from the preceding section describing the

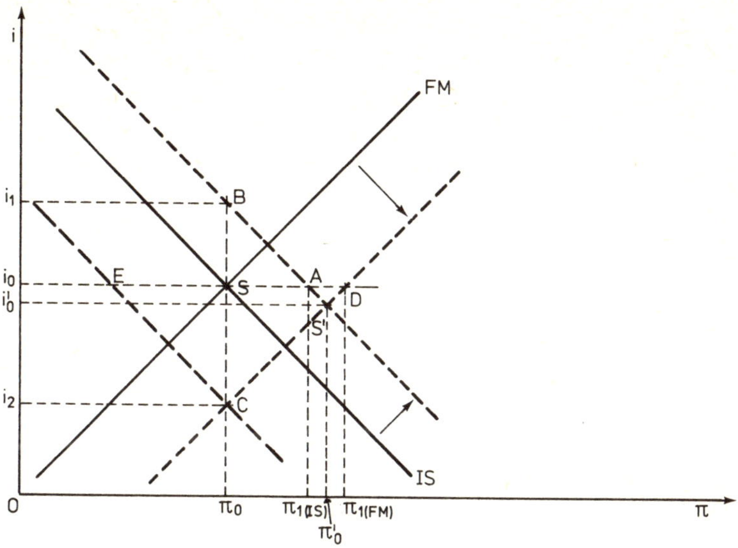

Figure 4

short-term model, the rate of inflation and the nominal rate of interest can now be expressed as an instigation for long-term problems as follows:

$$\pi = \pi(\pi^*, v, \ell; \mu, n) \tag{5}$$

$$i = (\pi^*, v, \ell; \mu, n) \tag{6}$$

With the aid of this system of equations, we will now examine how the equilibrium values of the nominal rate of interest and of the rate of inflation, will change when the different parameters, viz. labour intensity (ℓ), expected rate of inflation (π^*) and real cash-balances per unit of capital (v), change.

The values of the relevant partial derivatives will further be of essential significance in determining the impact of a change in the rate of monetary growth on the equilibrium values of the real variables.[31] The exogenous variables are the rate of growth of money (μ) and the rate of population growth (n).

31. See appendix to this chapter.

3.4.2. A change in the real cash-balances

An increase in real cash-balances per unit of capital (v) will influence the *IS*–curve as well as the *FM*–curve, given the other parameters ℓ and π^*.

On the one hand, an increase in real cash-balances will enlarge the excess-demand for goods by way of the wealth-effect in the savings function ($S_v < 0$). Given the nominal rate of interest (i_0) the *IS* curve will shift to the right and will bring about an increase in the rate of inflation (point A in graphs 2 and 4).

On the other hand, with a given rate of inflation (π_0) the nominal rate of interest will have to increase (i_1) in order to reduce investments and maintain the initial excess-demand for goods and consequently the rate of inflation (π_0) (point *B* in graphs 2 and 4).[32]

With regard to the influence of increased real cash-balances on the position of the *FM*-curve, the following can be observed. We can infer from the demand function for real cash-balances that an increase in real cash-balances per unit of capital brings about an increase in the excess-supply of real cash-balances ($1 > \hat{L}_4 > 0$)[33]. The outcome is that, given the rate of inflation (π_0), which in the Keynes-Wicksell analysis is proportionally related to the excess-demand for goods, the increase in the excess-supply is linked with a higher excess-demand for bonds, in accordance with Walras' law. In other words the excess-supply of real cash-balances will fully conform to the market for financial assets, in order to maintain the rate of inflation (Keynes-effect). This will cause the nominal rate of interest to decrease, restoring the equilibrium on the market for financial assets, and so Walras' law holds. This means that the *FM*-curve will shift downwards (point *C*, graphs 3 and 4). On the other hand – given the nominal rate of interest (i_0)–the increased excess-supply of real cash-balances will conform to the commodity market, by which the excess-demand for goods

32. J. Stein, 1971, op. cit. p. 101.
33. Patinkin has pointed out that upon enlargement of the real cash-balances, either by an increase in the nominal quantity of money, or by a decrease in the price level, the economic agents will use part of their additional funds to improve their liquidity position, i.e. part will be held (wealth elasticity of the demand for money is smaller than one), whereas the rest will be used to purchase goods (Pigou-effect or Fisher-effect) and to purchase financial assets (Keynes-effect). See in this context: D. J. Jüttner, Zur Geldtheorie Don Patinkins, *Untersuchungen über das Spar- Giro- und Kreditwesen*, Band 57, Bonn 1971, p. 74–79.

will increase (Pigou effect). The *FM*-curve will therefore shift to the right and the rate of inflation will increase $\pi_1 > \pi_0$ (point *D* graphs 3 and 4). From graph 3 it can be deduced that, if the increase of the excess-supply of real cash-balances is fully expressed on the bonds market, the nominal rate of interest will decrease, but the rate of inflation remains constant (π_0). However if the greater excess-supply follows the commodity market, the rate of inflation will increase (π_1), with a constant nominal rate of interest (i_0).

Further observation of graph 4 reveals that the shifts of both curves, as a consequence of increased real cash-balances per unit of capital, will increase the rate of inflation unambiguously (see point of intersection $S'(i_0', \pi_0')$). However, the impact on the nominal interest rate is not determined unambiguously. On the one hand, the negative wealth-effect in the savings function creates a rise in interest (shift of the *IS*-curve), on the other hand the monetary-effect in the form of a replacement of cash-balances by bonds has a negative impact on the nominal rate of interest (shift of the *FM*-curve)[34].

Shortly summarized, the partial derivative $\partial\pi/\partial v$ can be taken as positive and the value of $\partial i/\partial v$ is undetermined[35]. Apart from that, the operation of a relatively weak, negative wealth-effect in the savings function will ultimately result in a decrease in the equilibrium value of the nominal rate of interest. Otherwise expressed, the equilibrium value of the nominal rate of interest will have decreased relatively in the new equilibrium situation (point S') in as far as the operation of the Keynes effect-exceeds that of the Pigou-effect (graph 4). In those circumstances a greater part of the initial excess-cash-balances will follow the bonds market than the commodity market, with the interest-falling effect dominating. The reverse is very possible too, with the interest-rising effect dominating. In this context Nieuwenburg points out the significance of the credit market, which plays a central part in the monetarists' theoretical analyses; in their opinion it is connected with the other markets. According to the monetarists (Brunner, Meltzer, Friedman) an expansion of the supply of money should rather be associated with a rising than with a falling interest rate.

34. J. Stein, Journal of Political Economy, October 1966, op. cit. p. 456 and by the same author, 1971, op. cit. p. 102.
35. See appendix of this chapter.

Their reasoning then proceeds as follows. The enlarged supply of real cash-balances will lead to rising prices for existing physical assets as a result of substitution and wealth effects. If the price of existing capital goods rises above the production costs of new units of output, investment activity will be extended. This is the transmission-mechanism of the supply price of capital. Through the well-known multiplier-process an income will be generated, resulting in increased consumption expenditures with accelerator-effects on investments. The enlargement of economic activity which results from this, induces an upward revision of the expected rate of profit on capital goods, reinforcing further replacement of financial assets by physical assets. The monetarists point out that the foregoing development leads to an expansion of the public's demand for credit in order to finance the purchase of the newly-produced capital goods. In other words, revision of the expected rate of profit caused by the greater economic activity, which is set in motion by the expansive monetary impulse, leads to extension of the demand for credit by the public. This more than compensates the initial decrease in the interest rate (liquidity-effect). So there results a feed-back effect from the real sector on the credit market[36].

Though the relation between the rate of inflation and the nominal rate of interest will come up for discussion in detail in the following chapter in the context of the so-called 'Gibson-paradox' we should like to point out here that two other effects may be active. And these can result in enlargement of the supply of real cash-balances, having a positive effect on the nominal rate of interest. We refer to the classical Wicksell-effect and the Fisher-effect. The Wicksell-effect is most conceivable in our analysis, where we take the line of full employment.

After all, an excess-supply of real cash-balances, geared partly to the commodity market, generates a price rise which makes real cash-balances decrease again. This influence remains active until the price level has eliminated the initial excess-supply. The increased price level will again eliminate the initial decrease in the interest rate, which will return to its original level. So we see that

36. C. K. Nieuwenburg, Een vorm van modern monetarisme, *Maandschrift Economie*, University of Tilburg, September 1973, p. 542 and p. 548–550.

in the so-called 'transition-period', i.e. between two equilibrium situations, rises in prices and interests will occur at the same time. The Fisher-effect, which relates more to the long run, emphasizes the influence of the inflationary expectations and of the upward revision of this variable on the development of the rate of interest. Since we have considered the expected rate of inflation to be constant in this section, this effect will not set in.

3.4.3. A change in the expected rate of inflation

Next we shall analyse the influence of a change in the expected rate of inflation on the equilibrium value of the nominal interest rate and of the actual rate of inflation, given labour intensity (ℓ) and real cash-balances per unit of capital (v).

Given the nominal rate of interest (i_0) an increase in the expected rate of inflation will enlarge – if we take account of the supposed investment behaviour – the excess-demand for goods per unit of capital and consequently the current rate of inflation. For, influenced by the increase in the expected rate of inflation, the price of existing capital goods will exceed the price of newly-produced units, causing demand for new capital goods to increase. In other words, given the nominal rate of interest, the expected nominal rate of profit will increase ($r(\ell) + \pi^*$) and planned investments will be expanded. The *IS*-curve will consequently shift to the right (point *A* in graph 2 and 4).

If, on the contrary, the rate of inflation (π_0) is maintained, the nominal interest rate will have to increase in the same measure as the expected rate of inflation, so there will be no incentive to extend investment expenditure (point *B* in graphs 2 and 4).

An increase in the expected rate of inflation also has repercussions for the *FM*-curve. For the opportunity costs attached to the holding of real cash-balances ($r(\ell) + \pi^*$) will increase and so the demand for real cash-balances will decrease. ($\hat{L}_2 < 0$). An increase will occur in the excess-supply of real cash-balances, causing an increase in the excess-demand for goods and bonds, in accordance with Walras' law. Given the nominal rate of interest (i_0), the excess-demand for goods and consequently the rate of inflation will increase (point *D* in graphs 3 and 4). Conversely, given the rate of inflation (π_0) the influence of the greater excess-supply of the real cash-balances will be expressed in a decrease of the nominal rate of interest (point C in graphs 3 and 4). In both cases the FM-curve will shift to the right. Now too an increase in the expected rate of inflation has an unambiguously positive influence on the equilibrium value of the actual rate of inflation ($\delta\pi/\delta\pi^* > 0$), whereas the influence on the equilibrium value of the nominal rate of interest is again undetermined.[37] This last result arises from the fact that an increase in the expected rate of inflation on the one hand (as a result of expansion of investment activity) enlarges the excess-demand for goods, and on the other hand (due to increased opportunity costs for holding money) reduces the excess-demand for real cash-balances. These opposite effects mean that the influence on the excess-supply of financial assets and so on the nominal rate of interest can no longer be determined unambiguously. For, in accordance with Walras' law, the excess-supply of bonds is equal to the excess-demand for goods plus the excess-demand for real cash-balances.

Since we have started from a continuous equilibrium on the market for financial assets, given the nominal interest rate, the increase in the actual rate of inflation, as a result of the increased excess-demand for goods per unit of capital, will lead to a greater supply of bonds. These bonds are issued to finance new investments. This by itself already has the effect of increasing interest. However, purchase of bonds – given the nominal rate of interest – has become less attractive than before, in view of the increase in the expected rate of inflation. This will reduce the demand for bonds. The net-result then is an increase in the excess-supply of financial assets (bonds); the nominal rate of interest will have to increase in order to maintain the supposed equilibrium on the market ($\delta i/\delta\pi^* > 0$).

This situation again resembles the mechanism of the credit market described by Nieuwenburg.[38] However, in this analysis the greater demand for investment goods is financed by additional supply of bonds. The bonds market can, therefore, be considered as a reflection of demand for and supply of the required financial funds. Nieuwenburg, on the contrary, refers explicitly to the credit market, through which the public procures the required funds by appealing to bank credit. In the Keynes-Wicksell analysis it is rather a matter of the higher expected rate of inflation having led on the one hand

37. See appendix to this chapter.

38. C. K. F. Nieuwenburg, *Maandschrift Economie*, September 1973, op. cit. p. 550.

to an increase in the supply of bonds to finance the purchase of capital goods, on the other hand to the fact that bonds have become less attractive as a wealth asset. Both influences bring about the excess-supply of bonds mentioned above and the concomitant rise in interest.

3.4.4. A change in the labour-capital ratio

Finally we shall analyse the influences applying to the equilibrium values of the nominal rate of interest and of the actual rate of inflation of a change in labour intensity (ℓ), given the real cash-balances per unit of capital (v) and the expected rate of inflation (π^*). Now it will appear that the shifts in the relevant curves can no longer be determined unambiguously and that consequently the impact on the nominal rate of interest as well as on the rate of inflation is undetermined.[39] This can be explained as follows. The increase in the labour-capital ratio will lead – starting from the production function – to an increase in the rate of profit ($r'(\ell) > 0$) and in average capital productivity ($f(\ell) > 0$). Since the rate of profit has been inserted as an argument into the investment function and the average capital productivity as an argument into the savings function, an enlargement of planned investments and an increase in planned savings will set in ($S_\ell > 0$), if we start from the assumed behaviour of employers with regard to investments. It is clear that the influence on the excess-demand for goods per unit of capital and so on the actual rate of inflation can therefore not be determined unambiguously.

Now two cases can be distinguished. If the increase in investments (demand for savings) is greater than the increase in savings ($r'(\ell) > S_\ell$), an increase in the excess-demand for goods per unit of capital will arise. This means given the nominal rate of interest, an increase in the actual rate of inflation and a shift of the *IS*–curve to the right (point A in graphs 2 and 4). In the reverse case, which we will not discuss further here, the increase in savings will exceed the increase in investments, and a decrease in the excess-demand for goods per unit of capital will arise.

From this a deflationary influence will emanate on economic activity, given the nominal rate of interest, and the *IS*–curve will

39. J. Stein, 1971, op. cit. p. 106. See also the appendix of this chapter.

shift to the left (see point E in graph 2 and 4).[40] Stein remarks in this context 'The usual Keynesian assumption is that a rise in output and employment will raise planned savings relative to planned investment such that the *IS*–curve shifts to the left. But that is an arbitrary assumption'.[41]

The change in the labour-capital ratio also has repercussions for the demand for real cash-balances per unit of capital. On the one hand a positive income-effect will arise as result of increased capital productivity. The demand for real cash-balances for transaction purposes will increase in accordance with the assumed demand equation for real cash-balances from section 2 ($\hat{L}_1 f'(\ell) > 0$). On the other hand, we encounter a negative substitution effect, since the rate of return on real capital goods increases relatively, compared with the rate of return or real cash-balances ($\hat{L}_2 r'(\ell) < 0$). The demand for real cash-balances per unit of capital will therefore decrease. Given the supply of real cash-balances, the influence on the excess-supply of this variable can no longer be determined unambiguously.

Two cases can now be analysed with regard to the shift in the *FM*–curve. If the positive income-effect dominates – in algebraic terms, if $\hat{L}_1 f'(\ell) + \hat{L}_2 r'(\ell) > 0$ – an increase in the excess-demand for real cash-balances will come about. Given the rate of inflation (π_0) an increase in the excess-supply of financial assets will arise. The interest rate will have to increase to restore the equilibrium on the market for financial assets (points A and A' in graph 3). The *FM*–curve then shifts to the left.

Given the nominal rate of interest (i_0) (equilibrium on the bonds market) the excess-demand for real cash-balances per unit of capital will be expressed in an excess-supply of goods, with as a result, a decrease in the actual rate of inflation (π_2). Here too the *FM*-curve will shift to the left (points B and B' in graph 3).

If, on the contrary, the negative substitution-effect dominates, i.e. $\hat{L}_1 f'(\ell) + \hat{L}_2 r'(\ell) < 0$, the excess-supply of real cash-balances per unit of capital will increase. Given the nominal rate of interest

40. Partial differentiation of equation (1′) in section 3.3.1. to the labour intensity gives: $\partial i/\partial r = r'(\ell) - S_\ell$. From this it follows $\partial i/\partial \ell \gtrless 0$ if $r'(\ell) \gtrless S_\ell$.

41. J. Stein, 1971, op. cit. p. 103.

(i_0), this excess will be directed to the commodity market and lead to an enlarged excess-demand for goods, with, as a result, an increase in the rate of inflation (π_1). The *FM*-curve then shifts to the right (points *D* and *D'* in graph 3). In so far as the excess-supply of real cash-balances is merely directed to the bonds market, a fall in the rate of interest (i_2) will arise at the same, actual rate of inflation (π_0) with a shift of the *FM*-curve to the right (points *C* and *C'* in graph 3). If the greater excess-supply of the real cash-balances is directed to the commodity market as well as to the market for financial assets, the nominal rate of interest will decrease and the rate of inflation will increase. The *FM*-curve will again shift to the right.[42]

Resuming, we can distinguish between the following possibilities with regard to the impact of an increase in the labour-capital ratio on the equilibrium values of the nominal interest rate and of the rate of inflation:

1. The increase of planned investments is greater than that of planned savings, $r'(\ell) - S_\ell > 0$, and the substitution-effect with regard to the demand for real cash-balances dominates. The *IS*- and *FM*-curves both shift to the right and the equilibrium value of the rate of inflation will increase (π_1). The ultimate impact on the equilibrium value of the nominal rate of interest is undetermined in these circumstances (point *P* in graph 5).
2. The increase of planned savings exceeds that of planned investments $r'(\ell) - S_\ell < 0$ and the income-effect with regard to the demand for real cash balances dominates $\hat{L}_1 f'(\ell) + \hat{L}_2 r'(\ell) > 0$. The *IS*- and *FM*-curves both shift to the left, causing the equilibrium value of the rate of inflation to diminish unambiguously (π_2) and the influence on the equilibrium value of the nominal rate of interest is again undetermined (point *Q* in graph 5). All this can be illustrated graphically as on page 114.

42. For the analysis mentioned in the main text, readers are referred to J. Stein, 1971, op. cit. p. 103, and by the same author, *Journal of Political Economy*, October 1966, p. 457–458. Partial differentiation of equation (2) in paragraph 3.1. gives:

$$\frac{\partial i}{\partial \ell} = \frac{-(\hat{L}_1 f'(\ell) + \hat{L}_2 r'(\ell))}{\hat{L}_3}, \text{ from which follows } \frac{\partial i}{\partial \ell} \gtrless 0$$

if $\hat{L}_1 f'(\ell) + r'(\ell) \gtrless 0$ and $\hat{L}_3 < 0$

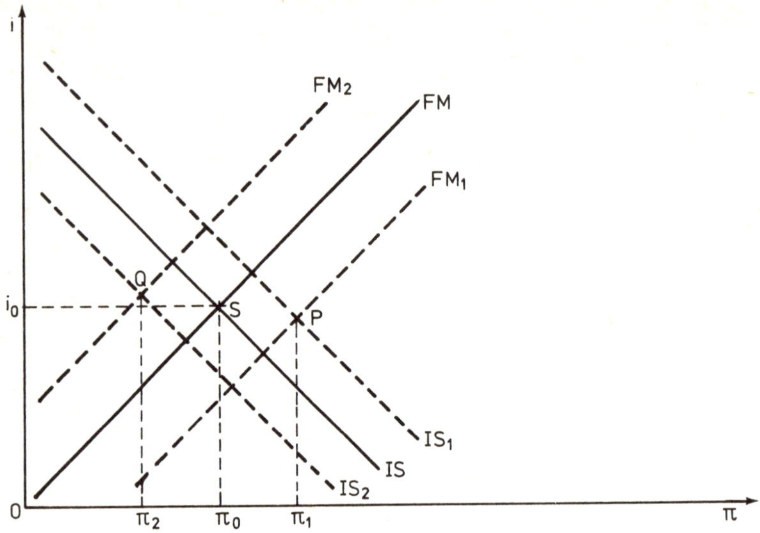

Figure 5

3. The increase of planned investments is greater than that of planned savings and the income-effect dominates. In these circumstances the *IS*-curve will shift to the right and the *FM*-curve to the left. This will lead to an increase in equilibrium value of the nominal rate of interest (i_1), whereas the influence on the equilibrium value of the rate of inflation is undetermined (point *R* in graph 6).
4. The increase of planned savings exceeds that of planned investments and the substitution-effect dominates. The *IS*-curve will shift to the left and the *FM*-curve to the right, causing the equilibrium value of the nominal rate of interest to decrease (i_2), whereas the influence on equilibrium value of the rate of inflation is again undetermined (point *T* in graph 6). The graphical presentation, applying to possibilities 3 and 4, looks as that on page 115.

These four possible shifts in the relevant curves and the ultimate effect on the nominal interest rate and the rate of inflation are presented in the appendix to this chapter in a more mathematical way.

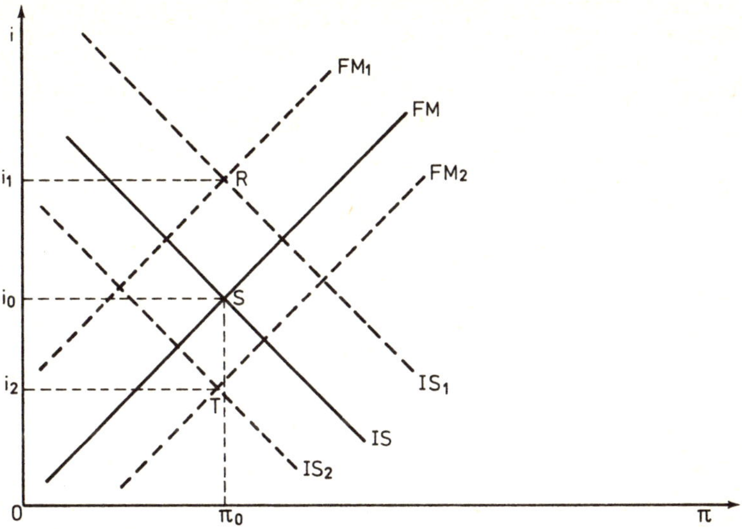

Figure 6

Schematically, the foregoing can be summarized as follows:

	$IE < SE$	$IE > SE$
$r'(\ell) > S_\ell$	π + i ?	π ? i +
$r'(\ell) < S_\ell$	π ? i −	π − i ?

3.5. Influence of a change in the rate of monetary expansion

3.5.1. Algebraic formulation

The preceding sections have already shown that two differential equations are of essential importance for analysis of the long-term equilibrium model. The relevant equations, obtained by logarithmic differentiation of the labour-intensity (ℓ) and the real cash-balances per unit of capital (v) (if we allow for equations (1) and (2) from section 4.1.) run as follows:

$$\frac{d\ell}{dt}\frac{1}{\ell} = n - \frac{dK}{dt}\frac{1}{K} = n - \frac{\gamma\pi}{\alpha} - S(\ell, v) \tag{1}$$

$$\frac{dv}{dt}\frac{1}{v} = \mu - \pi - \frac{dK}{dt}\frac{1}{K} = \mu - \pi - \frac{\gamma\pi}{\alpha} - S(\ell, v) \tag{2}$$

From equations (1) and (2) we can deduce that in the long-term equilibrium situation, when labour intensity and real cash-balances per unit of capital have become constant, the rate of inflation is equal to the growth rate of the nominal quantity of money per head.

$$\pi = \mu - n \tag{3}$$

The assumption with regard to the expected rate of inflation in section 2 is maintained, in other words the expected rate of inflation (π^*) is always equal to the equilibrium value, so that we can write

$$\pi^* = \pi = \mu - n. \tag{4}$$

If we substitute equation (5) from section 4.1. into basic equations (1) and (2) and allow for (4), the dynamic system can be reproduced by the following differential equations:

$$\frac{d\ell}{dt}\frac{1}{\ell} = n - \frac{\gamma}{\alpha}\pi\,(\ell, v; \mu, n) - S(\ell, v) \equiv F(\ell, v; \mu, n) \tag{5}$$

$$\frac{dv}{dt}\frac{1}{v} = \mu - \left(1 + \frac{\gamma}{\alpha}\right)\pi(\ell, v; \mu, n) - S(\ell, v) \equiv G(\ell, v; \mu, n) \tag{6}$$

[43]

These equations describe the development of the equilibrium system in the long run, under the assumption that at any moment a

43. Stein, 1971, op. cit. p. 108.

'short-term equilibrium' exists.[44] The positive long-term equilibrium values of the labour-capital ratio and the real cash-balances per unit of capital are represented by ℓ^* and v^* respectively given the growth rates of money (μ) and of population (n). The conditions for local stability of the equilibrium can be obtained by linearization of the dynamic system (5) and (6) around the equilibrium point (ℓ^*, v^*).[45]

We now assume that an equilibrium solution exists for the system, represented by equations (5) and (6), given the values for μ and n, the growth rate of the quantity of money and the growth rate of population respectively. In the equilibrium situation concerned it holds, that labour intensity and real cash-balances per unit of capital have become constant ($d\ell/dt\ 1/\ell = 0$ and $dv/dt\ 1/v = 0$).

We can formulate equations (5) and (6) as follows:

$$F(\ell^*, v^*; \mu, n) = 0 \tag{7}$$

$$G(\ell^*, v^*; \mu, n) = 0 \tag{8}$$

In order to examine the effects of a change in the rate of monetary expansion on the equilibrium values of the labour-capital ratio and of the real cash-balances per unit of capital equations (7) and (8) will have to be solved. This is the result:[46]

$$\frac{d\ell^*}{d\mu} = -\frac{F_\mu G_2^* + F_2^* G_\mu}{F_1^* G_2^* - F_2^* G_1^*} = -\frac{\frac{\gamma}{\alpha}\pi_v - S_v(1 - \pi_\mu)}{S_\ell \pi_v - \pi_\ell S_v} \tag{9}$$

$$\frac{dv^*}{d\mu} = -\frac{F_1^* G_\mu + F_\mu^* G_1}{F_1^* G_2^* - F_2^* G_1^*} = \frac{\frac{\gamma}{\alpha}\pi_\ell + S_\ell(1 - \pi_\mu)}{S_\ell \pi_v - \pi_\ell S_v} \tag{10}$$

in which $F_\mu = -\gamma/\alpha\pi_\mu$ and $G_\mu = 1 - (1 + \gamma/\alpha)\pi_\mu$.

44. This relates to a stability analysis in the sense of equilibrium dynamics, advanced by Hahn and Mathews. See F. Hahn and R. Mathews, *The theory of economic growth*, in *Surveys of Economic Theory*, part II 1965, p. 3. It is supposed that at any moment 'short-term equilibrium' exists. In other words a combination of the nominal rate of interest (i) and the rate of inflation (π) will always exist, for which equations (5) and (6) from section 3.1 hold.

45. See appendix to this chapter.

46. For the derivatives in (9) and (10) readers are referred to the appendix of this chapter. See Stein 1971, op. cit. p. 109.

As will be evident from the appendix, it will have to apply for the local stability that the denominators of equations (9) and (10) have a positive value. This means $S_l\pi_v - \pi_l S_v > 0$ or $S_l\pi_v > \pi_l S_v$. Since the wealth effect in the savings function is negative ($S_v < 0$) and partial derivatives S_l and π_v are both positive, the condition mentioned above implies that $\pi_l > 0$ must hold.

This positive influence of a change in labour intensity on the rate of inflation will arise if the negative substitution-effect with regard to the demand for real cash-balances exceeds the positive income-effect. All this has come up for discussion in the preceding section.[47]

In order to determine the influence of a change in the rate of monetary expansion on the equilibrium values of the real variables the sign of the numerator in equations (9) and (10) is of essential importance because of the assumed stability. If the value of term $(1 - \pi_\mu)$ is negative, an increase in the rate of monetary expansion (=expected rate of inflation) will enlarge the equilibrium value of the capital intensity, or conversely diminish the equilibrium value or the labour intensity. For in these circumstances it holds that $\pi_\mu > 1$, which implies that an increase of the rate of monetary expansion reduces the equilibrium value of the real cash-balances per unit of capital in the short run. As we have analysed in section 3.2., this is connected with the adjustment coefficient of the price level (α) in the assumed Walrasian excess-demand equation. If on the contrary the value of the term $(1 - \pi_\mu)$ is positive, it is no longer possible to determine unambiguously the sign of the numerator, and so the influence of a higher rate of monetary growth on the equilibrium value of capital intensity in equation (9). Further we can derive from equation (10) that if the value of the term $(1 - \pi_\mu)$ is positive, the equilibrium value of real cash-balances per unit of capital in the long run will increase as a result of an increase in the rate of monetary expansion. If on the contrary the value of the term $(1 - \pi_\mu)$ is negative, then the influence mentioned is undetermined.

47. This condition is also found in the literature, in M. Teubal's work, *Inflation, unemployment and economic growth*, Report 6616, Center for Mathematical Studies in Business and Economics, Chicago, June 1966, p. 8–9. By the same author *Monetary expansion, unemployment and economic growth*, Report 6607, Chicago, May 1966, p. 10–14.

Equations (9) and (10) express that, given the stability condition (see appendix), an unambiguous pronouncement cannot be made about the influence of a change in the rate of monetary expansion on the equilibrium values of capital intensity ($1/\ell$) and real cash-balances per unit of capital (v). Only the change in the growth rate of the price level has been determined unambiguously. Since the rate of population growth has been assumed to be constant, each increase (decrease) in the rate of monetary expansion will result in a higher (lower) equilibrium value of the rate of inflation.

3.5.2. A verbal interpretation

Let us now explain the mathematical results mentioned in the preceding section in a more verbal way.[48] We intend to examine which influences affect the equilibrium values of the real variables and which mechanisms are active, if the monetary expansion in the equilibrium situation is increased.

A rise in the rate of monetary expansion will lead first of all, to a higher equilibrium value of the rate of inflation, and, in view of the presupposition for price expectations, to an increase in the expected rate of inflation (π^*). Given the nominal rate of interest, an excess-demand for goods will be occasioned by the extension of planned investments (expected nominal rate of profit exceeds nominal rate of interest), increasing the actual rate of inflation as well. However, the question is how quickly will prices respond to possible changes in the excess-demand for goods per unit of capital, i.e. how quickly disequilibria on the commodity markets are passed down in price changes. This speed proves to be crucial for the development of the different variables in the Keynes-Wicksell growth model.

As we have already pointed out, the speed of price adjustment is determined by coefficient α. If prices respond slowly to commodity market disequilibria, with the actual rate of inflation increasing less than the rate of monetary expansion ($\pi_\mu < 1$), the real cash-balances per unit of capital will rise. Owing to a positive wealth-effect in the consumption function ($S_v < 0$), planned con-

48. J. Stein, 1971, op. cit. p. 112–114.

sumption expenditure will increase, further augmenting the existing excess-demand for goods, and consequently the actual rate of inflation. If the actual rate of inflation is still smaller than the rate of growth of the money supply per head, real cash balances will increase. The process of increased expenditure which this generates and the increase in the actual rate of inflation goes on until the existing rate of inflation has become equal to its equilibrium value and real cash-balances per unit of capital have become constant. Here we see that the causality runs from the expected rate of inflation to the actual rate of inflation. The quicker the actual rate of inflation adjusts to the higher equilibrium value of the expected rate of inflation, the quicker the fuel will as it were be burnt up which is implied in the induced excess-supply of real cash-balances.

The increase in the real cash-balances per unit of capital which arises during this adjustment process does, however, have repercussions for capital accumulation. On the one hand, in accordance with our previous assumptions, planned savings per unit of capital will decrease ($S_v < 0$), on the other hand the induced increase in the rate of inflation will reduce the real interest rate and enlarge investments. If actual capital accumulation is largely determined by planned savings per unit of capital, which is expressed in a small value of coefficient γ, the rate of growth of capital goods will decrease, as will the equilibrium value of capital intensity given the rate of population growth.

If $\gamma = 0$, i.e. the actual rate of growth of capital goods is determined by savings per unit of capital, we can deduce from equation (9) that the sign of the equation is determined by the term $-S_v(1 - \pi_\mu) < 0$. Because of the assumed slow adjustment of the actual rate of inflation $\pi_\mu < 1$, the sign will be positive in these circumstances, which implies that the equilibrium value of labour intensity has increased or the equilibrium value of capital intensity has decreased with respect to the path with a lower rate of monetary growth. If the actual rate of growth of capital goods is also determined by planned investments ($\gamma > 0$), we can deduce from equation (9) that the influence of a change in the rate of monetary expansion on the equilibrium value of capital intensity can no longer be determined unambiguously.

If the actual rate of inflation responds more quickly ($\pi_\mu > 1$) to changes in the excess-demand, the following effects will arise. An excess-demand for goods will come about initially, which however makes the existing rate of inflation increase quicker than the rate of monetary expansion (= expected rate of inflation). The real cash-balances per unit of capital decline resulting in a decrease in excess-demand for goods per unit of capital. The existing rate of inflation will thus be reduced and will adjust to the lower equilibrium value of this monetary variable. Besides, the decrease in real cash-balances will bring about a liquidity shortage during the adjustment process and an increase in the nominal rate of interest, which will further reinforce the decrease in excess-demand for goods and in the actual rate of inflation. The consequences of the lower equilibrium value of the real cash-balances for the development of capital intensity can be represented as follows. If under these circumstances planned savings are a determining factor for the actual rate of growth of capital goods ($\gamma = 0$), the decrease in equilibrium value of the real cash-balances will in this particular case lead to a higher rate of growth of capital goods ($S_v < 0$).

The equilibrium value of capital intensity will increase compared with the path with a lower rate of monetary growth. This result is evident in the neo-classical monetary growth model, where planned investments are always equal to planned savings per unit of capital.

If planned investments determine the actual rate of growth of the capital goods too, the equilibrium value of capital intensity will also increase. For in the Keynes-Wicksell model it holds that the actual rate of inflation (π) increases, as far as the excess-demand for goods is positive. Since real cash-balances per unit of capital decrease as a result of the assumed price adjustment, savings will increase, which means that investments must increase as well for a positive excess-demand for goods to exist. If $\gamma > 0$, the equilibrium value of capital intensity will increase compared with the path with a lower rate of monetary growth. In equation (9) section 5.1., we clearly see that in the case before us ($\pi_\mu > 1$) a higher rate of monetary growth implies a higher equilibrium value of capital intensity. This result does indeed appear to be independent of the question whether planned savings ($\gamma = 0$), or planned investments are also determining factors for the actual growth rate of capital goods ($\gamma > 0$). The preceding explanations can be summarized schematically as follows:

$\pi_\mu < 1$	$\gamma = 0$	$\gamma > 0$
$\frac{dl^*}{d\mu}$	+	?
$\frac{dv^*}{d\mu}$	+	+

$\pi_\mu > 1$	$\gamma = 0$	$\gamma > 0$
$\frac{dl^*}{d\mu}$	−	−
$\frac{dv^*}{d\mu}$	−	?

4. A synthesis of the neo-classical and the Keynes-Wicksell monetary growth theories

4.1. Introduction

The preceding two chapters have shown that the theoretical explanations in the framework of the neo-classical and the Keynes-Wicksell monetary growth theories lead to a number of widely different conclusions with regard to the influence of a change in the rate of monetary expansion on the equilibrium values of the real variables. This unsatisfactory result must be attributed to the models discussed and the suppositions concerned. Stein remarks in this context 'Since equally "reasonable" assumptions yield qualitatively different results monetary growth theory is an "Uncertain Trumpet": it cannot be used as a guide to policy'.[1] In his well-known, comprehensive article in the American Economic Review he says '... equally plausible models yield fundamentally different results' and concludes, 'The crucial question is: which is the correct monetary growth model'.[2]

Stein has tried to bring together the two models into one, which in the long-term equilibrium situation has the features of the neo-classical theory described in chapter 2, whereas in the analysis of the short run the features of the Keynes-Wicksell model are more prominent out. The synthesis model for the two approaches will be further indicated as the *S*-model.[3] In this chapter we have made use of the different equations from both preceding chapters, under the assumption that their interpretation is known. When the ana-

1. J. Stein, 'Neo-classical' and 'Keynes-Wicksell' monetary growth models, *Journal of Money, Credit and Banking*, May, 1969, p. 157.
2. J. Stein, Monetary growth theory in perspective, *American Economic Review*, March, 1970, p. 85 and p. 105.
3. J. Stein, *Money and capacity growth*, Columbia University Press, 1971, p. 120–162. For a comparison of the two models readers are also referred to S. Fischer, Keynes-Wicksell and Neo-classical models of money and growth, *American Economic Review*, December 1972, p. 880–892.

lysis deviates from the equations concerned, this will be clearly indicated.

4.2. The modified price change equation

We have already stated several times in the preceding analysis that the essential difference between the neo-classical and the Keynes-Wicksell models lies in the fundamental supposition on the growth rate of the price level. In the latter theory prices will change when there are disequilibria on the commodity market.[4]

The neo-classical variant of the monetary growth theory postulates, however, that there exists such a price flexibility that market disequilibria are immediately eliminated. This means that planned savings and investments per unit of capital are always equal (there is no independent investment function), as are the demand for and the supply of real cash-balances per unit of capital. The demand for real cash-balances is, as stated in chapter 2, dependent on the income per unit of capital and the expected rate of inflation. Since, at any moment, capital goods, expected rate of inflation, nominal quantity of money and population are given, the supposition of continuous equilibrium between demand for and supply of real cash-balances (portfolio-balance) will ensure that the price level is determined.

Stein introduces in the S-model a new equation for the actual rate of inflation which is influenced by price expectations in a direct (neo-classical) as well as in an indirect way (Keynes-Wicksell).[5]

This modified price change equation looks as follows:

$$\pi = \pi^* + \alpha\left(\frac{I}{K} - \frac{S}{K}\right) \text{ or } \frac{\pi - \pi^*}{\alpha} = \frac{I}{K} - \frac{S}{K} \qquad (1)$$

4. This supposition can also be found with D. Patinkin, *Money interest and prices*, 1965, p. 260–261, where demand is determined by the income, the nominal rate of interest and the real cash-balances.
5. J. Stein, 1971, op. cit. p. 122–123 and S. Fischer, *American Economic Review*, December 1972, op. cit. p. 881–882. The price formation equation mentioned was first advanced by R. Solow and G. Stiglitz in their publication, Output Employment and Wages in the short run, *Quarterly Journal of Economics*, November 1968, p. 537–560.

This equation implies that the actual rate of inflation is determined on the one hand by the expected rate of inflation (π^*) and on the other hand by the possibly-existing excess-demand for goods per unit of capital.

A change in the expected rate of inflation (π^*) will affect the actual rate of inflation (π) in an indirect way through a change in the excess-demand for goods. We might also say that the expected rate of inflation exercises a direct influence on the existing or actual rate of inflation (price-expectations effect) beside the indirect effect which operates through the commodity market.

The introduction of the equation mentioned above results in a slight change in the equations in the Keynes-Wicksell model from chapter 3.

The *IS* and *FM*-curves concerned can now be represented algebraically as follows:

$$\pi = \pi^* + \alpha[n + r(\ell) + \pi^* - i - S(\ell, v)] \tag{2}$$

$$\frac{\pi - \pi^*}{\alpha h} = v - L\left[f(\ell) + \frac{\pi - \pi^*}{\alpha}, r(\ell) + \pi^*, i, v\right] \tag{3}$$

The actual rate of growth of capital goods and of real cash-balances per unit of capital can be formulated, taking account of equation (1), as:

$$\frac{dK}{dt}\frac{1}{K} = \gamma\frac{I}{K} + (1 - \gamma)\frac{S}{K} = \frac{\gamma}{\alpha}(\pi - \pi^*) + S(\ell, v) \tag{4}$$

$$\frac{dv}{dt}\frac{1}{v} = \mu - \pi - \frac{dK}{dt}\frac{1}{K} \tag{5}$$

The development of the labour-capital ratio, the labour intensity, can be expressed as:

$$\frac{d\ell}{dt}\frac{1}{\ell} = n - \frac{dK}{dt}\frac{1}{K} = n - \frac{\gamma}{\alpha}(\pi - \pi^*) - S(\ell, v) \tag{6}$$

Regardless of which model is used, the actual rate of inflation (π) and the expected rate of inflation (π^*) are equal in the equilibrium situation. In other words, the change in the expected rate of inflation is zero. The neo-classical and Keynes-Wicksell analyses mostly assume, for the sake of simplicity, that the expected rate of inflation is equal to the equilibrium value of the rate of inflation, i.e. to the growth rate of the nominal quantity of money per head. Stein introduces in the *S*-model the well-known 'adaptive expectations function', an equation representing the adjustment of the expected rate of inflation.[6]

$$\frac{d\pi^*}{dt} = \beta(\pi - \pi^*) \text{ and } 0 < \beta < \infty \tag{7}$$

This equation implies that the existing rate of inflation is compared with the expected rate, and that expectations are revised accordingly with an 'expectations coefficient' if a deviation exists between the two variables. We saw in chapter 2 that this 'expectations coefficient (β) has a critical value which is of essential importance for the stability of the neo-classical monetary growth model.

The equations mentioned above form a dynamic model with six unknowns, viz. nominal rate of interest (i), actual rate of inflation (π), expected rate of inflation (π^*), real cash-balances per unit of capital (v), labour intensity (ℓ) and rate of growth of the capital goods ($dK/dt\ 1/K$). The rate of population growth (n) and the rate of monetary expansion (μ) are exogenously given and constant.[7]

Stein examines in the *S*-model first of all the influence of a change in the rate of monetary expansion on the equilibrium values of the real variables in the long run and further examines implications of the changed equations (1) and (7) for the equilibrium values of the real variables in the short-term analysis, when the labour-capital ratio is supposed to be constant.

6. We refer in this context to chapter 2 and further to Ph. Cagan. The monetary dynamics of hyperinflation, in Milton Friedman's *Studies in the quantity theory of money*, Chicago 1956, p. 25–117; Dean S. Dutton, The demand for money and the price level, *Journal of Political Economy*, 1970, p. 1162–1170, and, by the same author, A model of self generating-inflation, the Argentine case, *Journal of Money, Credit and Banking*, May 1971, p. 245–263.

7. J. Stein, 1971, op. cit. p. 123.

4.3. Long-term equilibrium analysis

4.3.1. An algebraic formulation of equilibrium

As the preceding analytical observations have shown, the equilibrium situation in the monetary growth theory is in the long run characterized by a constancy of capital intensity, of real cash-balances per unit of capital and of the expected rate of inflation.

This means that, if we take account of equations (5), (6) and (7), capital goods will grow at the same rate as natural growth, and the current rate of inflation in this equilibrium situation is equal to the growth rate of the nominal cash-balances per head. This can be represented as follows:

$$\pi_e = \mu - n \tag{8}$$

With regard to the adjustment equation of price expectations, it holds that in this equilibrium situation the change in the expected rate of inflation has become equal to zero, and the current rate of inflation tallies with the expected rate of inflation. ($\pi^* = \pi_e = \mu - n$)

Starting from equation (1) this means that the equilibrium situation in the *S*-model is characterized by the fact that discrepancy exists no longer between the demand for and the supply of goods per unit of capital.

Planned savings and investments are equal, the growth rate of the capital goods being equal to savings per unit of capital (see equation 4). In these circumstances the current rate of inflation develops continuously in accordance with its equilibrium value; and equilibrium on the commodity market is maintained at all time. This is based on the supposition (neo-classical) that possible disequilibria on the commodity market are eliminated directly and completely due to price flexibility. In the long-term equilibrium situation with equation (2) in mind, the following basic equation holds, implying at the same time an equilibrium on the commodity market:

$$n + r(\ell_e) + \pi_e - i_e = S(\ell_e, v_e) = n \tag{9}$$

Equation (9) enables us to deduce that in the equilibrium situation concerned the nominal rate of interest is equal to the nominal rate of profit ($i_e = r(\ell_e) + \pi_e$), and so the rate of return on bonds agrees with that on the physical capital goods.[8] From equation (3) we can further deduce that, in the equilibrium situation, the supply of real cash-balances per unit of capital equals demand.[9] This can be expressed as follows:

$$v_e = \hat{L}[f(\ell_e), r(\ell_e) + \pi_e, i_e, v_e], \tag{10}$$

by which $i_e = r(\ell_e) + \pi_e$

The above analysis illustrates that in the *S*-model the long-term equilibrium situation has the features of the neo-classical analysis, as presented in chapter 2. This means that the actual rate of growth of capital goods which is equal to the rate of population growth, is determined by savings per unit of capital.

Further, in this equilibrium situation, the demand for real cash-balances per unit of capital is equal to the supply of this monetary variable. This results from Walras' law and the assumed equilibrium on the bonds market. Equations (8), (9) and (10) enable us to solve the equilibrium values of labour intensity (ℓ_e), of real cash-balances per unit of capital (v_e) and of the rate of inflation (π_e) in terms of exogenous variables μ and n, the monetary rate of growth and the rate of population growth respectively.

4.3.2. A graphical interpretation of equilibrium

In this section we present a more verbal interpretation of the equilibrium solution in the long run.

Equation (9) from the preceding section can be represented graphically as an *IS*-curve for the long run, indicating the combinations of the equilibrium values of labour intensity and of real cash-balances per unit of capital, for which it holds that the savings (= investments) per unit of capital (= rate of growth of the capital goods) are equal to the given rate of population growth. Stein calls this the *LX*-curve. In the preceding chapter the *IS*-curve was defined on the one hand as combining the rate of interest and the rate of inflation on the other hand as combining the rate of interest and the

8. J. Stein, 1971, op. cit. p. 125–126.

9. This again assumes continued equilibrium on the bonds market.

real cash-balances per unit of capital, for which in both cases it holds that excess-demand for goods per unit of capital remains constant. The *IS*-curve defined in this section is better comparable with the *IS*-curve in the Hicks-Hansen diagram, since it relates to equilibrium on the commodity market.

Partial differentiation of equation (9) with respect to the equilibrium value of the labour intensity yields:

$$\frac{\partial v_e}{\partial \ell_e} = \frac{S_\ell}{-S_v} > 0 \tag{11}$$

The positively sloped curve can be explained as follows. A disturbance in equilibrium by an increased equilibrium value of the labour intensity will increase the average capital productivity and consequently the planned savings per unit of capital. All this results from the characteristics of the production function and from the savings function. The initially disturbed equilibrium (viz. the rate of growth of capital goods is larger than the natural rate of growth) will have been restored if the negative wealth-effect in the savings function has reduced savings sufficiently by way of increased real cash-balances per unit of capital. ($S_v < 0$).

The savings per unit of capital will increase under the influence of the induced increase in capital productivity. In order to maintain equilibrium growth, this increase in savings must be compensated. Therefore an increase in real cash-balances per unit of capital is required with the capacity of reducing savings sufficiently (by way of the wealth-effect) that the actual rate of growth of the capital goods develops in accordance with the exogenously given rate of population growth.

The *IS*-curve in the long-term equilibrium situation can be deduced graphically by the following system.

The second quadrant shows the operation of the wealth effect in the savings function, viz. the negative relation between real cash-balances and savings per unit of capital, whereas the equilibrium condition (equation 9) is represented in the third quadrant. In the fourth quadrant the negative relation is expressed between the rate of growth of capital goods and the equilibrium value of labour-intensity, given the natural rate of population growth (equation 6). As the rate of growth of the capital goods increases, given the rate

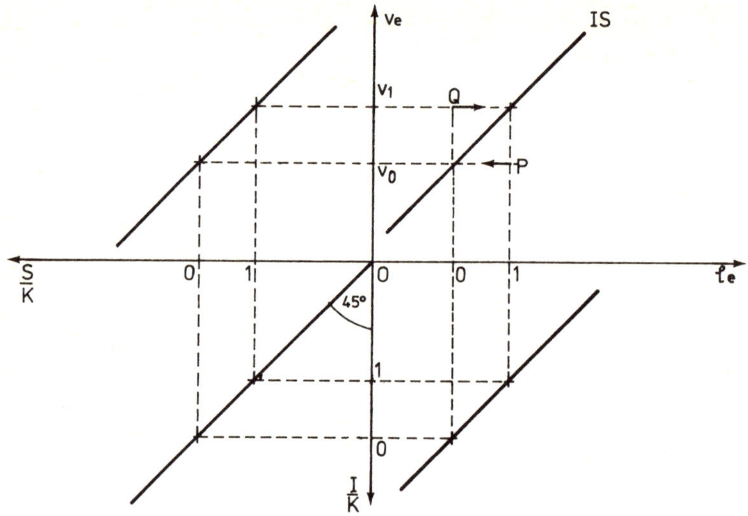

Figure 1

of population growth, the labour intensity will decrease through a technical substitution process, and vice versa. In the first quadrant the *IS*-curve results, with combinations of real cash-balances per unit of capital and labour intensity, for which it holds that savings per unit of capital are equal to the natural rate of growth.

The reasoning proceeds as follows. If we start from a specific amount of real cash-balances v_0, given the savings function, specific savings per unit of capital will result of $(S/K)_0$, and consequently a growth rate of capital goods of $(I/K)_0$. The fourth quadrant shows that, given the natural rate of growth, the corresponding equilibrium value of labour intensity will be equal to ℓ_0. If real cash-balances increase to the level v_1 savings per unit of capital and consequently the rate of growth of the capital goods will become $(S/K)_1 = (I/K)_1$. The corresponding equilibrium value of labour intensity in the fourth quadrant is then equal to ℓ_1.

On the other hand, equation (10) can be considered as the algebraic expression of the *FM*-curve in the long-term equilibrium situation. This curve (which Stein termed the *LV*-curve) represents the combinations of equilibrium value of labour intensity and of real cash-balances per unit of capital; here equilibrium exists between the supply of and the demand for real cash-balances per unit of capital. In the preceding chapter, the *FM*-curve was defined on the one hand as combining the rate of interest and the rate of inflation, on the other hand as combining the rate of interest and the real cash-balances per unit of capital, for which in both cases Walras' law holds.

In other words, given the equilibrium on the market for financial assets, excess-demand for goods equals excess-supply of real cash-balances. The *FM*-curve defined in this section can be compared with the *LM*-curve in the Hicks-Hansen diagram, because it now refers to equilibrium on the money-market (demand and supply of real cash-balances).

Partial differentiation of equation (10) with respect to the equilibrium value of labour intensity leads to:

$$\frac{\partial v_e}{\partial \ell_e} = \frac{1}{1 - \hat{L}_4}[\hat{L}_1 f'(\ell_e) + (\hat{L}_2 + \hat{L}_3)r'(\ell_e)] \tag{12}$$

The slope of this curve cannot be determined unambiguously, as appeared in the preceding chapter. This results from the fact that two opposite forces are operative, which determine the demand for real cash-balances. If, as a result of an increased equilibrium value of labour intensity, the increase in demand for transaction cash-balances on the basis of the positive income-effect ($\hat{L}_1 f'(\ell_e)$), exceeds the negative substitution-effect ($(\hat{L}_2 + \hat{L}_3)r'(\ell_e)$) the demand for real cash-balances per unit of capital will increase. The *FM* curve then has a positive slope. In the reverse case of a dominating substitution-effect, the curve concerned has a negative slope.[10] However, we must observe that the slope of the *FM*-curve is crucially determined by the wealth-elasticity of the demand for money ($\hat{L}_4$). For if wealth-sensitivity of the demand for money is larger than one, the above conclusions will be completely reversed. In those circumstances, a dominating income-effect will ultimately cause a decrease in the equilibrium value of the real cash-balances, whereas a dominating substitution-effect will enlarge the equilibrium value of this variable.

Empirical research for the Netherlands has proved that the wealth elasticity of money-demand is greater than one, in which case it is

10. J. Stein, 1971, op. cit. p. 126–127.

particularly clear that demand deposits at commercial banks are mainly related to wealth, whereas in the United States these deposits fluctuate far less with wealth.[11]

The following system enables us to derive the *FM*-curve.

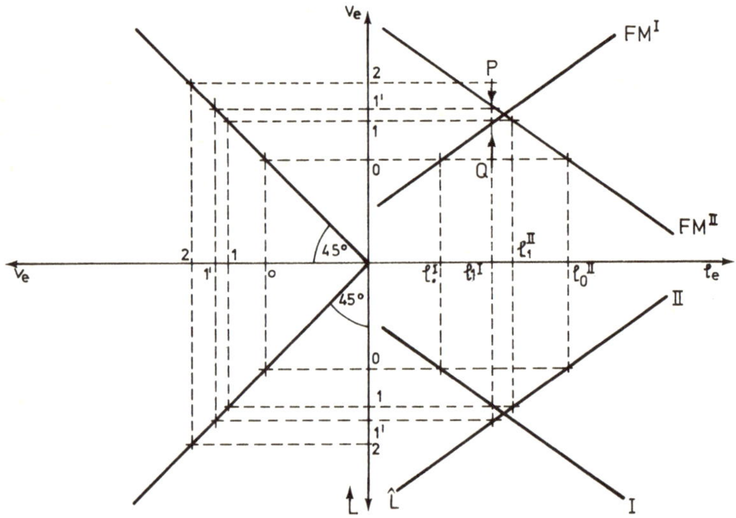

Figure 2

The second quadrant is self-evident; the third shows the equilibrium between supply of and demand for real cash-balances per unit of capital, in which it is supposed equilibrium always exists, on the market for financial assets (bonds).

The fourth quadrant expresses the relation between the development of labour intensity and the demand for real cash-balances per unit of capital. If the income-effect dominates the substitution-effect, a positive relation arises between the variables mentioned which is represented by curve-*I*.

An *FM*-curve with a positive slope results in the first quadrant (FM^I). If, however, the substitution-effect dominates, there is a negative relation between labour intensity and the demand for real

11. C. K. F. Nieuwenburg, *The ownership of liquidity by households in the Netherlands*, Kluwer-Deventer, 1969, p. 67–71.

cash-balances per unit of capital (curve *II*). And then the *FM*-curve follows a negative slope (FM^{II}). In the first quadrant we find the *FM*-curve representing the various combinations of real cash-balances and labour intensity, for which equilibrium exists on the money market (demand and supply of real cash-balances).

The reasoning now proceeds as follows.

If we start from a distinct amount of real cash-balances v_0 in the first and second quadrants, we obtain a demand for real-cash-balances amounting to $\hat{L}_0$, when there is equilibrium on the money market. Given the underlying model, this demand for real cash-balances of $\hat{L}_0$ will occur with a labour intensity value of ℓ_0^f. This will result if the income-effect dominates the substitution-effect in the demand for money.

If the real cash-balances increae to v_1 a demand for real cash-balances of $\hat{L}_1$ will results if there is equilibrium on the money market.

This demand for real cash-balances will be attained with a labour intensity value of ℓ_1^f. In the first quadrant the algebraically-derived positive relation between ℓ_e and v_e emerges. If the substitution-effect dominates, an analogous reasoning can be followed, resulting in a negatively sloped *FM*-curve in the first quadrant. Now both curves can be brought together in the following graph, in which the income effect dominates. We quote the graph on page 134 from Stein.[12]

Along the *IS*-curve the growth rate of savings and investments per unit of capital equals the exogenously given rate of population growth. This means that the points on the *IS*-curve represent combinations of the equilibrium values of the real cash-balances per unit of capital and of the labour intensity, for which it holds that equilibrium growth exists. A point to the right of the curve, e.g. point *P* in graph 1, represents a combination of real cash-balances per unit of capital and labour intensity (v_0, ℓ_1) from which a rate of growth of capital goods results exceeding that of population.

For, given the level of real cash-balances v_0, savings per unit of capital available for expanding capital goods total $(S/K)_0$. The rate of growth of the capital goods with the equilibrium value of labour intensity ℓ_1 is $(I/K)_1$ given the rate of population growth.

12. J. Stein, 1971, op. cit. p. 128.

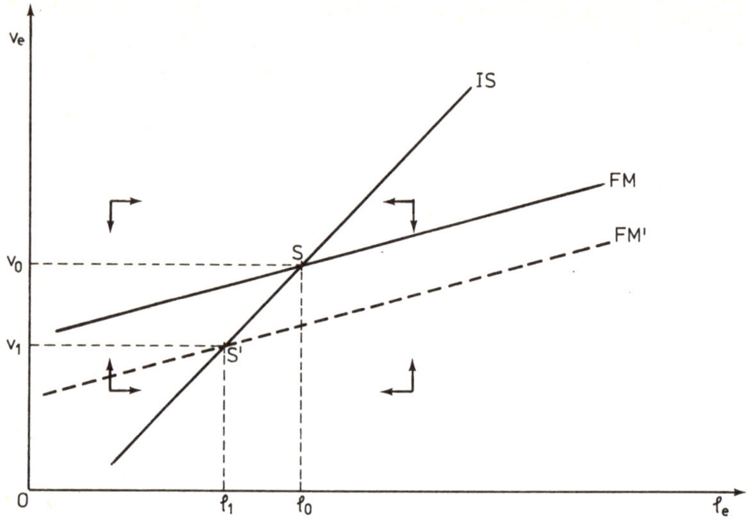

Figure 3

So we see that from that combination of real cash-balances and labour intensity the resulting actual rate of growth of the capital goods is greater than the equilibrium rate of growth (n). An adjustment process will come about as a result of this divergence, causing capital intensity to increase and labour intensity to decrease, and equilibrium will start to return.

For points to the left of the curve, e.g. point Q (v_1, ℓ_0) in graph 1, the opposite is valid. Given the level of real cash-balances (v_1) the resulting savings per unit of capital and growth rate of capital goods are smaller than with labour intensity ℓ_0. In other words, the rate of growth of capital goods is smaller than that of population, and so the equilibrium value of labour intensity will increase (ℓ_1) as a result of a technical substitution process. This is indicated by the direction of the arrows in graph 1.

Points on the FM-curve refer to combinations of the equilibrium values of real cash-balances per unit of capital and of labour intensity, for which it holds that the money market is in equilibrium. A point above the FM-curve, e.g. point P (v_2, ℓ_1^I) in graph 2, represents an excess-supply of real cash-balances per unit of capital $v_2 > \hat{L}_1^I$ (if the income-effect dominates), or $v_2 > \hat{L}_1^{II}$ (if the substitution-effect dominates). As a result of this disequilibrium in the monetary sector, a price rise will set in, by which the actual rate of inflation exceeds its equilibrium value ($\mu - n = \pi_e$). This means a decrease in the real cash-balances per unit of capital to v_1 or to $v_{1'}$.

For points below the *FM*-curve, e.g. point Q (v_0, ℓ_1^I) in graph 2, the opposite again applies.

Given the supply of real cash-balances v_0 and starting from labour intensity ℓ_1^I, with the corresponding demand for real cash-balances $\hat{L}_1^I$ or $\hat{L}_{1'}^{II}$ an excess-demand for real cash-balances per unit of capital results.

This disequilibrium will occasion a price drop, and real cash-balances will increase to (v_1) or ($v_{1'}$), given the supply of nominal cash-balances.

So we see forces in operation, which will ensure a restoration of the equilibrium when disturbances occur. All this is represented by the direction of the arrows in the graph mentioned above.[13] The point of intersection of the two curves, point S in graph 3, represents the combination of real cash-balances per unit of capital and labour intensity, for which an equilibrium exists simultaneously between the rates of growth of capital goods and of population on the one hand, and between supply of and demand for real cash-balances on the other hand.

4.3.3. Influence of a change in the rate of monetary expansion

Let us now examine the changes arising in the equilibrium values of labour intensity and real cash-balances per unit of capital when the rate of monetary expansion increases. Give the rate of population growth, a rise in the growth rate of the money supply (μ) means that the equilibrium value of the rate of inflation (π_e) increases. Since the rate of inflation has not been inserted as an argument into equation (9), S (ℓ_e, v_e) $= n$, the *IS* curve will not shift. As a consequence of the increased nominal rate of return on capital goods and bonds, the demand for real cash-balances will decrease (given the labour intensity) due to the substitution effect. This will shift the *FM* curve downwards, which means that with each capital or labour intensity the equilibrium value of real cash-

13. In the appendix to this chapter it is indicated that the stability of the system depends crucially on the slopes of the two curves.

balances per unit of capital is lower than in the initial situation.[14]

During the adjustment process an excess-supply for real cash-balances and an excess-demand for goods will arise, causing the actual rate of inflation to increase above its higher equilibrium value, so that the equilibrium value of the real cash-balances decreases (see equation (1)). The wealth-effect in the savings function will beget a rise in planned savings, the result being that the rate of growth of capital goods exceeds that of population. The economy is now in a situation, represented by a point to the right of the *IS*-curve in the *IS-S'-FM'* range (see graph 3). In accordance with the analysis in the preceding section this means a decrease in labour-intensity or an increase in capital intensity. In the new equilibrium situation (S') the rate of growth of the capital goods will again tally with the given rate of growth of population; the equilibrium value of the rate of inflation will be equal to the higher growth rate of the nominal quantity of money per head.[15]

In conclusion, we can observe that the long-term equilibrium situation in the *S*-model has the same features as the Tobin neo-classical monetary growth model. The current and expected rates of inflation are always equal, and an increased rate of monetary expansion will enlarge the equilibrium value of capital intensity unambiguously and reduce the equilibrium value of real cash-balances per unit of capital unambiguously, as compared with the equilibrium path with the lower rate of monetary growth. As chapter 2 elucidated, the above-mentioned result in Tobin's monetary growth theory is obtained by way of adjustments in portfolio composition (real cash-balances versus physical capital goods).

The savings from the concept of disposable income used by Tobin are not transformed automatically into physical capital goods. The division of total savings over the two assets depends on their real rates of return. The adjustments mentioned are induced in Tobin's analysis by a change in the expected rate of inflation resulting from

14. The shift in the *FM*-curve can be represented by the partial derivatives, deduced from equation (10):

$$\frac{\partial v_e}{\partial \pi_e} = \frac{\hat{L}_2 + \hat{L}_3}{1 - \hat{L}_4} < 0; 0 < \hat{L}_4 < 1.$$

15. J. Stein, 1971, op. cit. p. 131.

a change in the growth of the quantity of money per head. The relative change in the real rates of return on both wealth components starts up a substitution process within the portfolio, from which a distinct influence emanates on the equilibrium value of capital intensity.

In this particular analysis, as in the Keynes-Wicksell model in chapter 3, a change in the equilibrium value of the rate of inflation resulting from a change in the growth of the nominal money supply per head means that the commodity market is temporarily not in equilibrium (Walrasian excess-demand hypothesis). There are two reasons why a change in the growth rate of the nominal money supply will influence the equilibrium values of the real variables, even within the assumptions of the model. Firstly, the rate of profit, dependent on labour intensity, is inserted as an argument in the investment function. Secondly, labour intensity and real cash balances are included in the savings function.

As we have seen in the preceding chapter, this influence cannot be determined unambiguously in the Keynes-Wicksell analysis. In the *S*-model, a change in the rate of monetary growth will, however, affect the equilibrium value of the real variables in the long run unambiguously owing to the introduction of the modified price change equation.

4.4. Short-term dynamic analysis

The study of short-term economic phenomena is always based on a time period in which the capital intensity of the production process is given. In the preceding chapter detailed attention has been paid to the effects of a change in the rate of monetary expansion on the equilibrium values of the nominal interest rate, the real cash-balances per unit of capital and the expected and the current rates of inflation in the short run.

It was particularly clear that the influence on the short-term equilibrium value of the real cash-balances per unit of capital cannot be determined unambiguously. This must be attributed to the value of adjustment coefficient α. This coefficient indicates the speed at which disequilibria on the commodity market will be expressed in relative price changes (i.e. in changes in the rate of inflation), in accordance with the Walrasian excess-demand hypothesis. This ambiguous effect of a change in the rate of monetary expansion on the equilibrium value of real cash-balances per unit of capital has further repercussions for the long-term development of capital intensity.

Chapter 3 confirmed that in the long-term analysis two conclusions were possible, i.e. the neo-classical version of an increase in the equilibrium value of the capital intensity and a decrease in the equilibrium value of real cash-balances per unit of capital; as well as Stein's conclusion,[16] viz. an increase in the equilibrium value of the capital intensity and an increase in the equilibrium value of real cash-balances per unit of capital. All this is crucially dependent on the extent to which planned savings or planned investments determine the actual rate of growth of the capital goods.

However, in the current synthesis-model, an increase in the growth rate of the nominal quantity of money per head will reduce the short-term equilibrium value of the real cash-balances per unit of capital unambiguously and will enlarge the equilibrium value of the nominal interest rate.[17] This can be explained as follows: the short-term analysis can be represented by the following four equations:

$$\frac{\pi - \psi\pi^*}{\alpha} = n + r(\bar{l}) + \pi^* - i - S(\bar{l}, v) \tag{1}$$

In this equation, and in the preceding section, we see that the actual rate of inflation is determined on the one hand directly, by the expected rate of inflation (price expectations effect) and, on the other hand, more indirectly by the induced excess-demand on the commodity market. Factor ψ allows comparison between the Keynes-Wicksell model ($\psi = 0$) from chapter 3 and the S-model ($\psi = 1$).

With continuous equilibrium on the bonds market it holds, according to Walras' law, that excess-demand for goods equals excess-supply of real cash-balances per unit of capital. This is formulated

16. J. L. Stein, Money and capacity growth, *Journal of Political Economy*, October 1966, p. 461–462.
17. J. L. Stein, 1971, op cit. p. 132.

in the following expression:

$$\frac{\pi - \psi\pi^*}{\alpha h} = v - \hat{L}\left[f'(\bar{l}) + \frac{\pi - \psi\pi^*}{\alpha}, r(\bar{l}) + \pi^*, i, v\right] \tag{2}$$

The equation for the change in the expected rate of inflation will be:

$$\frac{d\pi^*}{dt} = \beta(\pi - \pi^*) \text{ and } 0 < \beta < \infty. \tag{3}$$

The development of real cash-balances per unit of capital, given the labour intensity, can be expressed as:

$$\frac{dv}{dt}\frac{1}{v} = \mu - \pi - \frac{dK}{dt}\frac{1}{K} = \mu - \pi - n. \tag{4}$$

The *IS* and *FM*-curves are represented algebraically by equations (1) and (2). These equations can be solved, as in the preceding chapter, for the nominal rate of interest (i) and the rate of inflation (π) in terms of the following two variables, viz. the expected rate of inflation (π^*) and the real cash-balances per unit of capital (v), given the labour intensity ($\bar{l}$) and the rate of population growth (n).[18]

From this the following equations are obtained:

$$\pi = \pi(\pi^*, v; n) \tag{5}$$

$$i = i(\pi^*, v; n). \tag{6}$$

In this synthesis-model ($\psi = 1$) an increase in the expected rate of inflation, as a result of an increase in the rate of monetary growth, will cause the actual rate of inflation to increase more than proportionally. ($\partial\pi/\partial\pi^* > 1$)[19] This is generated by two effects. On the

18. This is presented in graph 4 in the preceding chapter.
19. The relevant partial derivatives can be deduced in the same way as in the appendix to chapter 3, section 4. Only coefficient ψ must be taken into account; this is fixed at one. From this results:

$$\frac{\partial\pi}{\partial\pi^*} = \psi + \frac{(\hat{L}_2 + \hat{L}_3)}{\frac{1}{\alpha}\left[\hat{L}_3 - \left(\frac{1}{h} + \hat{L}_1\right)\right]} > 1$$

one hand, there is a direct influence by the higher expected rate of inflation on the actual rate of inflation owing to the assumed price-change equation in which the line is taken that the economic subjects anticipate expected price rises. On the other hand, the increase in the expected rate of inflation will bring about an excess-demand for goods through the investment equation, further reinforcing the primary impact (see equation (1)). This means that the difference between the actual and the expected rates of inflation becomes larger. In accordance with the theory of adaptive expectations (equation (3)), the expected rate of inflation will be revised in an upward direction and adjusted again. In this way an instable development, viz. a self-generating inflationary process can arise, unless adjustment of the expected rate of inflation is sufficiently sluggish.[20]

This can be demonstrated as follows. Substitution of equation (5) into equations (3) and (4) gives two differential equations, which represent the development of the expected rate of inflation and the real cash-balances per unit of capital in the short-term model.

$$\frac{d\pi^*}{dt} = \beta[\pi(\pi^*, v) - \pi^*] = J(\pi^*, v; \mu, n) \tag{7}$$

$$\frac{dv}{dt}\frac{1}{v} = \mu - \pi(\pi^*, v) - \frac{dK}{dt}\frac{1}{K} = \mu - n - \pi(\pi^*, v) = K(\pi^*, v; \mu, n) \tag{8}$$

The assumed positive equilibrium values of the expected rate of inflation and the real cash-balances in the short-term analysis are represented by π_e^* and v_e respectively, given the labour intensity, the rate of population growth and the growth rate of the money supply. From this it follows for equations (7) and (8):

$$J(\pi_e^*, v_e; \mu, n) = 0 \tag{9}$$

$$K(\pi_e^*, v_e; \mu, n) = 0. \tag{10}$$

The conditions for local stability of short-term equilibrium can be

20. In the neo-classical monetary growth model the value of 'expectations coefficient' β has also appeared to be of great significance for stability of the model.

derived by linearizing the dynamic system (7) and (8) around the equilibrium point (π_e^*, v_e). Partial differentiation of equations (7) and (8) with respect to the expected rate of inflation (π^*) and the real cash-balances per unit of capital (v) gives the following result:[21]

$$J_1 = J_{\pi^*} = \beta\pi_1 - \beta > 0; \text{(7a)} \quad J_2 = J_v = \beta\pi_2 > 0 \qquad \text{(7b)}$$

$$K_1 = K_{\pi^*} = -\pi_1 < 0; \text{(8a)} \quad K_2 = K_v = -\pi_2 < 0 \qquad \text{(8b)}$$

Given matrix $[M] = \begin{bmatrix} J_1 & J_2 \\ K_1 & K_2 \end{bmatrix}$ of the linearized system, the following conditions must be fulfilled for local stability:

$$\text{trace of matrix } [M]\text{: } J_1 + K_2 = \beta(\pi_1 - 1) - \pi_2 < 0 \qquad (11)$$

$$\text{determinant of matrix } [M]\text{: } J_1K_2 - J_2K_1 = \beta\pi_2 > 0 \qquad (12)$$

After these mathematical explanations we will proceed to a more verbal interpretation of the problems.

Starting from equation (3) and the short-term equilibrium situation (real cash-balances per unit of capital are constant and the actual and expected rates of inflation are equal to the growth rate of the nominal quantity of money per head) an increase in the rate of monetary growth will lead to a change in the expected rate of inflation. This process can be described as follows.

The increase in the rate of monetary expansion will manifest itself in the first place as an enlargement of real cash-balances, resulting in expansion of consumption expenditures. At the same time, investments increase as a consequence of the initial decrease in the nominal interest rate (labour intensity and rate of profit are given). Both are demand stimulating forces. The wealth-effect in the consumption function, and the interest-effect, or the Wicksell-effect, in the investment function will bring about an excess-demand for

21. For the partial derivatives $\pi_1 = \partial\pi/\partial\pi^*$ and $\pi_2 = \partial\pi/\partial v$ readers are referred again to the appendix to chapter 3. $\pi_2 = \partial\pi/\partial v > 0$, since it is supposed that $(1 - \hat{L}_4) > 0$. This means that an increase in real cash-balances per unit of capital brings about an increase in excess-supply of real cash-balances, because only part of the additional balances will be used to improve the individual's own cash-holdings ($\hat{L}_4 < 1$).

goods and will exercise an upward pressure on the actual rate of inflation. Adjustment of the expected rate of inflation, as a result of the difference between actual and expected rates of inflation, is equal to β-times the initial change in the actual rate of inflation.

In the model in question this adjustment of the expected rate of inflation will cause the actual rate to increase more than proportionally ($\beta\pi_1 > \beta$). This reinforcing influence results from the fact that, in the synthesis model, a higher expected rate of inflation has a direct, as well as an indirect effect on the actual rate ($\pi_1 = \pi_{\pi^*} > 1$). A direct effect, resulting from the modified price change equation, and an indirect effect occasioned by the Walrasian excess-demand equation. This means that an inflationary development will work cumulatively, and reinforces itself. Adjustment of the expected rate of inflation in an upward direction will further enlarge investment activity (the expected nominal rate of profit $r(\bar{\ell}) + \pi^*$, increases), thus advancing the actual rate of inflation further under the influence of an increased excess-demand for goods.

This cumulative movement of the price level is however slowed down to a certain extent by the real cash-balance-effect, inserted as an argument into the savings function. Clearly, continuous increase in the actual rate of inflation reduces the real cash-balances per unit of capital, if, during the adjustment process, the actual rate of inflation has become larger than the increase in the nominal quantity of money per head.

And so the excess-demand for goods will drop. Starting from the Walrasian excess-demand equation, the actual rate of inflation will consequently be mitigated to some extent ($\pi_2 > 0$)[22]. If the price expectations effect ($\beta\pi_1 - \beta$) dominates the real cash-balance effect ($\pi_2 = \pi_v$), the trace of the coefficient-matrix will be positive; the stability condition will no longer be fulfilled.

In other words, an initial disturbance in equilibrium will set a process going on the basis of the assumed behaviour with regard to adjustment of the expected rate of inflation. Each relative increase in the general price level will, consequently, lead to a further increase in the existing rate of inflation. This may produce an explo-

22. J. L. Stein, 1971, op. cit. p. 135. The author gives a graphic illustration of the short-run model, equations (7) and (8), with the aid of a 'phase-diagram', an important aid in analysing a dynamic process.

sive inflationary development.[23] An initial disturbance will lead the system even further from equilibrium. A strong wealth-effect and/or a sufficient lag in the adjustment of the expected rate of inflation (β) can take care of stability, by which a new equilibrium situation is attained. It is now clear that introduction of the modified price change equation in the synthesis model can lead to greater instability in development than in the Keynes-Wicksell model described in the preceding chapter. In the latter analysis the actual rate of inflation is merely influenced in an indirect way by the expenditure-effect which manifests itself on the commodity market.

4.5. The rate of inflation and the nominal rate of interest

4.5.1. The Gibson paradox

It is now interesting to examine how the nominal rate of interest will develop as a consequence of an increase in the rate of monetary growth. The more so as in the past decade almost continuous inflation is evident in the Western economies, which has exercised a distinct influence on the development of the nominal rate of interest. In an economic climate with almost permanent inflation, expectations with regard to the decline of the real purchasing power of money are bound to play a part in the decisions of the economic agents. In other words in these circumstances economic agents will become increasingly accustomed to the phenomenon of inflation and will adjust their behaviour accordingly.

The nominal rate of interest is dependent on the expected rate of inflation and the real cash-balances per unit of capital in the short-term analysis in question (see equation (6) from the preceding section).

In view of the economic agents' preference for liquidity, a higher rate of monetary growth will lead in the first instance to an increase in real cash-balances per unit of capital and accordingly to a fall in the nominal interest rate. This last result fits very well in the views of those who assume that a large supply of funds leads to a lower interest rate. With this we mean the operation of the well-

23. J. Koning, Inflatie in Zuid – Amerika, *Maandschrift Economie*, December, University of Tilburg, 1972, p. 66.

known Keynesian liquidity-effect, which refers to the initial short-term influence emanating from a higher rate of monetary growth. After all, the economic agents will adjust their portfolios as a result of the existing excess-supply of real cash-balances. This means that the demand for financial assets (bonds) increases, resulting in a drop in the interest rate. In this context Nieuwenburg and Leemreize point out that the adjustment process following a monetary impulse come about mainly in the short run in the bonds market sector and only in the long run in the sector of physical goods.

This is due to the fact that a portfolio adjustment is linked with information and transaction costs, which are relatively low for bonds, marginally speaking. In their empirical research they reach the conclusion that this liquidity-effect works very quickly, but is of relatively short duration.[24]

In antithesis to this liquidity-effect we see that the increase in the expected rate of inflation will, as we said before, bring about an excess-demand for goods. Employers who enlarge their investment activity will have more assets (bonds) to offer, or ask the banks for more credit in order to finance the purchase of capital goods. This generates an upward pressure on the interest rate which compensates the initial drop in the interest rate. This increasing demand for credit, or the greater supply of bonds, must be considered as the feed-back-effect of a monetary impulse from the real sector to the financial. Nieuwenburg and Leemreize's empirical study leads them to the tentative conclusion that nine to twelve months after the monetary impulse occurred the sign of the regression-coefficient turns from negative to significantly positive; the interest rate will start to rise again.[25] Moreover, the purchase of financial assets is less attractive than investment in real capital goods, owing to the increase in the expected rate of inflation.

From this an excess-supply of bonds will result, increasing the nominal rate of interest. This increase will further be reinforced on

24. C. K. Niewenburg and H. J. Leemreize, The long-term rate of interest in the Netherlands, an empirical study, Amsterdam-Rotterdam Bank, *Economic Quarterly Review*, March 1974, p. 13.

25. C. K. Nieuwenburg and H. J. Leemreize, Amsterdam-Rotterdam Bank, *Economic Quarterly Review*, March op. cit. pp. 14–15. The consequences of this issue for monetary policy is described in an article by Nieuwenburg, Een vorm van modern monetarisme, *Maandschrift Economie*, University of Tilburg, September 1973, p. 554–561.

the one hand by the decrease in real cash-balances, set in during the adjustment process owing to the increased actual rate of inflation (absorption of funds by a greater need for transaction-balances), and on the other hand by the upward movement of the expected rate of inflation. Since if an inflationary price development is expected, the credit-supply will decrease and the demand for credit will increase at each rate of interest. The lender expects a real decrease in principal and in the payments of interest, and the borrower expects that he can amortize his debt in the future with less real purchasing power. Both forces bring about a net-demand for funds and an increase in the nominal rate of interest. Boorman and Havrilesky state in this context, 'during periods of rising prices, for example, the premium component (based on expected changes in the price level) reflects an attempt on the part of lenders to recoup through an interest return an amount equal to the loss of real purchasing power which they expect to suffer from the deterioration of the real principle value of their assets'.[26] This means that lenders who expect a price rise, will try to secure themselves by claiming a sufficiently higher nominal rate of interest in order to compensate the capital loss on the principal. For the rate of interest can be considered as an expression of the exchange ratio between the current value of money and the claims on money in the future. Borrowers, on their part, expect an increase in the nominal value of the real assets which they purchase and will be very willing to pay a higher nominal rate of interest. If we assume that the synthesis model is stable (the real cash-balance effect exceeds the price expectations-effect), after the disturbance of the short-term equilibrium as a result of a higher rate of monetary growth, the actual rate of inflation and the nominal interest rate will both be higher in the new equilibrium situation than in the initial situation. This means that there is a positive relation between changes in the nominal rate of interest and the change in the growth rate of the nominal quantity of money (= rate of inflation).[27]

This positive relation between the development of the general price level and the nominal rate of interest, a phenomenon known

26. J. Boorman and Th. Havrilesky, *Money supply, money demand and macro-economic models*, 1972, p. 179.
27. J. L. Stein, 1971, op. cit. p. 114.

in economic literature as the 'Gibson-paradox', has been already described by the classical authors (Thomas Tooke, Wicksell, Fisher and others) and has drawn varying attention in the course of economic history.[28]

So Fisher writes: '. . . when prices are rising, the rate of interest tends to be high, but not so high as it should be to compensate for the rise; and when the prices are falling the rate of interest tends to be low, but not so low as it should be to compensate for the fall'.[29]

According to Fisher a partial and lagged adjustment will take place for the nominal interest rate to the rate of inflation and deflation. He ascribes this to the existence of a 'money-illusion' and to an imperfect foresight concerning future price development. The paradoxical issue lies in the fact that in the orthodox quantity theory it was always said that a high price level must be ascribed to an excess-supply of money and an accordingly low nominal rate of interest.

This view which has dominated post-war economic theory, assumes that a change in the supply of money influences the price level in the same direction, and the nominal rate of interest in an opposite direction. Fluctuations in the nominal interest rate are considered by defenders of this view as inidcators of the actual monetary policy.

In connection with the preceding analysis it can be assumed that a change in the growth rate of the nominal quantity of money has a short-term impact (liquidity-effect) and a more long-term impact (price-expectations-effect or Fisher-effect) on the development of the nominal interest rate. On the contrary the modern monetarist view focuses on the adjustment process in the short-run (the so-called 'transition-period'), described by Fisher, which follows on a monetary impulse. Monetarists today refer to this as the Fisher-effect too, without however appealing to the effects of inflationary expectations. They rather have in mind the direct relation between the monetary impulse and the conversion of the initial excess-cash-balances into goods and services. As we know, Keynes held the

28. M. Blaug, *Economic theory in retrospect*, Homewood Illinois 1968, p. 560. Keynes called this phenomenon 'the Gibson paradox' in his *Treatise on money*, referring to a number of empirical studies by A. H. Gibson in the twenties, in which Gibson found a close positive correlation between the rate of interest and wholesale prices over a period of more than 100 years in England.
29. I. Fisher, *The theory of interest*, New York, 1930, p. 43.

view that bonds are the only substitute for the holding of money, whereas Fisher considered the purchasing of goods and services as a substitute for holding real-balances. According to the theory of liquidity preference, a monetary impulse affects the nominal rate of interest direct, because the initial excess-cash-balances are eliminated via the bonds market. Fisher and the modern monetarists too (Brunner, Meltzer and Friedman) take the line that physical goods are a relatively better substitute for money than bonds. The influence of a monetary impulse on the nominal rate of interest rather manifests itself – according to the monetarists – in an indirect way via the commodity markets. The initial excess-cash balances are substituted for goods, followed, as we saw earlier, by a greater demand for credit, or a greater supply of bonds.[30]

This increased demand for funds then leads to an upward movement of the nominal interest rate.

The 'Gibson paradox' can be clarified with the aid of the Keynes-Wicksell analysis as follows. We have seen in the preceding explanations that short-term equilibrium will exist, given labour intensity ($\bar{\ell}$), if the expected rate of inflation (π^*) and the real cash-balances per unit of capital are constant (v). In other words in the equilibrium situation in the short run the actual and expected rates of inflation are equal to the rate of growth of the nominal money supply per head.[31] From equations (3) and (4) in the preceding section it then follows:

$$\pi^* = \pi_e \qquad (1)$$

$$\pi_e = \mu - n. \qquad (2)$$

Equation (1) from the preceding section enables us to derive an *IS*-curve representing the combinations of the nominal rate of interest (i) and the real cash-balances per unit of capital (v), for which it holds that investments and savings are equal. The algebraic expression of that curve runs as follows:

$$n + r(\bar{\ell}) + \pi_e - i = S(\bar{\ell}, v) \qquad (3)$$

30. C. K. Nieuwenburg and H. J. Leemreize, Amsterdam-Rotterdam Bank *Economic Quarterly Review*, March 1974, op. cit. p. 6–7 and Yung Chul Park, *Some current issues on the transmission process of monetary policy*, I.M.F. Staff Papers, May 1972, p. 31–36.
31. J. L. Stein, 1971, op. cit. p. 149–150.

The curve is positively sloped, since an increase in question in the nominal interest rate will reduce investments, necessitating an increase in real cash-balances to bring savings and investments in equilibrium. ($S_v < 0$ and $\partial i/\partial v = -S_v$)

On the other hand, from equation (2) from the preceding section we can derive an *FM*-curve also representing combinations of the nominal rate of interest and the real cash-balances per unit of capital, but for which it holds that the demand for and the supply of real cash-balances are in equilibrium. That equation can be formulated as:

$$v = \hat{L}[f(\bar{\ell}), r(\bar{\ell}) + \pi_e, i, v] \qquad (4)$$

This curve is negatively sloped $\left(\dfrac{\partial i}{\partial v} = \dfrac{1 - \hat{L}_4}{\hat{L}_3} < 0\right)$

For when the nominal rate of interest falls, the demand for real cash-balances per unit of capital will increase ($\hat{L}_3 < 0$) and ($1 - \hat{L}_4 > 0$). This means that the supply of real cash-balances will have to increase in order to maintain equilibrium. All this can be expressed graphically as follows:

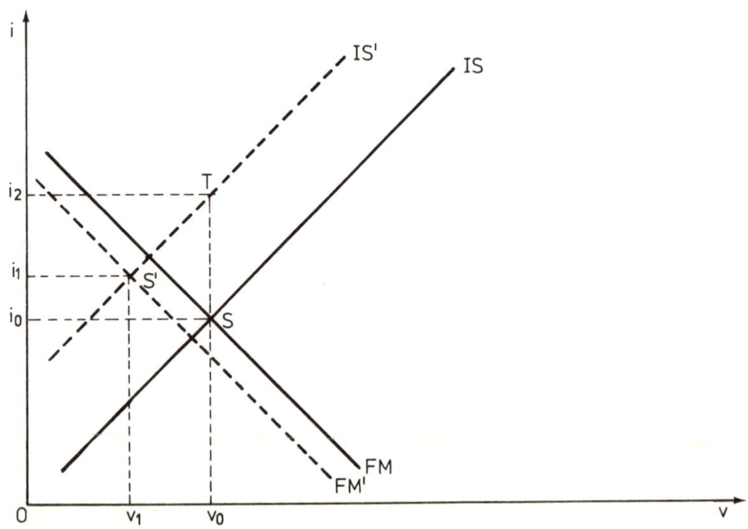

Figure 4

The short-term equilibrium is now represented by point S, a combination of the nominal rate of interest (i_0) and real cash-balances per unit of capital (v_0), for which it holds that a simultaneous equilibrium exists on the commodity and money markets.[32] If the equilibrium is disturbed as a result of an increase in the growth rate of the nominal money supply per head, and consequently the equilibrium value of the actual and expected rates of inflation increases, the following process will set in. In the first place the increase in planned investment will produce an excess-demand for goods, shifting the *IS*-curve upwards. In order to maintain equality between planned investments and planned savings, the nominal interest rate – given the real cash-balances per unit of capital (v_0) – will have to increase (i_2) as a compensation for the increased rate of inflation (ST). The real rate of interest ($i - \pi_e = r$) therefore will remain constant. Next, the increased equilibrium value of the rate of inflation will cause the opportunity costs for holding real cash-balances to increase and the demand for real cash-balances to decrease, given the nominal rate of interest.

The supply of real cash-balances per unit of capital will have to decrease in order to maintain the money-market equilibrium. In this particular case this means a shift of the *FM*-curve downwards. As the graph shows, a new equilibrium comes about in point S' (i_1, v_1), with a higher nominal rate of interest and lower real cash-balances per unit of capital compared with the initial situation.

If a wealth-effect applies in the savings and consumption function, the nominal rate of interest will increase less than the rate of inflation, causing the real rate of interest to decrease. In the graph mentioned above this is expressed as $i_0 i_1 < ST$. For the more savings increase as a result of a decrease in real cash-balances, the lower the ultimate rise in the nominal interest rate will be, in order to maintain equilibrium between savings and investments. This vies is expressed by Metzler, when he says that introduction of the wealth-effect in the savings function has consequences for the equilibrium value of the real rate of interest.[33]

32. J. L. Stein, 1971, op. cit. p. 150–152.

33. L. M. Meltzer, Wealth, saving and the rate of interest, *Journal of Political Economy*, April 1958, p. 93–116, See also W. A. Gibson, Interest rates and monetary policy, *Journal of Political Economy*, May-June 1970, p. 431–450.

Mundell also points out that the increase in the equilibrium value of the nominal interest rate depends on the operation of the wealth-effect in the savings function. Mundell uses the well-known Hicks-Hansen diagram in his analysis, replacing income on the horizontal axis by the monetary component of wealth, viz. real cash-balances. The point of intersection of the *IS* and the *LM*-curves now represents the combinations of the real and the nominal rates of interest on the one hand and the real cash-balances on the other hand, for which it holds that simultaneous equilibrium exists in the real sector and in the monetary sector at stable prices. Next he examines the influence of a higher expected rate of inflation on the equilibrium values of the interest rate and real cash-balances and concludes: 'We have seen that the money rate of interest rises by less than the rate of inflation and therefore the real rate of interest falls during inflation. The conclusion is based on the fact that inflation reduces real money balances and that the resulting decline in wealth stimulates increased saving. Real conditions in the economy are altered by the purely monetary phenomenon'.[34] Mundell assumes that anticipated fluctuations in the rate of inflation can be of real influence on economic activity. For when economic agents expect a price rise the nominal rate of interest will rise less than the rate of inflation, producing an incentive to extend investments as a result of the decrease in the real interest rate.

4.5.2. Empirical results

In recent years a great number of empirical studies have appeared, which support the analysis in the preceding section significantly. So Gibson comes to the conclusion in his empirical research that a strong positive correlation exists for the United States in the period 1952–1970, especially after 1959, between the expected rate of inflation and the interest on government securities. The positive correlation is stronger when related to short-term financial assets (6-months and 9–12 months).[35] This means that the time horizon concerned apparently also determines the number of periods in-

34. R. A. Mundell, Inflation, saving and the real rate of interest, *in Monetary Theory*, 1971, p. 18–21.
35. W. Gibson, Interest rates and inflationary expectations; new evidence, *American Economic Review*, December 1972, p. 854–863.

volved in the formation of inflationary expectations. The time horizon for short-term financial assets is shorter, which may mean that one does not look so far back in the past when building up inflationary expectations.[36] In this way recent price development receives more emphasis when inflationary expectations are formed than with long-term financial assets.

In another study by Gibson, which also refers to the United States, it emerges that in the years 1947–1966 a change in the nominal quantity of money resulted in a direct liquidity-effect, with the opposite impact on the market interest rate. It has appeared that this liquidity-effect was compensated by positive effects (income and price-expectations-effect) fairly shortly afterwards (3 to 5 months). The author concludes, referring to his empirical results, 'but the sequence clearly makes it hazardous to view the levels or changes of interest rates as indicators of monetary policy' and further '. . . interest rates can as well be regarded as reflecting an easier as a tighter monetary policy'.[37]

Nieuwenburg points out in this context that the Dutch Central Bank has never considered the increase of the capital market interest rate simply as a sign that the monetary situation was tightened. The Bank uses the quantity of money as a policy tool and tries to influence roughly the level of national expenditure through the liquidity-ratio. The interest level which results from a well-defined monetary policy is a resultant for the Dutch Central Bank and not an aim in itself.[38] From this it appears that the Bank's monetary philosophy is strongly based on views relating to the quantity theory. Unlike the American monetary authorities, who – under influence of the Keynesian theory – have considered the rate of interest as a dominating link between monetary impulses and economic activity. The use of the interest rate as an indicator for monetary policy can lead to a completely wrong judgment of the current monetary situation. Thus maintaining a lower nominal rate of interest in order to stimulate economic activity will necessitate a constant increase in the money supply. This expansionary

36. C. K. Nieuwenburg and H. J. Leemreize, Amsterdam-Rotterdam Bank, *Economic Quarterly Review*, March, 1974, op. cit. p. 12.
37. W. Gibson, *Journal of Political Economy*, May-June 1970, op. cit. p. 453.
38. C. K. Nieuwenburg, *Geld en economische activiteit*, University of Utrecht, Deventer 1973, p. 23.

monetary policy in itself generates an inflationary development and an expected price rise, which affect the nominal interest rate in a direction which was not aimed at by the monetary authorities. Monetarists for that reason reject the interest as an indicator for monetary policy. A rising interest rate can be an indication for the central bank that the desired monetary expansion has had no result, and the tendency exists to enlarge further the expansionary policy, which will only stimulate inflation.[39] Yohe and Karnosky conclude in their empirical research for the United States, that the risen nominal rate of interest in the 1952–1969 period must be explained for a great part by the rise in prices. Especially since 1961 the change in the nominal rate of interest can be almost fully ascribed to price changes.

It is worth noting that at present greater publicity is given to the development of the price level and that data on the price development are available more quickly than in the past. This gives economic agents better insight into the recent price development, enabling them to build up more exactly inflationary expectations. In this way the interest rate is greatly influenced by the economic subjects' dispositions.[40] The fact too that they have less money illusions has emphasized the 'Gibson paradox' more. The economic subjects are guided in their decisions more by real than by nominal variables, so that price changes from the recent past are expressed more completely in the nominal rate of interest. In other words the lag-structure of the price expectations to which Fisher refers becomes smaller. The phenomenon of the 'Gibson-paradox' has been verified empirically for the Netherlands by Fase, Nieuwenburg and Leemreize.[41] Fase examines the relation between the rate of return on bonds (perpetual government-bonds) and the price level during the 1901–1971 period; he comes to the conclusion that in this period the phenomenon concerned has occurred in the Netherlands too. He reaches for the total period, a correlation-coefficient between

39. C. K. Nieuwenburg, 1973, op. cit. p. 23.

40. W. Yohe and D. Karnosky, Interest rates and price level changes, 1952–1969, *Review, Federal Reserve Bank of St. Louis*, December 1969, p. 19–38.

41. M. M. Fase, Rate of return on bonds and inflationary expectations: a quantitative analysis of Dutch experiences, Amsterdam-Rotterdam Bank, *Economic Quarterly Review*, September 1972, p. 5–11, C. K. Nieuwenburg and H. J. Leemrezie, Amsterdam-Rotterdam Bank, *Economic Quarterly Review*, March 1974, op. cit. p. 5–16.

the rate of return on bonds and consumption-price-level of 0.68. Fase then tests statistically the theoretical explanation of the relation between the rate of interest and the rate of inflation, as was formulated earlier by Fisher, with monthly figures from the 1961–1970 period.

This research has revealed that the rise in the nominal interest rate in the decade concerned can be explained only partly by the expected price development. According to Fase, 1% expected additional price rise cause the interest rate to increase by 0.60 points in the long run. He concludes in fact that the adjustment will take place only partially because of the public's money illusion. Fase points out that his extremely simple formulation enables him to explain only 45% of the total interest variation from the sixties. This means that other factors have been operative beside the expected price rise, such as a trend rise in the real rate of interest.

Nieuwenburg and Leemreize have examined the development of a representative long-bond-interest rate in the Netherlands during the period 1961–1973, taking account of more variables than Fase in his research mentioned above. The main conclusions from their econometric study are as follows. The relation between money supply and the interest rate is only negative in the short run, but positive in the long run (after 9 to 12 months). This might point to the existence of a better substitution relation between money and goods than between money and bonds, a view which Fisher expressed in chapter IV of his well-known book. Nieuwenburg and Leemreize go on to conclude that 44% of the changes in the interest rate during the considered period can be attributed to a rate of interest, considered by the public as normal (Keynes 'safe level of interest rates'), 18% to an inflationary expectations-effect 'à la Fisher', whereas about 25% is accounted for by the price development on the markets competing with that for bonds (Eurodollars, short-term government securities, and shares). The rest can be attributed to changes in industrial production (10%) and to accelerations and decelerations of the growth rate of money and money-substitutes. (3%)

Finally they point out that, although inflation in the Netherlands in the considered period has had an accelerating character too, its effect on the development of the nominal interest rate has been smaller than emerges in comparable American empirical studies.

In most empirical studies concerning the relation between the development of the nominal interest-rate and the rate of inflation the line is taken that the real rate of interest is either constant or independent of the variable in the regression equation. The Fisher expectations-theory is generally applied in this research. The theory assumes that the nominal rate of interest is equal to the algebraic sum of the real rate of interest and the expected rate of inflation, the latter variable being considered as some weighted average of past inflation rates. This very expected rate of inflation also determines the real rate of interest in the framework of the monetary growth theory. If we take account of the analysis developed in the preceding chapters, we must assume that the supposition is not correct. For, a higher rate of monetary growth will cause the equilibrium value of the rate of inflation to increase, given the rate of population growth. The change in the real rate of return on real cash-balances will generate a substitution process (Tobin) in the portfolio, with the equilibrium value of the rate of profit (real rate of interest) decreasing in comparison with the growth path with the lower rate of monetary growth. The fact that this interdependency is abstracted in the regression equation might explain the sometimes extremely different results in the empirical studies.[42]

42. A. Santomero, A note on interest rates and prices in general equilibrium, *The Journal of Finance*, September 1973, p. 997–1000.

5. Evaluation, summary and conclusions

5.1. Introduction

In this chapter we intend to indicate how, in the course of time, views on the essence and importance of money in the economy have developed, and the consequences of this development for practical monetary policy.

We have attempted so far to make a clear distinction between the comparative-static aspects and the more dynamic aspects of monetary theory. The comparative static analysis of (neo)classical and Keynesian authors in the standard economic literature examines how an increase in money supply affects economic activity. This always entails comparison of two equilibrium situations. If, on the contrary, money is seen more against the background of growth theory or in a comparative-dynamic framework, the question arises how alternative rates of growth of money can influence the long-term equilibrium values of the real economic variables. And this very problem is of central interest in our study. Thorough knowledge of the standard economic literature is required, because on the one hand in modern analyses the classical and Keynesian conceptions and definitions are used very frequently; on the other hand the basis of the neo-classical and the Keynes-Wicksell monetary growth theories can be traced back to the monetary ideas developed by the classical authors and by Keynes.

5.2. Money from a medium of exchange to an asset

Theorists in the classical period merely considered money in its function of a medium of exchange. Although its wealth function or its function as an asset is recognized (Marshall and Pigou), money is not considered of essential importance for the issue of the real economic process. In classical theory, the neutrality of money in the long run is strongly emphasized, i.e. changes in the money supply have no influence on the equilibrium values of the real variables.

This view has always held a central place in the literature, in which case we refer to the 'classical dichotomy'. According to this conception, relative prices or exchange-ratios are determined in the real sector, and the general price level in the monetary sector of the economy. However we should like to point out here that the neo-classical authors, especially Fisher and Wicksell, did advance the dynamic adjustment processes which follow monetary impulse, in which situation money can be considered as non-neutral in the short run. The classical school takes the line that the individuals wish to retain a distinct, constant real cash-balance ratio. This implies that the general price level will vary in direct proportion to changes in the money supply. The causality or the transmission process proceeds from a change in money supply to a change in general price level. The underlying thought is that an expansive monetary impulse will lead initially to a surplus of real cash-balances, which will be eliminated by way of an increase in expenditures (Pigou-effect).

Starting from the supposition of market mechanism and consequently of full employment, the price level will move upwards until in the new equilibrium situation the original desired real cash-balance ratio has again been attained. Beside this more direct expenditure-effect (Cantillon and Hume) of a monetary impulse, the neo-classical authors (Thornton, and later especially Wicksell) brought out the indirect transmission mechanism, which operates by way of the interest rate.

With regard to the practical monetary policy the following can be observed in this context. Because long-term development is assumed to be determined in essence by real variables (the supply side of the economic process), the task of monetary policy in the classical period is reduced to stabilization of the price level, to maintaining the purchasing power of money. The monetary authorities are only able to influence the national income in a nominal sense through measures affecting the monetary policy, because the real system has been fully determined. So, in the classical period of monetary theory, we can speak of the absolute price level, where the possible inflation phenomenon is explained merely by the monetary sector (monetary-inflation theory). The nominal quantity of money is considered as an exogenous variable, whereas the real quantity of money has been determined fully endogenously owing to the supposed, constant, desired real cash-balance ratio.

This conception led in the 19th century to the well-known opposition between the adherents of the 'Currency Theory' and those of the 'Banking-Principle', an opposition which is still frequently encountered nowadays. We have in mind the controversy between the monetarists (Friedman, Brunner, Meltzer and others) who strongly advocate the views of the 'Currency Theory', and the post-Keynesians (Smith, Teigen and others) who favour more strongly the 'Banking Principle'. According to the 'Currency Theory', the money supply will have to be regulated to keep the danger of inflation under control. The 'Banking Principle' prefers the very opposite: great liberty with regard to the nominal quantity of money. The 'Banking School', advocating rather mechanical financing of the economic activity, takes the line that the money supply is determined by the needs of economic activity, in which situation no need exists for an active monetary policy. The views propounded in the quantity theory formed the framework in the nineteen-thirties, within which monetary problems were analysed and practical policy measures were formulated. As is known, it was Keynes who made a clear distinction between the barter economy and the money-economy. He emphasized expenditure (the demand side of the economic process) as the determinant of income and employment, and highlighted the wealth function of money. Private individuals can, after all, hoard the available purchasing power, through which certain withdrawals in the income-generating process appear. These are apparent in disequilibria on the commodity markets, with further consequences for the scope of employment. Keynes' conception of money as an asset, being the only alternative portfolio component, beside bonds, for individuals, turns the interest rate into a monetary variable. Liquidity preference now permits the theory of demand for money to make room for individual preference and decisions as regards portfolio composition.

The transmission process of an expansive monetary impulse to economic activity, or the real sector, now proceeds as follows.

The expansive impulse will lead initially to an increase of liquidity, evident in an excess-supply of real cash-balances. This excess-supply will not, however, be eliminated via the commodity market, as is the case in classical theory, but will be expressed in a greater demand for bonds, (Keynes-effect). This means that an interest fall will set in, which, with a certain interest sensitivity of investment demand, will stimulate economic activity via a multiplier and accelerator process. In other words, in the Keynesian view, monetary policy becomes significant for real economic development. The rate of interest can be used within certain limits as a policy-variable, in order to realize the goal of full employment.

Keynes and the post-Keynesians have never worried very much about the danger of inflation, which the classical authors classified as 'public enemy number one'. In our view, this must be ascribed to the fact that the years of depression caused unemployment to be feared more than inflation. The Keynesian view of macro-economic relations has had great influence on theoretical literature as well as on practical economic policy in the post-war period. The policy of low interest rates testifies to this, which – also prompted by the advantageous effect on the government budget – was pursued by the Federal Reserve System in the United States for a long period after World War II. The policy of full-employment was based upon the expenditure policy and the monetary phenomena which that entails. This means that according to the Keynesian income-expenditure theory, the money supply is rather an endogenous variable, with the causality running from the national income to the flow of purchasing power. So the Keynesians' monetary conceptions link up in this respect in essence with the view of the followers of the 'Banking Principle' in the classical period.

We refer deliberately to the flow of purchasing power, since the magnitude of expenditures in the economy is not solely determined by the available money, but equally by the number of times that a money-unit goes from hand to hand – in other words, by the circulation velocity of money. This conception of considerable flexibility in the financial system was sharply emphasized when the results of empirical research revealed that the rate of interest plays a less important part in expenditure decisions than it was supposed in theory. The Keynesian theory has advanced the idea of the purchasing power flow. For the velocity of money is not a purely institutional variable – as in the quantity theory – but rather depends also on the interdependencies between the different economic variables. As is known, Keynes links up fully with the classical authors in his conceptions about the transaction demand for money, because he considers this 'demand-for-money' component to be determined by the amount of nominal national income. This view was shown in another light in the fifties, since there are a great number of financial assets or wealth assets at present in the economy beside money. And with regard to the character of liquidity, they can be put on a level with money, and consequently are also of importance in a monetary respect.

Just think, in this context, of the strong development of the money-substitutes, including time deposits and, depending on the numerical value of circulation velocity, savings deposits with the commercial banks too. The change in opinion is closely linked with the radical institutional and functional changes which took place after the war, especially in the fifties, in the money and credit systems of the developed economies. The activities of the large group of non-bank financial intermediaries (especially the savings institutions) made it possible for economic agents' transaction balances to be partly held in interest-bearing substitutes instead of in non-interest bearing money. This means that the transaction demand for money is to some extent sensitive as regards interest, meaning that the tight Keynesian distinction between transaction balances on the one hand and speculative cash-balances on the other hand has become very blurred.

The institutional changes in the financial sector have also been of consequence for practical monetary policy. Briefly: if we start from incipient inflation (whatever the cause may be), and the monetary authorities wish to help combat this money-erosion via a restrictive monetary policy the effectiveness of their policy can be weakened. The liquidity squeeze in the economy will, in any event, lead to an upward movement of the interest rate. This means that the savings-banks will compete with the commercial banks and raise interest payment on savings deposits too. Thus an incentive arises for individuals to convert formerly hoarded balances into the higher-yielding money-substitutes of the non-bank financial intermediaries. Expressed in Keynesian terms, there is a decline in liquidity preference of the individuals. By these conversions the total supply of credit in the economy will increase. The savings banks will pass the attracted funds on again to the individuals, whose access to the credit of the commercial banks is closed by the authorities' very restrictive monetary policy. So we see that these 'near-banking' activities of the non-bank financial intermediaries can mobilize existing funds increasing the velocity of money. This activation of existing balances must be marked as a monetarily unfavourable development in overheated situations in the economy.

So a great number of other financial substitution-processes can come about, in which situation interest-bearing or other transaction balances can be converted in (higher) interest-bearing money-substitutes from the para-monetary financial institutions, as they are called. The problems described here have been of current interest in recent years in the Netherlands as well. The variant of the phenomenon of 'near-banking' also comes to mind in this context. Big firms will then provide each other with short-term loans and so take over the banking function in essence. This means that part of the credit activities occur outside the traditional financial circuits.

From the foregoing analysis we may conclude that the policy authorities ought to have good insight – within the framework of monetary policy – into the development of the more or less liquid financial assets of the various financial institutions, which are not admittedly part of the money supply but are marked as very liquid by private individuals. The Radcliffe-report (1959) also clearly discerned this development and pointed out that individual expenditures not only depend on the amount of existing cash-balances, but are essentially determined by the quantity and the structure of liquid assets in the economy. The consequence for monetary policy resulting from this view, can then be formulated as follows. The monetary authorities should no longer, according to a quantity-theoretical point of view, insert the money supply in a narrow sense (currency in circulation and demand deposits) as a strategic variable into the monetary policy, but rather the total liquidity-potential of the economy. The more so as the volume of total expenditure has become increasingly dependent on events which are independent of the extent of changes in the money supply (in a narrow sense).

We are now faced with the critical question how widely the concept of money must be defined. For in the economy there exist on the one hand kinds of liquidity, the creation of which leads to a change in money supply, on the other hand kinds of liquidity, the creation of which leads in most cases to a change in the circulation velocity of existing money. Authors like Gurley and Shaw, who favour the liquidity view (including the interest-bearing money-substitutes of the para-monetary institutions) draw the conclusion that the traditional distinction between monetary or money-creating institutions and non-bank financial intermediaries has not the importance which has been always attached to it.

The demand for speculative cash-balances in Keynes' money-bond model was further supported theoretically by Tobin in 1958. He took explicit account of risk and uncertainty variables in the portfolio composition, maintaining that investors desire compensation for the risk attached to the holding of bonds, with which a trade-off comes to the fore between the risk and the rate of return on the asset concerned. Tobin, and with him a number of economists from the University of Yale, have laid the basis with this 'portfolio-balance' theory for a wealth-theoretical approach in monetary theory. The traditional Keynesian suppositions that individuals can hold their wealth either in a non-interest bearing, but completely liquid form (money), or in interest-bearing bonds, are replaced in the 'portfolio-balance' theory by a more realistic hypothesis. This implies that in modern, financially highly-developed economies, the investor can choose from a spectrum of not totally substitutable assets, which – as we have indicated before – have a partly monetary character.

The Yale school has brought about a synthesis as it were between the traditional Keynesian approach to the demand for money (money versus bonds), and the views of the former Cambridge school, which considered an investment in physical capital goods the only alternative for the holding of cash-balances.

We must stress that Friedman, as well as the monetarists of the University of Chicago and of the research-department of the Federal Reserve Bank of St. Louis, did start from a re-formulation of the classical-quantity theory, but, like Tobin and others, focus on the function of money as an asset. They do not adopt the old doctrine without criticism, but integrate this into a general wealth theory of demand for money. So we see that the post-Keynesians (Tobin et al.) as well as the neo-quantity theorists (Friedman et al.) have emphasized the importance of money as an asset in their theoretical explanations about its influence on the outcome of the real economic process. The neo-quantity theory of the Chicago-school and the portfolio-theory of Yale have a fundamentally common characteristic, which manifests itself in the conception that monetary theory has evolved to a general theory of holding assets.

The distinction between the two approaches is expressed in the nature and the description of the transmission process via which the monetary impulse will influence ultimately economic activity. The central link between the monetary impulse and economic activity is found in the supply-price of capital, according to the views of the neo-Keynesian portfolio-theory. The underlying reasoning is as follows. When an expansive monetary impulse disturbs the portfolio equilibrium, an adjustment process will set in. As far as this process leads to a rise in the price of existing capital goods compared to that of newly produced units, investment activity will be enlarged.

Through the operation of multiplier and accelerator this investment impulse will further lead to greater economic activity. In other words, in the portfolio-theory the traditional Keynesian rate of interest (in the sense of a cost of capital) is replaced by the supply price of capital as the link between the monetary and the real sector of the economy.

The neo-quantity theorists, also referred to as the monetarists, centre their analysis on the view that changes in the money supply are the main determinant for changes in national income. This conception is strongly based on their empirical research. The monetary impulses act upon the real sector through a rather complicated portfolio-adjustment process, in which the relative rates of return on the different assets, the wealth-effects and mutual substitution relations play a strategic role. The monetarists, especially Brunner and Meltzer, can indeed agree in essence with the nature of the neo-Keynesian transmission-process, but add consumer durables to assets in the portfolio. They also consider this last category of wealth-assets as capital goods, which are then held by the households. This means that it is in effect merely a question of a difference in degree with regard to the transmission process between the neo-Keynesians and the monetarists.

In the fifties, orthodox Keynesianism, which had great influence in the post-war period, ripened for a counter-attack. This was started by Friedman, using his re-formulation of the quantity theory. Friedman holds the view that the Keynesian model is not able to solve the inflation problem.

The cheap-money policy, pursued in order to maintain expenditure on a sufficiently high level in view of the central objective of full employment, will lead to an inflationary development, which cannot be controlled in the long run by measures which emphasize expenditure. Friedman considers inflation purely as a monetary phenomenon, caused by an excessive creation of money. Excessive in that, given the economic agents' liquidity preference, the quantity of money grows more quickly than real production. This interpretation of inflation is connected with the fact that Friedman (and others) emphasize the manner of financing expenditure, whereas the neo-Keynesians merely pay attention to the income and employment-generating effect of expenditure. The controversy about the effectiveness of the monetary and fiscal policy still exists to the full extent nowadays, though in recent years the neo-Keynesians have started paying more attention to the importance of monetary policy as an instrument of business-cycle policy. We hold the view that the relative significance of the monetary and fiscal policy is empirical rather than purely theoretical. The solution to the controversy should be sought in further development of econometric research in the monetary field.

We hope in the preceding analysis to have made clear that money has evolved in the course of time from a medium of exchange in the classical period, which in essense was not very interesting for real economic development, via the conception of liquidity preference in the Keynesian model, to a significant asset, beside the other real and financial assets in the economy. In this way money has acquired a new dimension, which has formed the basis for the monetary growth theory developed in the past decade. As observed at the beginning of this chapter, the meaning of money in its function of a medium of exchange, as well as in that of an asset, was until recently only analysed in a comparative-static framework. The same conclusion will then always emerge: that in the short run the changes in money supply are certainly of importance for the real sector, in view of the influence of the interest rate and of the real cash-balance effect on expenditures, but that in the long run the outcome of the real economic process will not be affected fundamentally in any way by the monetary variable. In other words: in the long run money is neutral.

5.3. A critical analysis of the present monetary growth theory

Before we summarize and evaluate the present monetary growth theory, we believe it is worth indicating very briefly the state of affairs with regard to the development of the real growth theory after the war. We assumed in chapters 2, 3 and 4 that our readers were acquainted with the real growth theory. It is a well-known fact that Harrod and Domar were the pioneers in the field of modern growth theory in the post-war period. They were inspired by Keynes' views on the importance of demand and of equilibrium between savings and investments for the development of the national income. In this way Keynes cleared the way, as it were, for analysis of the dynamic problems in economic theory. Harrod and Domar drew special attention to the capacity-increasing effect of investments as an expenditure-component, after the demand-stimulating effect of investment activity had been emphasized rather one sidedly for too long.

Domar points out that investments will indeed lead to enlarged production possibilities, but it is of an essential importance that effective demand also expands accordingly. Here we see the Keynesian influence: that effective demand must be sufficient to bring about an income-equilibrium with full employment.

He also concludes that the economic system is unstable, since it is a pure coincidence that the increase in effective demand will tally with the increase in production. The consequence of this for the economic policy is (fully in accordance with the orthodox Keynesian conceptions) that the government will have to ensure the correct fiscal policy in order to achieve full utilization of the available resources. Harrod, who assumes a complementarity of factors of production, also has a pessimistic opinion on the structural development of the economy, on the basis of his theoretical analysis. In his model the rate of population growth, possibly of labour potential too, only happens by chance to develop in accordance with the warranted rate of growth of capital goods. He also advocates government intervention in order to realize an equilibrium economic development in the long run.

The growth theoretical conceptions of this post-Keynesian authors have been liable to strong criticism, directed particularly at the crucial assumptions of a rigid price system according to Keynes and of the complementarity of factors of production. In the fifties and especially in the sixties a great number of authors, including Solow, Swan and Meade in the Anglo-Saxon world, and Schouten and de Roos in the Netherlands, developed a real growth theory, in which the central importance of the autonomous supply factors (production function) in the growth process was emphasized. They take the line of technical substitution of factors of production, induced by a change in the relative prices of factors of production. This change is determined by the relative scarcity of these factors on the markets.

This neo-classical approach is thought to achieve a more optimistic view of the structural development of the economy, appealing to the operation of the market mechanism, than the post-Keynesian authors Harrod and Domar. Harrod and Domar base their arguments on a fundamental instability of the structural economic development. The government must, to their mind, take regulatory measures. On the other hand, the neo-classical authors believe that in society forces are active which ensure stability of economic development and an automatic regulation. We should like to recall that Kaldor, as a post-Keynesian, believes in a stable economic development in the long run, though he bases himself on the complementarity view, but assuming the operation of the price system. This results from the stabilizing-effect which emanates from the different savings-ratios of the various groups of income-recipients. As we observed in the first chapter, these real growth models have been further refined by allowing for more sectors in the economy, for the impact of technological change on the price-structure of factors of production and employment, and so on.

Beside the post-war development of the real growth theory briefly described here, a rather advanced monetary theory was developed, as we have just explained. We should now ask ourselves whether it is possible and appropriate to include these modern monetary conceptions in the real growth theory, integrating them into a monetary growth theory. We must stress that in the real growth theory a money-economy really has been supposed, but that the monetary variable is not involved in the analyses in an explicit way. In the real growth theory it is always assumed, in accordance with the ideas of the 'Banking Principle', that the monetary authorities will take care of the required quantity of money to finance real economic development in the long run.

If this is not the case, it is assumed that the financial system is so flexible (velocity of money) that the monetary sector will not cause a restriction to real economic growth. In the last extremity when a liquidity crisis arises, the monetary authorities will give priority to the objective of full employment over maintenance of the real purchasing power of money, and the required funds will be provided. It was Tobin, the pioneer of the portfolio-theory, who was the first to be engaged in research into the influence of money as an asset in the growth theory in 1955 and later on in 1965. One may wonder in this respect whether money can be considered as neutral in a comparative-dynamic sense too; i.e. whether alternative growth rates of the money supply will influence the structural equilibrium values of the real variables in comparison with a growth path with another rate of monetary growth. Tobin's analysis, as we saw in the second chapter, laid the basis for the monetary growth theory as was developed in the second half of the sixties. Tobin's monetary growth theory is characterized by Keynesian, as well as by neo-classical elements. The Keynesian element is found in the consumption-savings decision, and in the decision on use of these accumulated savings, (the latter applying views developed in the portfolio-theory). For the rest, the analysis is neo-classical in all respects, evident for instance in the fact that the production function is the focal point and that the market mechanism will ensure full employment of all available resources in the economy.

Tobin proceeds from a two-asset model: on the one hand money or real cash-balances, and on the other physical capital goods. Money must compete with capital goods in order to secure, as it were, a place in the portfolio of the individuals. Tobin than introduces money as an asset, in which case 'outside money' is always involved. This in fact means a non-interest bearing-financial debt of the monetary government to the private sector, without any debt from the individuals to the issuer, i.e. the government. So changes in this money supply will lead to a change in the individuals' net-wealth. On the basis of this view Tobin introduces a new income concept, viz. disposable income, which is equal to the sum of the traditional income from current production and the change in the real cash-balances held (wealth-change). In our view, he wishes to indicate with this that expenditure depends on the total disposable funds of the individuals, so including the change in the holding of real cash-balances as a monetary wealth-component.

Taking the line of a very special aggregation-method in which the households and firms are not considered as separate decision units, Tobin comes to the following analysis. The savings ratio out of disposable income is constant, resulting in greater savings than in the real growth theory. In his model the individuals have a 'wealth-illusion,' in that they consider the holding of real cash-balances in their portfolios as a perfect substitute for physical capital goods. Tobin argues that savings formed from disposable income will not be completely transformed into capital goods (physical capital), as was the case in the traditional real neo-classical growth model, since part will be directed towards increasing real cash-balances (monetary-wealth).

This division (portfolio-balance) depends crucially on the real rate of return on both wealth-assets. This means that the pure introduction of money as an asset will lead to a lower material savings ratio than in the pure, real model, with all the consequences for the growth rate of capital goods and for the other real variables. This is the 'Tobin-paradox', well-known in the literature. Further, the question emerges what will happen if the rate of growth of the money supply changes. A higher rate of monetary growth, which will be attended by a higher equilibrium value of the rate of inflation, will reduce real cash-balances as a wealth-component on the basis of the supposed portfolio-behavior. In Tobin's views, the difference which arises between the real rates of return on both assets will be expressed in more physical capital goods. We have described this substitution process within the wealth-sector as the portfolio-effect of Tobin. So we see that in this analysis, the monetary authorities can influence the material savings ratio through a regulation of the growth rate of the money supply (i.e.: equilibrium value of the rate of inflation). An upper limit exists when the inflation rate is such that money as an asset disappears from the economy. Disposable income is again equal to the traditional income from current production, meaning there is no longer a difference between the savings ratio in the Tobin sense and the material savings ratio from the real growth theory. The amount of material savings which will be directed towards expanding capital goods will then correspond with savings in the real growth model. To sum up, in Tobin's monetary economy savings out of disposable income can be expressed ultimately either in physical goods or in purely monetary savings, so in an expansion of the real cash-balances.

Johnson goes a step further, assuming that the holding of 'outside money' yields the owner a non-physical return in the form of convenience, safety, liquidity and so on. The utility derived from real cash-balances can then be considered as a kind of imputed income, comparable with house-ownership, which is fully consumed. Johnson follows in Tobin's footsteps and appeals to the trick of a wealth-illusion on the side of the economic agents. However, he introduces another new element, viz. the immaterial consumption-effect. He takes the line that the imputed income in question is fully consumed, a kind of immaterial consumption, through which the individuals will change the consumption of material goods and services accordingly. On the basis of this view, not only Tobin's portfolio-effect, but the material savings ratio can be influenced too. As we demonstrated in the second chapter, a change in the rate of monetary growth will not, in Johnson's analysis, have an unambiguous effect on material savings and so on the equilibrium values of the real variables. This results from the fact that Tobin's portfolio-effect and the immaterial consumption-effect have opposite consequences for material savings.

The authors Patinkin and Levhari examined the 'Tobin-paradox' critically and also implicated in their analysis the functions of money as a medium of exchange and as an asset. In a methodological respect they link up with the monetary views of the Chicago-school (Friedman et al.) and present a couple of models, in which a distinction is made between money as a consumer good and as a producer good.

In their first analysis focusing on money as a consumer good, they take the line of a more realistic saving-hypothesis, in that the savings ratio out of disposable income (including Tobin's wealth-component and Johnson's imputed income component) is variable and dependent on the respective real rates of return on the two wealth-assets.

They reach the same conclusion as Johnson: that an unambiguous opinion is impossible on the influence of a change in the rate of monetary expansion on the equilibrium values of the real variables, or capital intensity. This must be ascribed to the fact that a great many, often opposite effects are in operation which hampers the verbal interpretation strongly as well. This influence proves in the end to depend crucially on the effects of a changed rate of inflation for the development of the material savings-ratio.

However, if the constant savings ratio according to Tobin applies, an increase in the rate of monetary expansion will affect the equilibrium value of capital intensity positively in comparison with the growth path with the lower rate of monetary growth. For, if the savings ratio is constant, a higher rate of monetary growth (read: equilibrium value of the rate of inflation) will reduce the desired cash-savings and more savings will be directed towards expanding physical capital goods. The same conclusion applies when a positive relation exists between a change in the rate of inflation and a change in the savings ratio out of disposable income. This will arise if the individuals do not accept the decrease in monetary wealth (real cash-balances) as a result of a higher rate of inflation.

One might imagine that these economic agents would want to compensate the decrease in wealth at the expense of consumption expenditure, in fact resulting in more material savings. The hub of the analysis of money as a producer good is the view that money provides productive services, in that the search and transaction costs attached to the exchange process in a barter economy are reduced. The introduction of money as a generally-accepted medium of exchange makes it possible to organize the exchange of goods and services in a better way and leads to more efficient allocation of the available resources in the economy.

Patinkin and Levhari now include real cash balances as an argument in the production function and revert to Tobin's income definition, so including the monetary-wealth component, because the productive services of the cash-balances are now expressed in current production. The authors appeal to the principle of marginal productivity with regard to the demand for real cash-balances as a producer good, and then also come to the conclusion that the influence of a change in the rate of monetary growth on the equilibrium values of the real variables is undetermined. As we saw in the second chapter, anything and everything can happen in the analysis concerned. What we mean is that with expansion of the functions of money compared with those described in Tobin's analysis, a change in the rate of monetary growth brings about a number of often opposite effects, the ultimate result of which is hard to interpret in a verbal way. However, we must observe that if the marginal productivity of the real cash-balances as a producer good is negligible which is not an unrealistic supposition in our economies, highly developed in a monetary and financial respect, Tobin's conclusion with regard to the influence of a change in the rate of monetary growth can be maintained.

In the attempt to assess the significance of the neo-classical analysis of money in a growth theoretical framework for concrete monetary policy, one runs up very soon against a critical analysis of the suppositions of the model.

In the first place, it is worth noting that Tobin confines himself in his theoretical analysis to 'outside money' (currency in circulation), which means that he completely neglects the very important feature of a monetary economy, being the function of money to facilitate transactions and to diminish the transaction and information costs attached to the exchange process. All this can be clarified as follows. The functions in question above are taken over in our economies to an increasing degree by 'inside money' (demand deposits), which is, however, offset by a debt from the individuals to the issuer i.e. the monetary or money-creating financial institutions. However, according to modern conceptions in the literature, this 'inside money' does not generate the wealth-effect, which forms a critical link in Tobin's analysis between the changes in the rate of monetary growth and in the equilibrium values of the real variables. From this point of view, a theory aiming at integrating the monetary and growth theories and confining itself to a component of the money supply (currency in circulation) which in a quantitative respect is not very large will, in our opinion, be of little significance for the practical monetary policy.

The theoretical distinction between 'outside' and 'inside money' and the concomitant question to what extent these money-components form part of the individuals' net-wealth have often been discussed in economic literature. No-one (except Pesek and Saving) has worked out this question in detail in the frame-work of his theory. We should like to dwell on this matter, because in our analysis the function of money as an asset has been emphasized. Very generally we can define 'outside' money as the money-component which implies a form of net-wealth for the individuals (excluding the government and the money-creating financial institutions). In other words, it is a completely liquid financial asset of the issuer (government and monetary institutions) with no debt from the individuals in question to the issuer. This description means that the non-interest bearing 'outside money', meant by Tobin which is brought into circulation through government transfers, implies a change in net-wealth for the individuals.

Now the question arises whether the interest-bearing government bonds owned by individuals might also be considered as a net-wealth component. The literature is not always unequivocal in this respect either. Some authors, particularly the monetarists, take the line that financing the budget-deficit with the aid of bonds does contribute to an increase in net-wealth of the private sector. On the contrary, other authors assume that the individuals capitalize the future tax-obligations completely or partially on behalf of interest and redemption, only partly creating net-wealth, if at all. In other words, according to the latter conception the holding of government bonds means both an asset and a liability for the individuals, through which only a partial net-wealth effect is generated, if at all. Still, this question has more radical consequences than one might think at first sight. It is known that an openmarket-transaction between the Central Bank and the private sector, expressed in Bank purchase of government bonds, will result in creation of money. If the private individuals do not capitalize future tax-obligations, this operation will lead neither to a fall, nor to a rise in their net-wealth, with all that that entails for consumption expenditure, etc. The original holder of the government bonds now gets higher demand deposits – as far as the transaction is carried out by demand deposits – though he has no debt to the issuer, i.e. the commercial bank. Consequently his net-wealth position has not changed. If there is indeed a question of capitalization of future tax-obligations, the openmarket-purchase by the Central Bank will also lead to creation of money, but at the same time produce a positive contribution to the net-wealth of the individuals. The original holder of the government bonds now replaces a financial asset of the government (which was not considered as a net-wealth component) by a completely liquid financial asset of the monetary institutions, for which he has no debt to the issuer.

Let us go even further and assume that every monetization of government financial assets, so including those with the character of liquidity, (short-term government securities) will lead to creation of money (currency in circulation or demand deposits), but that the net-wealth position does not change. This still assumes, of course, that the economic agents do not capitalize the future tax-obligations. We can extend our criticism of the identification of 'outside money' with currency in circulation with the following remark. Government purchase of goods and services not financed with tax-returns or funds from the capital market, will also lead to creation of 'outside money' and to a change in the individuals' net-wealth. This money creation might well be expressed in an increase of demand deposits with the commercial banks. We can well imagine that a government which pays its officials from its balances at the Central Bank, does contribute to an increase in the net-wealth of the individuals. If the government has drawn a credit from the Central Bank in order to procure the funds required for payment, this will not influence the conclusion described for the change in net-wealth. All this depends crucially on the way in which asset and liability positions are consolidated when the changes in net-wealth are determined. We have taken the government and the monetary institutions together, as opposed to the private individuals, the more so as the government is not guided in its expenditure by the amount of its existing debt; this does hold for the private individuals.

The foregoing explanation leads us to conclude that we cannot support identification of 'outside money' with currency in circulation, as the relevant literature often propounds. We must also conclude that financing of the budget-deficit with long-term bonds can no longer be considered as neutral, in a monetary sense, as is generally the case in the monetary analysis of the Nederlandsche Bank. In the past the financing-criterium was used in assessing the monetary consequences of the government deficit, in which case the line was taken that this financing resulted from current savings, with a corresponding decrease in individual expenditure. But neutrality need not be the case at all from the criterium of the change in net-wealth. Financing with the aid of treasury bills continues to maintain its inflationary character in our view because this method implies moreover a creation of money-substitutes.

If the above-mentioned conceptions are taken into account, 'inside money' will be reserved for the monetary-component which implies no net-wealth for the individuals. This is due to the fact that against the completely liquid financial asset of the issuer, the same debt exists between individual and the issuer. We have in mind in particular demand deposits and the currency in circulation which arise from the credit granting activities of the monetary institutions to the private sector and from the purchase of private financial assets.

According to our conception, the monetization of a government bond then means creation of 'outside money' – in the supposition that future tax-obligations will not be capitalized. Whereas monetization of private financial assets implies creation of 'inside money'. Open-market transactions between the Central Bank and the private sector, in which the Bank purchases private financial assets mean creation of 'inside money' and also no change in net-wealth. Transactions between the government and the monetary institutions have no effect for the individuals' wealth in view of our conception of consolidation.

On the basis of the preceding analysis, we believe that limitation of 'outside money' to non-interest bearing government money (currency in circulation), which is often applied in the literature, is incorrect. This naturally has important consequences for the operation of the monetary growth-models described earlier. For the more the government calls on the available resources in the economy and financing takes place with government bonds, the more the net-wealth position of the private individuals will increase. This increase will set in if individuals do not capitalize the future tax-obligations resulting from the debt-financing. As far as these government bonds can be considered as perfect substitutes for physical capital goods in the portfolio of the individuals, the foregoing interpretation of the concepts of 'inside' and 'outside money' will lead according to

Tobin's view, to a continuous reduction of material capital goods and a fall in the equilibrium value of capital intensity.

Further in the neo-classical analysis a bold supposition is made, introducing households and firms as one decision unit. This suspends the action of the financial markets and the central significance of financial assets in the process of saving and investment. However, in a modern industrialized economy a proliferation of financial institutions exists which channel the savings from sectors with supplies to sectors with deficits by issuing financial assets with a different rate of liquidity.

In our opinion these financial assets are as good a substitute for capital goods in the portfolio as Tobin's 'outside money'. This omission of a market for financial assets forces Tobin to the rather unrealistic supposition that the marginal product of capital plays a strategic part in the equilibrium composition of the portfolio. However, in actual fact the saver is interested in the rate of return on shares (claims on the physical capital goods) and not in the physical marginal product of capital. On the contrary the investor entrepeneur pays more attention to the expected returns on the invested funds. If the portfolio is now increased with more financial assets it is possible to take account of the institutional developments in the financial field, making for a more realistic analysis. Johnson's extension of Tobin's theories, taking explicit account of the immaterial consumption which could be attached to the holding of real cash-balances, cannot be spared criticism either. We may assume here that the holding of demand deposits can also provide the holder with the same immaterial consumption in the sense they give it. We shall go even further and also include money substitutes in the analysis on the basis of the Radcliffe-committee's views on liquidity.

These interest-bearing-liquid financial assets (saving and time deposits, treasury bills and so on) provide the holder the same utility in the form of liquidity, convenience, safety as the 'outside money' mentioned by Johnson and Tobin. However, 'inside money' – as we defined it – and the money-substitutes generate only partly a net-wealth effect according to Tobin, if at all, but we are of the opinion that for significant integration of monetary and growth theories, the importance of 'inside money' and monetary substitutes cannot be neglected. If we add this liquidity concept to Johnson's analysis, the consluion will be that the immaterial consumption derived from the holding of liquid financial assets (money plus money-substitutes) increases, which has a favourable effect on material savings. This approach links up with the views of Gurley and Shaw that the post-war development of the financial structure of the economy, especially the growth of the liquidity-creating institutions, had a stimulating impact on real economic development.

We do not find it unrealistic to suppose that introduction of money as a medium of exchange leads to a more efficient use of the available resources. Is it an admissible working hypothesis, however, to consider money explicitly as an argument in the production function, in the same way as labour and capital? In our opinion the introduction of money is rather a kind of financial-economic invention for employers as well as for the whole economy comparable with the technological development in the real sector. Besides, the influence of money on the efficiency and the organization of production can be viewed in an empirical light.

Finally we indicated the consequences of an assumed continuous equilibrium between demand for and supply of real cash-balances (portfolio-balance) for the stability of the neo-classical monetary growth model. We saw that in the theory of adaptive expectations, in which the individuals revise their expectations with regard to the rate of inflation again and again, stability is greater with a more sluggish revision of the expected rate of inflation. If, however, the individuals notice that there is a difference between the actual and the expected rates of inflation and adjust their expectations more quickly, a self-generating inflationary process will be possible. Difficulties will arise as regards calculation, and money will no longer properly perform its function of a unit of account. This phenomenon, when the economic agents will flee from money to goods to an increasing degree, is extremely current nowadays in the western economies with an almost permanent and sometimes accelerating rate of inflation.

In the third chapter a model was discussed which is indicated in economic literature as the Keynes-Wicksell monetary growth model. One might expect it to concentrate on the demand side, but that is not at all the case. For this analysis is founded on a neo-classical production function and the supposition of continuous equilibrium on the labour market. It differs from the neo-classical monetary growth theory in various respects. The first difference is of a methodological nature and lies in the fact that the neo-classical analysis emphasizes equilibrium dynamics and supposes a continuous equilibrium on all markets. In the Keynes-Wicksell model on the contrary, dis-equilibrium situations are emphasized more, and are found particularly in disequilibria on the commodity markets, but not on the labour market or on the market for financial assets (bonds). It is a well-known fact that the neo-classical analysis starts from continuous equality of the actual and equilibrium values of the rate of inflation which is determined by the rate of monetary growth. But in the Keynes-Wicksell analysis the actual or current rate of inflation is a reflection of an existing disequilibrium on the commodity market. The Keynesian element in the analysis comes to the fore in the introduction of a separate savings and investment function, and in a market for financial assets (bonds). This obviates part of our criticism of Tobin's approach. After all, room is now made for separate decision units, enabling an explicit division of the economy into households and firms – to be included in the model. The Wicksellian element is implied in the investment equation. For the demand for planned investments is assumed to be related positively to the difference between the real rate of capital and the real rate of interest (= nominal interest on bonds minus the expected rate of inflation). Unlike the neo-classical analysis, the Keynes-Wicksell model contains no market for existing homogeneous capital goods, which are purchased and sold, and/or of which the services can be rented and let. The independent investment equation in the Keynes-Wicksell analysis indicates that a possible difference between desired and actual capital goods will be eliminated through a change in investment activity.

Otherwise formulated, in the Keynes-Wicksell model the difference referred to above is eliminated through a change in investment activity as a flow-variable, whereas in the neo-classical model this difference is eliminated by way of a change in the existing stock of capital goods as a stock-variable. An expansive monetary impulse will manifest itself in the Keynes-Wicksell model in the first instance in an excess-demand for bonds. Next the nominal rate of interest will fall, until the continuously supposed equilibrium on the bonds market has been restored again.

The upward movement of the price level will now be expressed in a more indirect way, i.e. through the induced commodity market disequilibria. On the one hand as a result of the interest – induced investment demand, on the other hand as a result of the wealth – effect with regard to consumption expenditure.

Unlike the neo-classical two-asset-model, the Keynes-Wicksell model starts from three assets: money, private bonds and capital goods. For the operation of the model the supposition is of critical importance that, an excess-demand for goods and services, when the plans of consumers and producers, or of savers and investors, cannot be fully honoured, the actual rate of growth of the capital goods is some linear combination of planned investments and savings. This is a rather arbitrary matter. For it is more than likely that in the case of excess-demand and an upward movement of the price level, the individuals will not be willing to accept less real consumption, meaning that the forced savings mentioned in chapter three will not set in.

The actual rate of growth of capital goods is then determined by planned savings. It is also possible that the individuals will not accept the fall of real cash-balances as a result of the higher rate of inflation and will increase their savings at the expense of consumption expenditures. Then the producers' plans will be honoured to a stronger degree. As the third chapter shows, this division is essential for determination of the ultimate influence of a change in the rate of monetary growth on the equilibrium values of the real variables.

In the short-term analysis of the Keynes-Wicksell model an *IS*-curve and a *FM* curve can be constructed which are analogous in a formal respect to the traditional *IS*-*LM* curves from the well-known Hicks-Hansen diagram.

The *IS*-curve now represents the combinations of the nominal rate of interest and real cash-balances, for which it holds that the excess-demand or the excess-supply of goods is constant. Next the *FM*-curve represents combinations of the nominal rate of interest and real cash-balances for which it holds that the sum of the excess-demand for goods and for real cash-balances is equal to zero, given equilibrium on the bond and labour market. In order to fully appreciate the variables and mechanisms which play a part in the effects of change in the rate of monetary expansion on the equilibrium values of the real variables in the long run, we have expressed the rate of inflation and the nominal rate of interest in the third chapter in terms of labour intensity, real cash-balances per unit of capital and expected rate of inflation. This is connected with the fact that the rate of inflation, as well as the nominal rate of interest form the essential transmission-variables through which the influence of change in the rate of monetary growth will manifest itself in the real sector. The followers of the Keynes-Wicksell model come to the conclusion, as do a number of authors representing the neo-classical school (Patinkin and Levhari), that alternative rates of growth of the money supply do not have an unambiguous influence on the equilibrium values of the real variables. This non-unambiguity links up with a built-in lag in the commodity market and, at the same time, with the rather arbitrary choice which can be made as to whether planned investments or planned savings will ultimately determine the actual rate of growth of the capital goods. The lag gives an indication for the speed at which the existing commodity market disequilibria will be expressed in a change in the rate of inflation. In the neo-classical model this question is left out of consideration because one starts from the supposition that possible disequilibria on the commodity market will be eliminated directly and completely.

We should like to point out specifically that the authors who represent the Keynes-Wicksell view as a counterpart of the neo-classical analysis violate the orthodox Keynesian analysis with their suppositions. Keynes would never have shared their view on a change in the rate of inflation as a result of disequilibria on the commodity market. The Walrasian general equilibrium model would appear to lurk in the background, although with changes in demand and supply situations on the commodity markets a new equilibrium will not immediately come about in the Keynes-Wicksell model through adequate price adjustments. The supposition at issue with regard to a change in the rate of inflation also implies that in times of excess supply of goods, the price level will fall. This is not at all the case in the traditional Keynesian analysis, because in the first instance an adjustment will set in from the transaction side. In other words, disequilibria on the commodity market are more likely to have repercussions for the employment situation, and so for the other real variables. This consequence is not analysed in the Keynes-Wicksell model, since it starts from continuous equilibrium on the labour market.

In other words a possible feed-back of the disequilibria on the commodity market to the labour market is not implicated in the analysis, making it less realistic. In this way many current problems of our western economies are neglected.

We can continue in this vein, since the Keynes-Wicksell model only has room for demand-inflation, in which prices rise as a result of an excess-demand for goods and services. In this respect the analysis is indeed closer related to Keynes. However, no attention is paid, for example, to cost-inflation, in which prices are more likely to be moved upwards by factors on the supply side of the economic process. We have in mind the attempts by the different social groups to improve their real income or to maintain a distinct real income. These attempts can very well lead to the well-known wage-price spiral. If this process of rising prices continues for a long time, as in the western economies in the past years, private individuals will expect price rises for the future and therefore find a motive to adjust their dispositions accordingly. Everybody tries to safeguard his real income, which is evident in continuously higher nominal income rises, giving the inflation an autonomous and a self-generating character. When this point has been reached, the monetary authorities will have to be prove their strength in contributing to restriction of accelerating inflation by breaking the wage-price spiral. In these circumstances the same question recurs whether the objective of full employment and the concomitant additional financing, or the stability of the real purchasing power of money and the attendant restrictive monetary policy must be emphasized (inflation-unemployment trade-off).

So we see that the Keynes-Wicksell model leaves no room for either income-inflation or the simultaneous appearance of inflation and unemployment, a situation with which the western economies are being confronted to an increasing degree of late. Since the consequences of disequilibria on the commodity market for labour market developments are omitted, the Keynes-Wicksell model is only able – in our opinion – to explain a small part of the extremely complicated economic reality. Consequently it is hardly surprising that many authors engaged in the monetary growth theory remark that no useful recommendations for practical economic policy can be expected with these theoretical models.

Should one wish to include the operation of the labour market in the model, there is a simple, initial procedure. The growth of the nominal wage rate depends on the excess-demand for labour and on the expected rate of inflation. In this way the underlying view to the Phillips-curve can be implicated in the analysis. At the same time we can construct a Phillips-curve for each given value of the expected rate of inflation. At present this question is particularly topical now we are confronted with a continuously higher rate of nominal wages with an equal and/or increasing rate of unemployment.

This situation is also referred to as 'stag-flation', a decline in the economic activity connected with a money-erosion, a decline in the real purchasing power of money. If the social-economic groups have no money-illusion during wage-negotiations (which implies that they are purely guided by real variables) each increase in the expected rate of inflation can lead to an immediate and complete corresponding increase in the rate of nominal wages. We say 'can', because the honouring of the claims depends on the power of the different social partners during wage-negotiations.

Let us deal with this in more detail. The simple relation between changes in the nominal wage-rate and in the rate of unemployment, expressed in the traditional Phillips-curve, had become less realistic since the sixties. The operation of the free-market and price-mechanism in the wage field which leads back the Phillips-curve, is nowhere to be seen in practice.

The power of trade-unions, and also political factors play a strategic and growing role in wage-negotiations. At the same time, pressure groups are increasing their influence too. Moreover, as we can see in practice, the Phillips-curve is defined in real terms; this means that the social partners aim to maintain or improve the real income position by way of price-compensations. The greater the elasticity of the rate of nominal wages compared with the general price level, the greater the likelihood of a shifting-process and the well-known wage-price spiral. The automatic price-compensation through higher nominal wages then serves to 'anchor' the wage-price spiral. In a period with continuous, even accelerating inflation this shifting-process will force the responsible authorities to choose between reducing unemployment in the short-run and allowing inflation to go on rising in the future.

Finally, another critical remark involves the use of money in the economy. This is in essence based on the one hand upon the existence of uncertainty and transaction costs attached to the exchange process, and on the other hand upon the absence of complete information for the various market participants with regard to demand and supply situations on the different markets. These questions are not implicated in the existing monetary growth theories. In the neo-classical analysis with the Walrasian 'tâtonnement-process' always in the background, this omission might even be justified. For according to the equilibrium conception and the idea of the 'auctioneer', transactions will only take place at equilibrium prices so the factors mentioned above do not play a part. At the same time this might explain why Tobin restricts the function of money in a growth theoretical framework to that of an asset. Tobin pays no explicit attention to the function of money as a medium of exchange, which is far more connected with the information and transaction costs mentioned above and uncertainty in the exchange process.

The significance of this omission is however cogently apparent in the Keynes-Wicksell model, in which the very disequilibria on the commodity markets are emphasized and so transactions can take place at non-equilibrium prices. In that model the interaction between participants on the different markets is not regulated by a Walrasian 'auctioneer', and consequently not all markets are always in equilibrium. Disequilibrium is then determined by or is critically dependent on the value of the various adjustment coefficients. The inclusion of money in such a model is most tenable, because money as a medium of exchange replaces the Walrasian paradigm of the 'tâtonnement-process'.

The neo-classical and Keynes-Wicksell models were combined in one model in the fourth chapter conveyed in the supposition that the current or actual rate of inflation can now be influenced in two ways by the expected rate of inflation, which itself depends on the rate of monetary growth. The first way is direct (direct price-expectations effect) in that the economic agents take the expected price rise into account when determining prices. The second way is more indirect: through disequilibria on the commodity market induced by the expected rate of inflation.

This implies that in the synthesis model the actual rate of inflation can still change, even though equilibrium exists on the commodity market, i.e. as long as the expected rate of inflation is not equal to zero. When the actual and expected rates of inflation are equal, equilibrium will exist at the same time on the commodity market, in that planned savings are equal to planned investments.

We can now construct an *IS*-curve for the long run, representing the different combinations of labour intensity and real cash-balances, for which it holds that the savings (= investments) per unit of capital are equal to the given rate of population growth. This curve links up better with the Hicksian interpretation of the *IS*-curve because it also relates to equilibrium in the real sector, unlike in the Keynes-Wicksell model in the third chapter where the very disequilibria in the real sector are centred. The *FM*-curve also fits better in the basic ideas behind the traditional *LM*-curve, because combinations of labour intensity and real cash-balances are involved, for which it holds that the demand for and the supply of real cash-balances are in equilibrium (equilibrium in the monetary sector). A higher rate of monetary growth will now increase the equilibrium value of capital intensity and reduce real cash-balances in an unambiguous way, in comparison with the equilibrium growth path with the lower rate of monetary growth. This conclusion corresponds with that of Tobin in his neo-classical two-asset model.

In the short-term analysis, in which the labour intensity is supposed to be constant, and disequilibria on the different markets can arise, the Keynes-Wicksell analysis in the third chapter appears to be better qualified to describe the monetary growth process in the economy. The introduced supposition of direct and indirect influence of the expected rate of inflation on the actual rate of inflation proves however to have remarkable consequences for the stability of the model. Starting from the theory of adaptive expectations, a higher rate of monetary growth can lead to a cumulative, self-generating inflationary process, unless adjustment of the expected rate of inflation takes place in a sufficiently sluggish way. This stability condition also occurred in the neo-classical analysis. Besides, stability is increased as the wealth-effect is stronger, which mitigates expenditure and so the rise in the actual rate of inflation somewhat.

Finally in chapter 4 a matter was discussed which has received a great deal of attention since the second half of the sixties. It concerns the simultaneous upward movement in the rate of inflation and the nominal rate of interest, which can be observed in practice and which is indicated in the literature as the 'Gibson-paradox'. In an economy with almost permanent inflation the individual's expectations on money-erosion are bound to play a role at a given moment. In these circumstances they will become familiar with the phenomenon of inflation, and adjust their economic behaviour accordingly. All this also has consequences for the development of the nominal interest rate which can be briefly described as follows. As is known from the orthodox-Keynesian analysis, an expansive monetary impulse will be expressed in the first instance in an excess-supply of money, which leads to a lower nominal rate of interest. Empirical research has shown that this effect is of relatively short duration. For the increased investment activity which the drop in interest induced and the related income-rise and greater demand for transaction balances, will then lead to a liquidity-squeeze, causing another rise in the interest rate. However, the interest remains below the initial level. This is the traditional view. But in recent years the reasoning has changed. If we take the line that the individuals take account of the inflation expectations in accordance with Fisher, lenders will try to secure themselves in loan-contracts by claiming an inflation-compensation, expressed in a sufficiently higher nominal interest rate to compensate the capital-loss on interest and redemption.

Borrowers, on their side, expect a rise in the nominal value of the real assets (houses etc.) purchased with borrowed funds. This last group, will therefore be very willing to pay a higher nominal rate of interest. Through the operation of this classical Fisher-effect, the interest can rise above the initial level. Besides during the process of income-expansion, set going by the initial fall in the nominal rate of interest, a feed back-effect arises from the real to the financial sector. This effect manifests itself in a greater demand for credit, which contributes again to a rise in the nominal rate of interest. In the section concerned in the fourth chapter we saw that a relatively strong operation of the wealth-effect in the consumption function will lead to a situation with the nominal rate of interest rising less than the rate of inflation, and so the real rate of interest will fall ultimately. The higher rate of inflation, as a result of the higher rate of monetary growth, will reduce the amount of real cash-balances. This will provide counter-pressure again, due to the relative decrease in expenditure, causing the nominal rate of interest needs to rise less quickly in order to restore equilibrium between planned savings and investments.

And now a last word on the money-concept used in the monetary growth models. We hold the view that it is much more interesting for practical monetary policy to see the desired amount and rate of growth of money in a broad perspective (including money substitutes) than in terms of the narrow traditional money-concept (currency and demand deposits).

This approach coincides strongly with that of the Dutch Central Bank. The line is taken in its monetary analysis that there are assets which are held primarily for liquidity considerations, and assets with which primarily the investment-motive is significant. We include in the first category money-substitutes (e.g. short-term government securities held by the public) as defined by the Bank, plus the money-substitutes issued by the so-called paramonetary institutions (savings-banks). In our opinion, it is of crucial importance to know which assets have a potentially 'money-character', in other words which assets can be used as a medium to meet a distinct payment-obligation within a fairly short period, without costs and capital-loss.

This view will not be found in the theoretical explanations within the framework of the monetary growth theory, making it very difficult to give practical recommendations for the monetary policy based on the models concerned. The existing theory on the effects of monetary variables for the development of the real variables in the long run, assumes a given financial structure, i.e. a given 'financial production-function'. This gives no scope for the 'financial inventions' which have a strongly institutional character. These are comparable with the technical inventions in the real sector and may refer to the used money or liquidity definition, to the velocity of circulation of the money supply in the traditional sense, to the more or less flexible operation of the financial markets, to the individuals' liquidity preference, to the demand for money in a narrow sense, and so on.

In our opinion there is a need for a classification of the 'financial inventions', which can be compared with the classification of technological development in the production sector.

If we follow in this case the modern theory with regard to the micro-economic foundation of the use of money in an economy, we believe that all 'financial inventions' have an induced character. As has previously been observed, the pure introduction of money as a medium of exchange has been induced by the substantial transaction and information costs in a barter economy. When money is introduced into the community, this can be considered as a capital and labour-saving invention, increasing the productivity of these factors of production. The origin and development of the interest-bearing money-substitutes in the economy which lead to more intensive utilization of the existing money supply in a narrow sense, might then be characterized as a pure cash-saving invention. And this very category of 'financial inventions', receives hardly any attention in the existing monetary growth theory, meaning that there is no link with monetary practice.

5.4. Suggestions for extension of the present monetary growth theory

Our central problem in fact amounts to determining the influence which monetary variables can exert in a growing economy on the equilibrium values of the real variables in the long run. We have reached our final conclusion, partly in the light of existing views in the relevant literature.

In Tobin's neo-classical analysis, we can recognize the unambiguous influence of a change in the growth rate of money on the long-term equilibrium values of the real variables.

However, in our opinion, this theory is too far removed from reality for conclusions to be drawn for practical monetary policy. The same applies for the equally abstract variant of the analysis in question, indicated by Levhari, Patinkin and Johnson. The Keynes-Wicksell analysis appeals to us more for the following reasons. First of all, this model makes room for the operation of the financial markets in the relation between the monetary and the real sectors. And this clearly reveals the significance of financial as well as physical assets. Next the practical importance of this monetary growth theory is augmented, since market disequilibria are taken into account, although they are still limited to the commodity and money markets in the Keynes-Wicksell model.

Admittedly, present monetary growth theory proceeds on a rather abstract level and is perhaps less significant for concrete monetary policy. Nevertheless, we are of the opinion that this new field of economic theory must be extended. We are aware that the existing theory needs some modification in order to increase its practical importance and operational character. In this context we should like to make the following suggestions.

First of all, it is necessary that the used money and liquidity-concepts link up better with concepts which are relevant in practice. We refer in particular to a widening of the traditional definition of money in view of the importance which can be attached to money-substitutes (for instance as created by the government, commercial banks and para-monetary institutions, e.g. savings-banks, building-societies). For these fairly liquid wealth-components can in effect perform a number of functions traditionally attached to money. In this way it is possible to insert into the analysis the institutional developments which have come about in the financial field and might still come about in the near future.

This suggestion is especially important, because it has become clear since the fifties that not only the quantity of money and certainly not only 'outside money' according to Tobin, but also the liquid-assets created by the para-monetary institutions, have started to play a strategic part in concrete monetary policy.

We are also of the opinion that the concepts of 'outside' and 'inside money' indeed can be used, but that the distinction should emphasize the criterion of the possible net-wealth formation which will set in with changes in the amount of monetary components at issue. Consequently, the identification of 'outside money' with currency in circulation, which is frequently encountered in the literature, will be a thing of the past. The criterion of net-wealth formation also enables the significance of at least a great part of the demand deposits in modern economies to be expressed. This point brings us to a third suggestion, which is connected with the influence of government activities and the monetary consequences resulting from the financing of the government budget. Our study has shown that the government only takes part in the existing monetary growth theory in its role as a monetary institution ensuring the supply of (outside) money. This supposition is wide of the mark as regards economic practice. After all in our society the government is given all kinds of tasks to raise the citizens' prosperity and welfare. This is connected with an increasing monopolization of the resources, which means that the government's activities are extremely important for real economic development. However, these government activities do not only affect expenditure. The monetary consequences of government financing must also be taken into consideration, the more so as the manner of financing has consequences for the net-wealth formation and/or the liquidity-holdings of private individuals.

We have already raised these questions in our criticism of Tobin's analysis. We are aware that, although the analysis is more realistic in view of the introduction of government activities, the links between the monetary and the real sectors become more complicated. In all probability the tentative conclusions from the monetary growth theory described in this study will have to be adjusted or fundamentally changed.

A fourth suggestion relates to the labour-market-mechanism. In existing monetary growth theory attention is paid only briefly to this aspect. The practical importance of the theory can now also be increased if, starting from the Keynes-Wicksell model, possible disequilibria on the commodity markets are, for instance, fully or partially reflected in disequilibria on the labour market. We have two mechanisms in mind. Situations of an excess-demand can be expressed first of all in an eating into the stocks and only in a later phase in tension on the labour market with its consequences for wages and prices. However it is also possible that the excess-demand in question will not lead to corresponding changes in the stocks, but will manifest itself directly and completely on the labour market. The possible adjustment through changes in stocks will mean that the disequilibria on the commodity market need not be shifted direct to the labour market for the full extent. It is obvious that in the short run the stock-mechanism is more relevant, whereas in the long run the disequilibria on the commodity market are more likely to manifest themselves in disequilibria on the labour market. The same reasoning can be applied for situations of excess-supply and a decline in economic activity.

With these views in mind, we believe it will be possible to include phenomena like income-inflation and stag-flation in the considerations, whereas no starting points will be found for that in the Keynes-Wicksell analysis of chapter 3.

The present monetary growth theory can subsequently be

extended, by inclusion of the influence of international economic relations. It is clear that this is more important for a country with a strong open economy, such as the Netherlands, than for a country like the United States, where the economy has a rather closed character. Just think of the influence of the balance of payments position on the domestic money supply and money-substitutes in a system of fixed exchange rates and hence on the development of interest rates, of the monetary influence of short-term capital movements, and so on. This extension will make the analysis more realistic on the one hand, but apparently more complicated, on the other.

A final suggestion concerns the inclusion of a money supply theory in the existing monetary growth theory. This is particularly relevant since the monetary growth theory emphasizes the theory on money demand rather unambiguously due to the fact that the portfolio-analysis was focused in the transmission process. By introducing a theory which represents the money-supply process, it is also possible to review the various tools of monetary policy with which the money supply can be influenced by regulating the base-money and the variables which have been inserted into the money-multiplier. We should like to go further still, referring even to a theory of liquidity-supply. We can then allow for the 'near-banking' activities of the para-monetary institutions too. In this way the monetary consequences of fluctuations in the velocity of money in a narrow sense can also be implicated in the analysis. These fluctuations are hard to control in practice.

With this we refer specifically to the impaired effectiveness of a distinct monetary policy, which can be caused by fluctuations in the circulation velocity of money. The views mentioned above will of course have consequences for the scope of the Central Bank's existing tools of monetary policy which has so far applied to the monetary institutions in particular, and scarcely to the para-monetary institutions if at all.

We believe that if the existing monetary growth theory is extended on the basis of the foregoing suggestions, we shall be in a better position to make practical recommendations for the monetary policy in a growing economy. Henceforth monetary growth theory will no longer be, as Stein terms it, an 'Uncertain Trumpet: it cannot be used as a guide to policy.'

Appendix, chapter 2, section 2.5.

In equations 1 and 2 below for capital intensity development (k) and the development of the expected rate of inflation (π^*) respectively, functions f and $\hat{L}$ have the non-negative real numbers as a definition set.

They also have the following differentiability properties: f and $\hat{L}$ are twice, respectively once continuously differentiable:

$$f(k) > 0 \qquad k > 0$$
$$f(O) = 0$$
$$f'(k) > 0 \qquad f''(k) < 0$$

Notice moreover that $f'(k)k < f(k)$ for $k > 0$. The following differential equations are taken as the starting points:

$$\frac{1}{k}\frac{dk}{dt} = \frac{\sigma_B f(k)}{k} - (1 - \sigma_B)(\mu - \pi^*)\frac{m}{k} - n \tag{1}$$

$$\frac{d\pi^*}{dt} = \beta(\pi - \pi^*) \tag{2}$$

in which:

$m = \dfrac{M}{PL}$ = real cash-balances per head

$\mu = \dfrac{dM}{dt}\dfrac{1}{M}$ = growth rate of the nominal quantity of money or rate of monetary expansion.

$\pi = \dfrac{dP}{dt}\dfrac{1}{P}$ = actual rate of inflation.

$n = \dfrac{dL}{dt}\dfrac{1}{L}$ = rate of population growth.

$\pi^* = \pi^*(t)$ = expected rate of inflation.
$0 < \sigma_B < 1$ = savings ratio out of disposable income
$0 < \beta < \infty$ = 'expectations coefficient' of price expectations
$k = k(t)$ = capital intensity
t = time

The demand function for real cash balances:

$$\frac{M}{PK} = \frac{m}{k} = \hat{L}(f'(k) + \pi^*) \text{ and } \hat{L}' < 0 \tag{3}$$

Because $m = M/PL$, it holds:

$$\frac{1}{m}\frac{dm}{dt} = \mu - \pi - n. \tag{4}$$

Further it holds, according to (3): $m = m[k(t), \pi^*(t)]$.

$$\frac{dm}{dt}\frac{1}{m} = \frac{\partial m}{\partial k}\frac{dk}{dt} + \frac{\partial m}{\partial \pi^*}\frac{d\pi^*}{dt} = \tag{5}$$

$$\{\hat{L}(f'(k) + \pi^*) + k\hat{L}'(f'(k) + \pi^*)f''(k)\}\frac{dk}{dt} +$$

$$+ k\hat{L}'(f'(k) + \pi^*)\frac{d\pi^*}{dt}$$

Hence

$$\frac{dm}{dt}\frac{1}{m} = \frac{\eta}{k}\frac{dk}{dt} + \frac{\hat{L}'(f'(k) + \pi^*)}{\hat{L}(f'(k) + \pi^*)}\frac{d\pi^*}{dt} \tag{6}$$

where η represents elasticity of the demand for real cash-balances with regard to capital intensity.

$$\eta = 1 + \frac{k\hat{L}'(f'(k) + \pi^*)f''(k)}{\hat{L}(f'(k) + \pi^*)} > 1.$$

From (4) and (6) it follows:

$$\pi = -\frac{\eta}{k}\frac{dk}{dt} - \frac{\hat{L}'(f'(k) + \pi^*)}{\hat{L}(f'(k) + \pi^*)}\frac{d\pi^*}{dt} + \mu - n. \tag{7}$$

After substitution of (7) into (2), (1) and (2) change into the following basic equations:

$$\frac{dk}{dt} = \sigma_B f(k) - (1 - \sigma_B)(\mu - \pi^*)\, m - nk \tag{8}$$

$$\frac{d\pi^*}{dt} = \frac{\beta}{1 + \beta\dfrac{\hat{L}'(f'(k) + \pi^*)}{\hat{L}(f'(k) + \pi^*)}}\left[\mu - n - \pi^* - \frac{\eta}{k}\frac{dk}{dt}\right] \tag{9}$$

By definition for an equilibrium $[k_e(t), \pi_e^*(t)]$ it holds:

$$\frac{dk_e}{dt} = \frac{d\pi_e^*}{dt} = 0$$

In the equilibrium situation it holds that $\pi_e^* = \mu - ..$

Assume (k_e, π_e^*) is such an equilibrium. In order to investigate the asymptotical stability of this equilibrium we consider the following system:

$$\text{(a)}\ \frac{dk}{dt} = F(k, \pi^*) \tag{10}$$

$$\text{(b)}\ \frac{d\pi^*}{dt} = G(k, \pi^*)$$

where

$$\text{(a)}\ F(k, \pi^*) = \sigma_B f(k) - (1 - \sigma_B)(\mu - \pi^*)k\hat{L}[f'(k) + \pi^*] - nk \tag{11}$$

$$\text{(b)}\ G(k, \pi^*) = \frac{\beta}{1 + \dfrac{\beta\hat{L}'(f'(k) + \pi^*)}{\hat{L}(f'(k) + \pi^*)}}\left[\mu - \pi^* - n - \frac{\eta}{k}F(k, \pi^*)\right]$$

Thus $F(k_e, \pi_e^*) = G(k_e, \pi_e^*) = 0$
From (11) it follows:

$$\text{(a) } \frac{\partial F}{\partial k}(k_e, \pi_e^*) = \sigma_B f'(k_e) - (1 - \sigma_B)n(\hat{L} + k_e\hat{L}'f'') - n < 0 \qquad 12(a)$$

for from (11a) it follows: $(1 - \sigma_B)\, n\hat{L} = \dfrac{\sigma_B f(k_e) - nk_e}{k_e}$

$$\frac{\partial F}{\partial k}(k_e, \pi_e^*) = \sigma_B f'(k_e) - \frac{(\sigma_B f(k_e) - nk_e)}{k_e} - (1 - \sigma_B)nk_e\hat{L}'f'' - n$$

$$= \frac{\sigma_B\left[k_e f'(k_e) - f(k_e)\right]}{k_e} - (1 - \sigma_B)nk_e\hat{L}'f'' < 0$$

$$\frac{\partial F}{\partial \pi^*}(k_e, \pi_e^*) = k_e(1 - \sigma_B)(\hat{L} - n\hat{L}') > 0 \qquad 12(b)$$

$$\frac{\partial G}{\partial k}(k_e, \pi_e^*) = \frac{-\beta\eta}{\left(1 + \dfrac{\beta\hat{L}'}{\hat{L}}\right)} \frac{\partial F}{\partial k}(k_e, \pi_e^*) \qquad 12(c)$$

$$\frac{\partial G}{\partial \pi^*}(k_e, \pi_e^*) = \frac{-\beta}{\left(1 + \dfrac{\beta\hat{L}'}{\hat{L}}\right)} \left[1 + \frac{\eta}{k}\frac{\partial F}{\partial \pi^*}(k_e, \pi_e^*)\right] \qquad 12(d)$$

The real parts of the 'eigen'-values of the matrix:

$$J = \begin{bmatrix} \dfrac{\partial F}{\partial k}(k_e, \pi_e^*) & \dfrac{\partial F}{\partial \pi^*}(k_e, \pi_e^*) \\ \dfrac{\partial G}{\partial k}(k_e, \pi_e^*) & \dfrac{\partial G}{\partial \pi^*}(k_e, \pi_e^*) \end{bmatrix}$$

are negative if

the trace of $[J] < 0$
the determinant of $[J] > 0$

Because the trace of $[J] < 0$ if $0 < \beta < -\dfrac{\hat{L}}{\hat{L}'}$

and the determinant of $[J] = \dfrac{-\beta \dfrac{\partial F}{\partial k}(k_e, \pi_e^*)}{1 + \dfrac{\beta \hat{L}'}{\hat{L}}} > 0$, if and only if

$$0 < \beta < -\frac{\hat{L}}{\hat{L}'}, \text{ the equilibrium } (k_e, \pi_e^*)$$

is stable asymptotically if $0 < \beta < -\hat{L}/\hat{L}'$.

Appendix, chapter 3

I. Appendix to section 4

The values of the different partial derivatives described in the main text can be derived as follows. The basic equations are:

$$\frac{\pi}{\alpha} = n + r(\ell) + \pi^* - i - S(\ell, v) \tag{1}$$

$$\frac{\pi}{\alpha h} = v - \hat{L}\left[f(\ell) + \frac{\pi}{\alpha}, r(\ell) + \pi^*, i, v\right] \tag{2}$$

where: $r'(\ell) > 0, S_\ell > 0, S_v < 0, \hat{L}_1 > 0, \hat{L}_2 < 0, \hat{L}_3 < 0,$
$0 < \hat{L}_4 < 1, 0 < \alpha < \infty, 0 < h < \infty.$

Consider now functions F and G defined by

$$F(\pi, i, \pi^*, \ell, v; \mu, n) = n + r(\ell) + \pi^* - i - S(\ell, v) - \frac{\pi}{\alpha}$$

$$G(\pi, i, \pi^*, \ell, v; \mu, n) = v - \hat{L}\left[f(\ell) + \frac{\pi}{\alpha}, r(\ell) + \pi^*, i, v\right] - \frac{\pi}{\alpha h}$$

From (1) and (2) it follows that in our model:

$$F(\pi, i, \pi^*, \ell, v; \mu, n) = 0 \tag{1a}$$
$$G(\pi, i, \pi^*, \ell, v; \mu, n) = 0 \tag{2a}$$

Because: $$\begin{bmatrix} \frac{\partial F}{\partial \pi} & \frac{\partial F}{\partial i} \\ \frac{\partial G}{\partial \pi} & \frac{\partial G}{\partial i} \end{bmatrix} = \frac{1}{\alpha}\left(\hat{L}_3 - \hat{L}_1 - \frac{1}{h}\right) < 0$$

we can resolve π and i from (1a) and (2a) in terms of π^*, ℓ and v, given the exogenous parameters μ and n, and write therefore:

$$\pi = \pi(\pi^*, \ell, v; \mu, n) \tag{3}$$

$$i = i(\pi^*, \ell, v; \mu, n) \tag{4}$$

If we take account of equations (3) and (4) we can write for (1a) and (2a):

$$F[\pi(\pi^*, \ell, v; \mu, n), i(\pi^*, \ell, v; \mu, n), \pi^*, \ell, v; \mu, n] = 0 \tag{5}$$

$$G[\pi(\pi^*, \ell, v; \mu, n), i(\pi^*, \ell, v; \mu, n), \pi^*, \ell, v; \mu, n] = 0 \tag{6}$$

Now it holds:

I. $F_\pi \pi_{\pi^*} + F_i i_{\pi^*} + F_{\pi^*} = 0$
$G_\pi \pi_{\pi^*} + G_i i_{\pi^*} + G_{\pi^*} = 0$

II. $F_\pi \pi_\ell + F_i i_\ell + F_\ell = 0$
$G_\pi \pi_\ell + G_i i_\ell + G_\ell = 0$

III. $F_\pi \pi_v + F_i i_v + F_v = 0$
$G_\pi \pi_v + G_i i_v + G_v = 0$

With the aid of equations I, II and III and (1a) and (2a) above, the partial derivatives mentioned in the main text can be derived.

From I: $$\pi_{\pi^*} = \frac{\hat{L}_3 + \hat{L}_2}{\frac{1}{\alpha}\left[\hat{L}_3 \; \left(\frac{1}{h} + \hat{L}_1\right)\right]}; \quad i_{\pi^*} = -\frac{\hat{L}_1 + \frac{1}{h} + \hat{L}_2}{\hat{L}_3 - \left(\frac{1}{h} + \hat{L}_1\right)}$$

From II: $$\pi_\ell = \frac{\hat{L}_3[r'(\ell) - S_\ell] + [L_1 f'(\ell) + \hat{L}_2 r'(\ell)]}{\frac{1}{\alpha}\left[\hat{L}_3 - \left(\frac{1}{h} + \hat{L}_1\right)\right]}$$

$$i_\ell = \frac{-\left(\hat{L}_1 + \frac{1}{h}\right)\left(r'(\ell) - S_\ell\right) + [\hat{L}_1 f'(\ell) + \hat{L}_2 r'(\ell)]}{\hat{L}_3 - \left(\frac{1}{h} + \hat{L}_1\right)}$$

From III: $\pi_v = \dfrac{-\hat{L}_3 S_v - (1 - \hat{L}_4)}{\dfrac{1}{\alpha}\left[\hat{L}_3 - \left(\dfrac{1}{h} + \hat{L}_1\right)\right]}$

$$i_v = \frac{-S_v\left(\hat{L}_1 + \dfrac{1}{h}\right) - (1 - \hat{L}_4)}{\hat{L}_3 - \left(\dfrac{1}{h} + \hat{L}_1\right)}$$

II Appendix belonging to section 5

Production function $Y = F(K, L)$ which is supposed linear homogeneous. (1)

Production per unit of capital $y = \dfrac{Y}{K}$ (2)

Labour intensity $\ell = \dfrac{L}{K}$ (3)

From (1) it follows for the *production per unit of capital:*

$y = f(\ell)$ where $f' > 0$ and $f'' < 0$ (4)

Real rate of capital

$r = \dfrac{\partial y}{\partial K} = f(\ell) - \ell f'(\ell)$, where $r'(\ell) > 0$ (5)

Savings equation:

$\dfrac{S}{K} = S^*[f(\ell), v] = S(\ell, v)$, where $S_\ell > 0$ and $S_v < 0$ (6)

Investment equation

$\dfrac{I}{K} = n + r(\ell) + \pi^* - i$ (7)

Walrasian excess-demand hypothesis:

$\pi = \alpha\left(\dfrac{I}{K} - \dfrac{S}{K}\right)$, where $0 < \alpha < \infty$ (8)

Rate of growth of capital

$\dfrac{dK}{dt}\dfrac{1}{K} = \gamma\dfrac{I}{K} - (1 - \gamma)\dfrac{S}{K}$, where $0 < \gamma < 1$ (9)

Demand function for real cash-balances

$$\hat{L} = \hat{L}\left[f(\ell) + \frac{\pi}{\alpha}, r(\ell) + \pi^*, i, v\right]$$

where $\hat{L}_1 > 0$, $\hat{L}_2 < 0$, $\hat{L}_3 < 0$ and $0 < \hat{L}_4 < 1$. (10)

Walras' Law

$$\frac{\pi}{\alpha h} = v - \hat{L}[f(\ell) + \frac{\pi}{\alpha}, r(\ell) + \pi^*, i, v] \quad (11)$$

In the equilibrium situation it holds

$$\pi^* = \pi = \mu - n \quad (12)$$

Rate of growth of labour intensity

$$\frac{d\ell}{dt}\frac{1}{\ell} = n - \frac{dK}{dt}\frac{1}{K} \quad (13)$$

Rate of growth of real cash-balances per unit of capital.

$$\frac{dv}{dt}\frac{1}{v} = \mu - n - \frac{dK}{dt}\frac{1}{K}. \quad (14)$$

From (8), (7) and (6) it follows:

$$\pi = \alpha[n + r(\ell) + \pi^* - i - S(\ell, v)] \quad (15)$$

Solution of (11) and (15), for π and i in terms of ℓ and v, taking account of equation (12) and given exogenous variables μ and n yields:

$$\pi = \pi(\ell, v; \mu, n) \quad (16)$$

$$i = i(\ell, v; \mu, n) \quad (17)$$

From (9), (13), (15), and (16) follows:

$$\frac{d\ell}{dt}\frac{1}{\ell} = n - \frac{\nu}{\alpha}\pi(\ell, v; \mu, n) - S(\ell, v) = F(\ell, v; \mu, n) \quad (18)$$

From (9), (13), (14) and (16) follows:

$$\frac{dv}{dt}\frac{1}{v} = \mu - \left(1 + \frac{\nu}{\alpha}\right)\pi(\ell, v; \mu, n) - S(\ell, v) = G(\ell, v; \mu, n)$$

It is assumed that for given values of μ and n there exist positive equilibrium values, ℓ^* and v^*, so that $F(\ell^*, v^*; \mu, n) = 0$ and $G(\ell^*, v^*; \mu, n) = 0$. The stability conditions for the dynamic system, represented by equations (18) and (19) can be derived by linearization of the system around the equilibrium point. From this it results:

$$F_1^* = \frac{\partial F}{\partial \ell} = -\frac{\nu}{\alpha}\pi_\ell - S_\ell \tag{20}$$

$$F_2^* = \frac{\partial F}{\partial v} = -\frac{\nu}{\alpha}\pi_v - S_v \tag{21}$$

$$G_1^* = \frac{\partial G}{\partial \ell} = -\left(1 + \frac{\nu}{\alpha}\right)\pi_\ell - S_\ell \tag{23}$$

$$G_2^* = \frac{\partial G}{\partial v} = -\left(1 + \frac{\nu}{\alpha}\right)\pi_v - S_v. \tag{24}$$

The real parts of the 'eigen'-values of the matrix

$$J = \begin{bmatrix} F_1^* & F_2^* \\ G_1^* & G_2^* \end{bmatrix} \text{ are negative if}$$

$$\text{the trace of } [J] = F_1^* + G_2^* < 0 \tag{25}$$

$$\text{the determinant of } [J] = F_1^* G_2^* - F_2^* G_1^* > 0 \tag{26}$$

From equations (18) and (19) the comparative-dynamic properties of the equilibrium can now be derived. If we start from the functions:

$$F(\ell, v; \mu, n);\ G(\ell, v; \mu, n);\ \ell = \ell(\mu, n) \text{ and } v = v(\mu, n) \tag{27}$$

it can be written:

$$F_\mu + F_\ell \ell_\mu + F_v v_\mu = F_\mu + F_1^* \ell_\mu + F_2^* v_\mu = 0 \tag{28}$$

$$G_\mu + G_\ell \ell_\mu + G_v v_\mu = G_\mu + G_1^* \ell_\mu + G_2^* v_\mu = 0 \tag{29}$$

From (28) and (29) follows:

$$\frac{d\ell^*}{d\mu} = \frac{-F_\mu G_2^* + F_2^* G_\mu}{F_1^* G_2^* - F_2^* G_1^*} = \frac{-\dfrac{\gamma}{\alpha}\pi_v - S_v(1 - \pi_\mu)}{S_\ell \pi_v - \pi_\ell S_v} \tag{30}$$

$$\frac{dv^*}{du} = \frac{-F_1^* G_\mu + F_\mu G_1^*}{F_1^* G_2^* - F_2^* G_1^*} = \frac{\dfrac{\gamma}{\alpha}\pi_\ell + S_\ell(1 - \pi_\mu)}{S_\ell \pi_v - \pi_\ell S_v} \tag{31}$$

where $F_\mu = -\frac{\gamma}{\alpha}\pi_\mu$, $G_\mu = 1 - \left(1 + \frac{\gamma}{\alpha}\right)\pi_\mu$ and $\pi_\mu > 0$

Appendix, chapter 4, section 4.3.

Differentiate equations (9) and (10) mentioned below from the main text with regard to the equilibrium value of the rate of inflation: $\pi_e = \mu - n$.

$$S(\ell_e, v_e) = n \tag{9}$$

$$v_e = \hat{L}[f(\ell_e), r(\ell_e) + \pi_e, r(\ell_e) + \pi_e, v_e] \tag{10}$$

From this the following system results:

$$\begin{bmatrix} S_\ell & S_v \\ -\hat{L}_1 f'(\ell) + (\hat{L}_2 + \hat{L}_3)\, r'(\ell); & (1 - \hat{L}_4) \end{bmatrix} \begin{bmatrix} \ell_{\pi e} \\ v_{\pi e} \end{bmatrix} = \begin{bmatrix} 0 \\ \hat{L}_2 + \hat{L}_3 \end{bmatrix}$$

Solution with the aid of Cramers' rule:

a) $$\frac{d\ell_e}{d\pi_e} = \frac{-S_v(\hat{L}_2 + \hat{L}_3)}{D} < 0$$

b) $$\frac{dv_e}{d\pi_e} = \frac{S_\ell(\hat{L}_2 + \hat{L}_3)}{D} < 0$$

where determinant $D = S_\ell(1 - \hat{L}_4) + S_v[\hat{L}_1 f'(\ell) + (\hat{L}_2 + \hat{L}_3) r'(\ell)]$ or otherwise expressed:
$D = (-S_v)(1 - \hat{L}_4)[\alpha - \beta] > 0$ where α and β represent the slopes of the *IS* and *FM*-curves respectively.

$$\alpha = \frac{S_\ell}{-S_v} \text{ and } \beta = \frac{1}{1 - \hat{L}_4}[\hat{L}_1 f'(\ell) + (\hat{L}_2 + \hat{L}_3)\, r'(\ell)]$$

For stability the slope of the *IS*-curve must be greater than that of the *FM*-curve ($\alpha > \beta$).

List of the main symbols used in chapters 2 up to and including 4

Y	volume of production
Y_B	disposable income
K	stock of capital goods
L	labour
k	capital intensity
ℓ	labour intensity
S_B	total savings out of disposable income
S_M	material savings
S_K	monetary savings
S	planned savings
I	planned investments
C_T	total consumption (material consumption plus the immaterial consumption)
C_M	material consumption
M	nominal quantity of money
P	price level
r	real rate of capital or rate of profit
σ_B	savings ratio out of disposable income
σ_M	material savings ratio
μ	rate of growth of the nominal quantity of money
n	rate of population growth
g	rate of growth of the national income
π	rate of growth of the price level (the current rate of inflation)
π^*	expected rate of inflation
i	nominal rate of interest
i^*	expected real rate of interest
m	real cash-balances per head $\left(\frac{M}{PL}\right)$
v	real cash-balances per unit of capital $\left(\frac{M}{PK}\right)$

W	total real wealth of the private sector
λ	real cash-balance ratio $\left(\frac{M}{PY}\right)$
U	total utility
u	utility per head
c	consumption per head
∂	subjective rate of time preference
ε	interest sensitivity of the demand for real cash-balances
η	elasticity of the demand for real cash-balances with regard to capital intensity
β	expectations coefficient
$\hat{L}$	demand for real cash-balances
α	price adjustment coefficient
h	a coefficient which links up the disequilibria on the money market with the commodity market
γ	coefficient which indicates the extent to which planned investments or planned savings determine the actual rate of growth of the capital goods
ψ	coefficient enabling comparison between the Keynes-Wicksell model and the synthesis model
t	time

Bibliography

Abele, H., Uber geldwirtschaftliche Wachtumsmodelle, *Zeitschrift für Nationalökonomie, Band* 30, 1970.

Archibald, G. and R. Lipsey, Monetary and Value Theory: a critique of Lange and Patinkin, *Review of Economic Studies*, October 1958.

Aschheim, J. en Ching-Yao Hsieh, *Macroeconomics*; *income and monetary theory*, 1969.

Bailey, M., The welfare cost of inflationary finance, *Journal of Political Economy*, April 1956.

Bailey, M., *National income and the price level, a study in macrotheory*, 1962.

Bailey, M., Comment: optimum monetary growth, *Journal of Political Economy*, July-August 1968.

Ball, R., *Inflation and the theory of money*, London 1973.

Baumol, W., The transactions demand for cash: an inventory theoretic approach, *Quarterly Journal of Economics*, November 1952.

Baumol, W., Monetary and value theory: Comments, *Review of Economic Studies*, 1960–1961.

Baumol, W., *Economic theory and operation analysis*, Prentice-Hall, 1961.

Becker, G. and W. Baumol, The classical monetary, the outcome of the discussion, *Economica*, 1952.

Beckmann, M., A Wicksellian model of growth, *Revista Internazionale di Scienze Economiche e Commerciale*, March 1965.

Bieri, H., Der Streit um die 'klassische Dichotomie', Ein Bericht über die Patinkin-Kontroverse, *Schweizerische Zeitschrift für Volkswirtschaft und Statistik*, 1963.

Black, F., Active and passive monetary policy in a neo-classical model, *Journal of Finance*, 1972.

Black, F., Uniqueness of the price level in monetary growth models with rational expectations, *Journal of Economic Theory*, January 1974.

Blaug, M., *Economic theory in retrospect*, 1968.

Bolle, M., Kurz- und langfristige Analyse ungleichgewichtiger makroökonomischer Angebot – Nachfrage – Systeme, Duncker Humblot, 1971.

Bolle, M., Geld, Wachstum und Beschäftigung, Zeitschrift für die gesamte Staatswissenschaft, March 1973.

Boorman, J., and Th. Havrilesky, Money supply, money demand and macro-economic models, 1972.

Bosman, H., *La théorie monétaire qualitative*, Bulletin de documentation et d'information, Banque Nationale de Belgique, November 1958.

Bosman, H., Amerikaanse opvattingen over monetaire politiek. *Uitgave van het Instituut voor Sociale Wetenschappen*, Den Haag 1963.

Bosman, H., De monetaire betekenis van de niet-geldscheppende instellingen, *Bank- en Effectenbedrijf*, December 1965.

Brainard, W., and J. Tobin, Pitfalls in financial model building, *Cowles Foundation Paper, No. 279*, Yale University, 1968.

Bronfenbrenner and Th. Mayer, Liquidity functions in the American Economy, *Econometrica*, October 1960.

Brunner, K., Inconsistency and indeterminacy in classical economics, *Econometrica*, April 1951.

Brunner, K., The role of money and monetary policy, *Review, Federal Reserve Bank of St. Louis*, July 1968.

Brunner, K., A survey of selected issues in monetary theory, *Schweizerische Zeitschrift für Volkswirtschaft und Statistik*, no. 1, 1971.

Brunner, K. and A. Meltzer, Some further evidence on supply and demand functions for money, *Journal of Finance*, May 1964.

Brunner, K. and A. Meltzer, Liquidity traps for money, bank credit and interest rates, *Journal of Political Economy*, February 1968.

Brunner, K. and A. Meltzer, The uses of money: in the theory of an exchange economy, *American Economic Review*, December 1971.

Brunner, K. and A. Meltzer, Money, debt and economic activity, *Journal of Polital Economy*, September-October 1972.

Brunner, K. and A. Meltzer, Mr. Hicks and the 'Monetarists', *Economica*, February 1973.

Burmeister, E. and A. Dobell, *Mathematical theories of growth*, 1970.

Burmeister, E. and E. Phelps, Money, public debt, inflation and real interest, *Journal of Money, Credit and Banking*, May 1971.

Cagan, Ph., The monetary dynamics of hyperinflation, in *Studies in the quantity theory of money*, Chicago, 1956.

Cagan, Ph., The non-neutrality of money in the long run: A discussion of the critical assumptions and some evidence, *Journal of Money, Credit and Banking*, May 1969.

McCarthy, N., Money as net wealth, *Oxford Economic Papers*, November 1972.

Cassel, F. Theory of social economics, London 1923.

Chandavarkar, A., Money and economic growth, *Economia Internazionale*, 1965.

Chetty, V., On measuring the nearness of nearmoneys, *American Economic Review*, June 1969.

Claasen, E., *Probleme der Geldtheorie*, 1970.

Clower, R., Classical monetary theory revisited, *Economica*, 1963.

Clower, R., The Keynesian counterrevolution: a theoretical appraisal, in F. Hahn and F. Brechling, *The theory of interest rates, Institute of Economic Affairs*, 1965.

Clower, R., A reconsideration of the micro-foundations of monetary theory, *Western Economic Journal*, December 1967.

Clower, R., Comment: the optimal growth rate of money, *Journal of Political Economy*, July-August 1968.

Clower, R., Is there an optimal money supply? *Journal of Finance*, May 1970.

Cohen, B., The Johnsonian savings function and the rate of inflation, *Economia Internazionale*, February 1971.

Committee on the working of the monetary system, London 1959.

Controlling monetary aggregates II: The implementation, Federal Reserve Bank of Boston, September 1972.

Crouch, R., *Macroeconomics*, New York 1972.

Crouch, R., A new approach to the monetisation of neo-classical growth models, in A. Powell and R. Williams, *Econometric studies of macro and monetary relations*, 1973.

Dahmén, E., Inflation: Economics or politics? *Quarterly Review, National Westminster Bank*, November 1973.

Davidson, P., Money, portfolio balance, capital accumulation and economic growth, *Econometrica*, April 1968.

Davidson, P., *Money and the real world*, London 1972.

Dernburg, T. and D. McDougall, *Macro-economics, the measurement, analysis and control of aggregate economic activity*, 1968.

Dillard, D., The theory of a monetary economy, *Post-Keynesian Economics*, ed. bij K. Kurihara, New Jersey 1954.

Domar, E., Expansion and employment, *American Economic Review*, March 1944.

Dornbusch, R. and J. Frenkel, Inflation and growth: alternative approaches, *Journal of money, Credit and Banking*, February 1973.

Dutton, D., A model of self-generating inflation, the Argentine case, *Journal of Money, Credit and Banking*, May 1971.

Dutton, D., The demand for money and the price level, *Journal of Political Economy*, September 1971.

Duwendag, D., Theoretische Grundlagen der monetären Stabilisierungspolitik, *Zeitschrift für Nationalökonomie*, 1971.

Enthoven, A., A neo-classical model of money, debt and economic activity, in J. Gurley and E. Shaw, *Money in a theory of finance*, 1960.

Fair, R., Aggregate price changes and price expectations, *Review, Federal Reserve Bank of St. Louis*, November 1970.

Fand, D., Keynesian monetary theories, stabilization policy and the recent inflation, *Journal of Money, Credit and Banking*, August 1969.

Fand, D., Some issues in monetary economics, *Review; Federal Reserve Bank of St. Louis*, January 1970.

Fand, D., Geldtheorie und ökonometrische Grossmodelle, *Kredit und Kapital*, 1972.

Fase, M., The rate of return on bonds and inflationary expectations, a quantitative analysis of Dutch experiences. *Amsterdam-Rotterdam Bank N.V. Economic Quarterly Review*, March 1974.

Feige, E. and M. Parkin, The optimal quantity of money, bonds commodity inventories and capital, *American Economic Review*, June 1971.

Fischer, S., Keynes-Wichsell and neo-classical models of money and growth, *American Economic Review*, December 1972.

Fischer, S., Money, income, wealth and welfare, *Journal of Economic Literature*, 1972.

Fischer, S., A neo-classical monetary growth model, a comment, *Journal of Money, Credit and Banking*, May 1973.

Fisher, I., *The purchasing power of money*, New York 1911.

Fisher, I., *The theory of interest*, New York 1930.

Floyd, J. and J. Hynes, The contribution of real money balances to the level of wealth, *Journal of Money, Credit and Banking*, May 1972.

Foley, D. and M. Sidrauski, *Monetary and fiscal policy in a growing economy*, New York 1971.

Foster, E., Cost and benefits of inflation, studies in monetary economics, *Research Department, Federal Reserve Bank of Minneapolis*, 1972.

Fried, J., Money, exchange and growth, *Western Economic Journal*, September 1973.

Friedman, M., Discussion of the inflationary gap, *American Economic Review*, June 1942.

Friedman, M., The demand for money: some theoretical and emperical results, *Journal of Political Economy*, August 1959.

Friedman, M., *A program for monetary stability*, New York 1960.

Friedman, M., The role of monetary policy, *American Economic Review*, March 1968.

Friedman, M., *The optimum quantity of money and other essays*, Chicago 1969.

Friedman, M., The optimum quantity of money, in *The optimum quantity of money and other essays*, Chicago 1969.

Friedman, M., The quantity theory of money: a restatement, in *The optimum quantity of money and other essays*, Chicago 1969.

Friedman, M., The counter-revolution in monetary theory, *The Institute of Economic Affairs, First Wincott Memorial Lecture*, September 1970.

Friedman, M., A theoretical framework for monetary analysis, *Journal of Political Economy*, March-April 1970.

Friedman, M. A monetary theory of nominal income, *Journal of Political Economy*, March-April 1971.

Friedman, M. and A. Schwartz. *A monetary history of the United States, 1867–1960,* National Bureau of Economic Research, 1963.

Friedman, M. and A. Schwartz, The definition of money: net wealth and neutrality as criteria, *Journal of Money, Credit and Banking*, February 1969.

Fukuoka, M., Monetary growth à la Keynes, *Keio Economic Studies*, no. 1, 1969.

Gibson, W., Interest rates and monetary policy, *Journal of Political Economy*, May-June 1970.

Gibson, W., Price-expectations effects on interest rates, *Journal of Finance*, March 1970.

Gibson, W., Interest rates and inflationary expectations: new evidence, *American Economic Review*, December 1972.

Goldman, S., Hyperinflation and the rate of growth in the money supply, *Journal of Economic Literature*, January 1972.

Gramm, W., Laissez-faire and the optimum quantity of money, *Economic Inquiry*, March 1974.

McGregor, L. and A. Walters, Real balances and output: a productivity model of a monetary economy, in *A. Powell and R. Williams*, 1973.

Gurley, J. and E. Shaw, *Money in a theory of finance*, Washington D.C. 1960.

Haan, H. de and S. Kuipers, Een onderzoek naar de invloed monetaire factoren op het van reële groeiproces in enkele traditionele theorieën van economische groei, *De Economist*, March-April 1969.

Hadjimichalakis, M., Equilibrium and disequilibrium growth with money; The Tobin models, *Review of Economic Studies*, October 1971.

Hadjimichalakis, M., Money, expectations and dynamics, an alternative view, *International Economic Review*, October 1971.

Hahn, F., Money, dynamic stability and growth, *Metroeconomica*, August 1961.

Hahn, F., On money and growth, *Journal of Money, Credit and Banking*, May 1969.

Hahn, F. and R. Matthews, The theory of economic growth, a survey, *The Economic Journal*, December 1964.

Hamberg, D., *Models of economic growth*, 1971.

Hamburger, N., The demand for money bij households, money substitutes and monetary policy, *Journal of Political Economy*, December 1966.

Hansen, B., *S survey of general equilibrium systems*, 1970.

Harkness, J., The role of money in a simple growth model: comment, *American Economic Review*, March 1972.

Helmstädter, E., Das Walras-Gezetz und Oscar Langes Kritik an der neo-klassischen Geldtheorie, *Studien zur Geldtheorie und monetäre Okonometrie*, G. Bombach, Basel 1972.

Hester, D. and J. Tobin, *Financial markets and economic activity*, New York-London 1967.

Hicks, J., Mr. Keynes and the 'Classics'; a suggested interpretation, *Econometrica*, April 1937.

Jaeger, K., Ein einfaches monetäres Wachstumsmodel mit Produkt- und Prozessinnovationen, *Zeitschrift für die Gesamte Staatswissenschaft*, August 1973.

Johnson, H., Monetary theory and policy, *American Economic Review*, June 1962.

Johnson, H., Monetary theory and Keynesian economics, *Readings in money, national income and stabilization policy*, 1965.

Johnson, H., The neo-classical one-sector growth model: a geometrical exposition and extension to a monetary economy, *Economica*, August 1966.

Johnson, H., *Essays in monetary economics*, 1967.

Johnson, H., Money in a neo-classical one sector growth model, in *Essays in monetary economics*, 1967.

Johnson, H., Recent developments in monetary theory, *Essays in monetary economics*, 1967.

Johnson, H., A comment on Pesek and Savings' theory of money and wealth, *Journal of Money, Credit and Banking*, August 1969.

Johnson, H., Inside money, outside money, income, wealth and welfare in monetary theory, *Journal of Money, Credit and Banking*, February 1969.

Johnson, H., Is there an optimal money supply?, *Journal of Finance*, May 1970.

Johnson, H., *Macro economics and monetary theory*, *Lectures in economics I*, 1971.

Johnson, H., Richard Ely Lecture: the Keynesian revolution and the monetarist counter-revolution, *American Economic Review, Papers and Proceedings*, May 1971.

Johnson, H., *Further essays in monetary economics*, London 1972.

Johnson, H., Inflation and the monetarist controversy, *Professor Dr. F. de Vries Lectures*, Amsterdam 1972.

Jong, F. de, Het begrip monetair evenwicht en zijn verband met de post-Keynesiaanse economie, *Monetaire Theorie*, *Monetaire Opstellen I*, Agon Elsevier, 1965.

Jong, F. de, Don Patinkin's integratie van geldtheorie en prijstheorie, *Orbis Economicus*, December 1966–March 1967.

Jordan, J., Money, interest rates, prices and output, *Review, Federal Reserve Bank of St. Louis*, November 1967.

Jüttner, D., Zur Geldtheorie Don Patinkin's, *Untersuchungen über das Spar-, Giro- und Kreditwesen*, *Band 57*, 1971.

Kaufman, G., Current issues in monetary economics and policy; a review, New York University, *The Bulletin*, nr. 57, May 1969.

Keynes, J. M., *The general theory of employment, interest and money*, London 1946.

Klundert, Th. van de, Enkele opmerkingen over de theorie van Patinkin, *De Economist*, January-February, 1967.

Koning, J., Inflatie in Latijns-Amerika, *Maandschrift Economie*, December 1972.

Koopmans, J. G., Zum Problem des 'neutralen' Geldes, in *Beiträge zur Geldtheorie*, F. A. von Hayek, Wenen 1933.

Korteweg, P., De rentegevoeligheid van de vraag naar geld. Een beknopt theoretisch overzicht, *Selecte studies over sparen, omloopsnelheid, geldvraag*, Coöperatieve Centrale Raiffeisenbank, Utrecht 1969.

Korteweg, P., *De monetaire sector, het aanbod van geld en de instrumenten van de monetaire politiek*, Leiden 1971.

Kregel, J., *Rate of profit, distribution and growth*; *two views*, Manchester 1971.

Laidler, D., Some evidence on the demand for money, *Journal of Political Economy*, February 1966.

Laidler, D., The rate of interest and the demand for money-some empirical evidence, *Journal of Political Economy*, December 1966.

Laidler, D., *The demand for money: theories and evidence*, 1973.

Lange, O., Say's Law, a restatement and criticism, *Studies in mathematical economics and econometrics*, Chicago 1942.

Latané H., Cash balances and the interest rate – a pragmatic approach, *Review of Economics and Statistics*, November 1954.

Lee, T. H., Substitutability of non-bank intermediary liabilities of money, *Journal of finance*, September 1966.

Leontief, W., The fundamental assumption of Mr. Keynes' monetary theory of unemployment, *Quarterly Journal of Economics*, November 1936.

Levhari, D. and D. Patinkin, The role of money in a simple growth model, *American Economic Review*, September 1968.

Levhari, D. and D. Patinkin, The role of money in a simple growth model: reply, *American Economic Review*, March 1972.

Leyonhufvud, A., *On Keynesian Economics and the Economics of Keynes*, Oxford 1968.

Leyonhufvud, A., Keynes and the classics, *The Institute of Economic Affairs*, *Occasional Paper*, *30*, London 1971.

Lloyd, C., Classical monetary theory and the velocity of circulation, *Canadian Journal of Economics*, February 1970.

Lucas, R. Expectations and the neutrality of money, *Journal of Economic Literature*, 1972.

Lundberg, E., How harmful is inflation, *Skandinaviska Enskilda Banken*, *Quarterly Review*, nr. 4, 1973.

Malliaris, A., *Monetary growth theory: criticism and models*, Oklahoma University, 1971.

Marty, A., The optimal rate of growth of money, *Journal of Political Economy*, July-August 1968.

Marty, A., Inside money, outside money and the wealth effect, A review essay, *Journal of Money, Credit and Banking*, February 1969.

Marty, A., Notes on money and economic growth, *Journal of Money, Credit and Banking*, May 1969.

Marty, A., Growth, satiety, and the tax revenue from money creation, *Journal of Political Economy*, October 1973.

Mauer, L. J., The Patinkin controversy: a review, *Kyklos*, 1966.

Meade, J., *A neo-classical theory of economic growth*, 1961.

Meade, J., The effect of savings on consumption in a state of steady growth, *Review of Economic Studies*, June 1962.

Meltzer, A., Money, intermediation and growth, *Journal of Economic Literature*, March 1969.

Metzler, L., Wealth, saving and the rate of interest, *Journal of Political Economy*, April 1951.

Mill, J. S., The principles of political economy, London 1871.

Mill, J. S., *Essays on some unsettled questions of political economy*, London 1948.

Minabe, S., A note on post-Keynesian monetary theory, *The American Economist*, 1971.

Modigliani, F., Liquidity preference and the theory of interest and money, *Econometrica*, January 1944.

Möller, H., Money as an economic good – a contribution to the foundations of monetary theory, *The German Economic Review*, nr. 3, 1972.

Moroney, J., The current state of money and production theory, *American Economic Review, Papers and Proceedings*, May 1972.

Mundell, R., Inflation saving and the real rate of interest, in *Monetary Theory*, 1971.

Nagatani, K., A monetary growth model with variable employment, *Journal of Money, Credit and Banking*, May 1969.

Nagatani, K., A note on Professor Tobin's 'Money and economic growth', *Econometrica*, January 1970.

Newbery D. and A. Atkinson, Investment, savings and employment in the long-run, *International Economic Review*, October 1972.

Niehans, J., Efficient monetary and fiscal policies in balanced growth, *Journal of Money, Credit and Banking*, May 1969.

Niehans, J., The neo-classical dichotomy as a controlled experiment, *Journal of Political Economy*, 1969.

Niehans, J., Money and barter in general equilibrium with transaction costs, *American Economic Review*, December 1971.

Nieuwenburg, C. K., *Het liquiditeitsbezit van gezinshuishoudingen in Nederland*, 1969.

Nieuwenburg, C. K., Friedman and monetary policy, Amsterdam-Rotterdam Bank N. V., *Economic Quarterly Review*, June 1970.

Nieuwenburg, C. K., Een vorm van modern monetarisme, *Maandschrift Economie*, September 1973.

Nieuwenburg, C. K., *Geld en economische activiteit*, University of Utrecht, Kluwer-Deventer, 1973.

Nieuwenburg, C. K. and H. J. Leemreize, The long-term rate of interest in the Netherlands, an empirical study, Amsterdam-Rotterdam Bank N.V., *Economic Quarterly Review*, March 1974.

Olivera, J., Passive money, inflation and economic growth, a comment, *Journal of Money, Credit and Banking*, February 1971.

Park, Y. Ch., Some current issues on the transmission process of monetary policy, *I.M.F. Staff Papers*, May 1972.

Park, Y. Ch., The transmission process and the relative effectiveness of monetary and fiscal policy in a two sector neo-classical model, *Journal of Money, Credit and Banking*, May 1973.

Patinkin, D., The indeterminacy of absolute prices in classical economic theory, *Econometrica*, January 1949.

Patinkin, D., The invalidity of classical monetary theory, *Econometrica*, 1951.

Patinkin, D., *Money, interest and prices, an integration of monetary and value theory*, New York 1965.

Patinkin, D., The Chicago tradition, the quantity theory and Friedman, *Journal of Money, Credit and Banking*, February 1969.

Patinkin, D., Inside money, monopoly bank profits and the real-balance effect, a comment, *Journal of Money, Credit and Banking*, May 1971.

Patinkin, D., Money and growth in a Keynesian full-employment model, in D. Patinkin, *Studies in Monetary Economics*, 1972.

Perlman, M., The role of money in an economy and the optimum quantity of money, *Economica*, August 1971

Pesek, B. and T. Saving, *Money, wealth and economic theory*, New York 1967.

Phelps, E., The golden rule of accumulation, a fable for growthmen, *American Economic Review*, September 1961.

Phelps, E., Second essay on the golden rule of capital accumulation, *American Economic Review*, September 1965.

Phelps, E., Notes on optimal monetary growth, comment, *Journal of Political Economy*, July-August 1968.

Phelps, E., The optimal rate of growth of money: comment, *Journal of Political Economy*, July-August 1968.

Phelps, E., *Microeconomic foundations of employment and inflation theory*, London 1971.

Phillips, A., A simple model of employment, money and prices in a growing economy, *Economica*, November 1961.

Pigou, A., The classical stationary state, *Economic Journal*, December 1943.

Powell, A. and R. Williams, *Econometric studies of macro and monetary relations*, Amsterdam 1973.

Purvis, D., Introducing useful money into a growth model, *Canadian Journal of Economics*, August 1971.

Rakshit, M., Classical monetary theory revisited: a comment, *Economica*, February 1965.

Ramanathan, R., The role of money in a simple growth model: comment, *American Economic Review*, March 1972.

Riese, H. Gleichgewichtswachstum und optimales Wachstum in der Neoklassischen Wachstumstheorie, *Kyklos*, 1964.

Robinson, J., A neo-classical theorem, *Review of Economic Studies*, June 1962.

Roos, F. de, Complementaire interest theorieën, monetaire theorieën, *Monetaire theorie, Monetaire Opstellen I*, Agon Elsevier, 1900.

Roos, F. de and D. Schouten, *Groeitheorie*, 1962.

Rose, H., Unemployment in a theory of growth, *International Economic Review*, September 1966.

Rose, H., Real and monetary factors in the business cycle, *Journal of Money, Credit and Banking*, May 1969.

Rousseas, S., *Monetary theory*, 1972.

Samuelson, P., Nonoptimality of money holdings in 'laissez-faire', *Canadian Journal of Economics*, May 1969.

Santomoro, A., A note on interest rates, and prices in general equilibrium, *The Journal of Finance*, September 1973.

Sargent, Th., Interest rates and prices in the long run, *Journal of Money, Credit and Banking*, February 1973.

Saving, Th., Portfolio – choise and monetary theory; a review essay, *Journal of Money, Credit and Banking*, May 1970.

Schneider, E. Patinkin über Geld und Güterpreise, *Festschrift für Frederik Zeuthen*, Kopenhagen, 1958.

Schouten, D., De economische groei in de Westerse wereld, *Praeadvies voor de Vereniging van Staathuishoudkunde*, 1962.

Schouten, D., *Dynamische macro-economie, conjunctuurtheorie*, Leiden 1967.

Schouten, D., *Dynamische macro-economie, structuurtheorie*, Leiden 1967.

Schouten, D., Over macht en wet in het economisch gebeuren, *Maandschrift Economie*, May-June 1973.

Shane, M., Capital markets and the dynamics of growth, *American Economic Review*, March 1974.

Sheshinski, E., Is there an optimal money supply? Discussion, *Journal of Finance*, May 1970.

Sidrauski, M., Inflation and economic growth, *Journal of Political Economy*, December 1967.

Sidrauski, M., Rational choice and patterns of growth in a monetary economy, *American Economic Review*, May 1967.

Sijben, J., De betekenis van de niet-geldscheppende financiële instellingen en de effectiviteit van de monetaire politiek, *Maandschrift Economie*, January 1969.

Sijben, J., 'Near-banking' and monetary policy, Amsterdam-Rotterdam Bank N.V., *Economic Quarterly Review*, December 1972.

Silber, W., Fiscal policy in IS-LM analysis, a correction, *Journal of Money, Credit and Banking*, November 1970.

Sinai, A. and H. Stokes, Real money balances: an omitted variable from the production function?, *Review of Economics and Statistics*, January 1972.

Smith, W., On the effectiveness of monetary policy, *American Economic Review*, September 1956.

Smith, W., A graphical exposition of the complete Keynesian-system, *Southern Economic Journal*, October 1965.

Smith, W., A neo-Keynesian view of monetary policy, in *Controlling monetary aggregates, Monetary Conference, Federal Reserve Bank of Boston*, June 1969.

Smith, W., Is there an optimal money supply? Discussion, *Journal of Finance*, May 1970.

Smith, W., On some current issues in monetary economics, an interpretation, *The Journal of Economic Literature*, 1970.

Smith, W. and R. Teigen, The theory of income determination, Introduction, in *Readings* in *money, national income and stabilization policy*, 1965.

Solow, R., *Growth theory, an exposition*, Oxford 1970.

Solow, R. and G. Stiglitz, Output, employment and wages in the short-run, *Quarterly Journal of Economics*, November 1968.

Sontheimer, K., On the determination of money prices, *Journal of Money, Credit and Banking*. August 1972.

Spencer, R., The relation between prices and employment; two views, *Review, Federal Reserve Bank of St. Louis*, March 1970.

Spencer, R. and W. Yoke, The 'crowding out' of private expenditure bij fiscal policy actions *Review, Federal Reserve Bank of St. Louis*, October 1972.

Stein, J., Money and capacity growth, *Journal of Political Economy*, October 1966.

Stein, J., Rational choice and patterns of growth in a monetary economy, comment, *American Economic Review*, September 1968.

Stein, J., Introduction, *Journal of Money Credit and Banking*, May 1969.

Stein, J., 'Neo-classical' and 'Keynes-Wicksell' monetary growth models, *Journal of Money, Credit and Banking*, May 1969.

Stein, J., Stabilisation policies in a growing economy, *Review of Economic Studies*, April 1969.

Stein, J., Monetary growth theory in perspective, *American Economic Review*, March 1970.

Stein, J., The optimum quantity of money, *Journal of Money, Credit and Banking*, November 1970.

Stein, J., *Money and capacity growth*, New York-London 1971.

Stein, J., and E. Infante, Optimal stabilization paths, *Journal of Money, Credit and Banking*, February 1973.

Takahashi, F., Money supply and economic growth, *Econometrica*, March 1971.

Tanner, J., Empirical evidence on the short-run real-balance effect in Canada, *Journal of Money, Credit and Banking*, November 1970.

Teigen, R., Demand and supply functions in the United States, some structural estimates, *Econometrica*, October 1964.

Teigen, R. The demand for and supply of money, *Readings in money, national income and stabilization policy*, 1965.

Teigen, R., A critical look at monetarist economics, *Review, Federal Reserve Bank of St. Louis*, January 1972.

Teubal, M., Inflation unemployment and economic growth, *Report 6616, Center for mathematical studies in Business and Economics, Chicago*, June 1966.

Teubal, M., Monetary expansion, unemployment and economic growth, *Report 6607*, Chicago, May 1966.

Thorn, R., *Monetary theory and policy*, 1966.

Tobin, J., A dynamic aggregative model, *Journal of Political Economy*, April 1955.

Tobin, J., The interest-elasticity of transactions demand for cash, *Review of Economics and Statistics*, August 1956.

Tobin, J., Liquidity preference as behavior towards risk, *Review of Economic Studies*, February 1958.

Tobin, J., Money, capital and other stores of value, *Papers and Proceedings, American Economic Review*, May 1961.

Tobin, J., Money and economic growth, *Econometrica*, October 1965.

Tobin, J., The neutrality of money in growth models; a comment, *Economica*, February 1967.

Tobin, J., Notes on optimal monetary growth, *Journal of Political Economy*, July-August 1968.

Tobin, J., A general approach to monetary theory, *Journal of Money, Credit and Banking*, February 1969.

Tobin, J., Money wage rates and employment, in *Readings in macro economics*, ed. by M. Mueller, 1969.

Tobin, J., *Essays in economics, Volume I, macroeconomics*, Amsterdam 1971.

Tobin, J., Inflation and unemployment, *American Economic Review*, March 1972.

Tsiang, S., A critical note on the optimum supply of money, *Journal of Money, Credit and Banking*, May 1969.

Uzawa, H., Towards a Keynesian model of monetary growth, in *Models of Economic Growth*, ed. by J. Mirrlees and N. Stern, London 1973.

Valavanis, S., A denial of Patinkin's contradiction, *Kÿklos*, 1955.

Vermaat, A., De Wet van Walras, *De Economist*, July-August 1968 en September-October 1968.

Vermaat, A., De Patinkin-puzzle, *De Economist*, January-February 1971.

Villanueva, D., A neo-classical monetary growth model with independent savings and investment functions, *Journal of Money, Credit and Banking*, November 1971.

Villanueva, D., A neo-classical monetary growth model, a reply, *Journal of Money, Credit and Banking*, May 1973.

Visser, H., Neutraal geld, een overzicht, *De Economist*, Nr. 4, 1971.

Visser, H., Keynes en de neo-klassieken: een herinterpretatie, *De Economist*, January-February 1972.

Visser, H., *The quantity of money*, London 1975.

Vogt, W., Zinssatz, Preisniveau und 'optimale inflationsrate' in einer wachsenden Wirtschaft, *Weltwirtschaftliches Archiv, Heft 2*, 1970.

Vosgerau, H., *Über optimales wirtschaftliches Wachstum*, 1965.

Wallich, H., Money and growth: A country cross-section analysis, *Journal of Money, Credit and Banking*, May 1969.

Wan, H., Extensions of the neo-classical model: the inclusion of monetary assets, in *Economic Growth*. Cornell University, 1971.

Weiszächer, C. von, *Wachstum, Zins und optimale Investitionsquote*, 1963.

Wicksell, K., The influence of the rate of interest on commodity prices, in *Selected Papers in Economic Theory*, Cambridge, Mass. 1958.

Williamson, J., A simple Neo-Keynesian growth model, *Review of Economic Studies*, April 1970.

Willms, M., Das Gleichgewichtsproblem in der klassischen und neo-klassischen Geldtheorie, *Jahrbuch für Sozialwissenschaft*, 1966.

Yohe, W., and D. Karnosky, Interest rates and price level changes, 1952–1969, *Review, Federal Reserve Bank of St. Louis*, December 1969.

Zwick, B., The adjustment of the economy to monetary changes, *Journal of Political Economy*, February 1971.

Index